...kira Yoshida
...Paul Smith
Inker (Issues #4-6): Joe Rubinstein
...istina Strain
Letters: Virtual Calligraphy's Randy Gentil...
Assistant Editor: Sean Ryan
Associate Editor: Nick Lowe
Editor: Mike Marts

Collection Editor: Jennifer Grünwald
Assistant Editor: Michael Short
Senior Editor, Special Projects: Jeff Youngquist
Director of Sales: David Gabriel
Production: Jerry Kalinowski
Book Designer: Jhonson Eteng
Creative Director: Tom Marvelli

Editor in Chief: Joe Quesada
Publisher: Dan Buckley

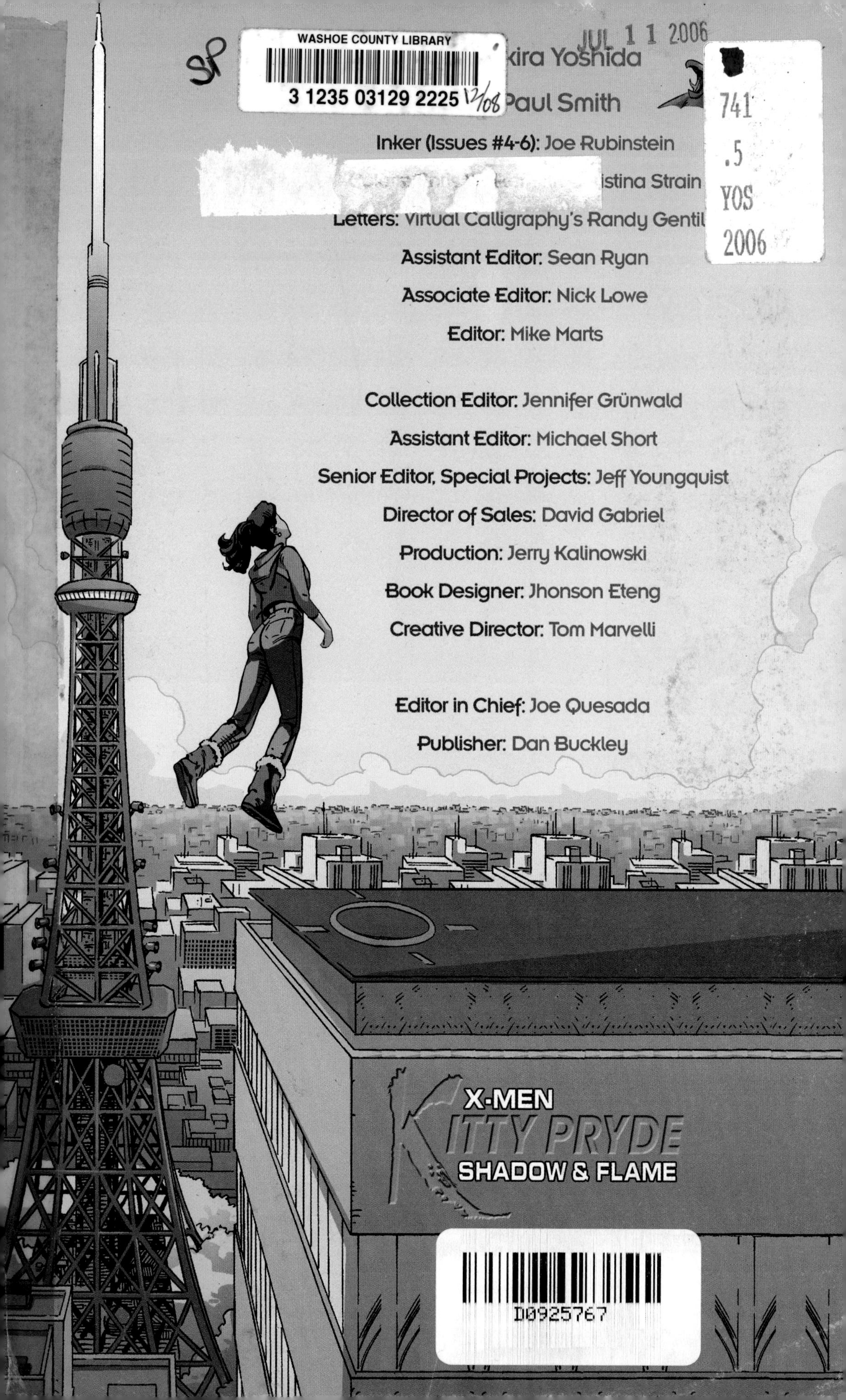
X-MEN
KITTY PRYDE
SHADOW & FLAME

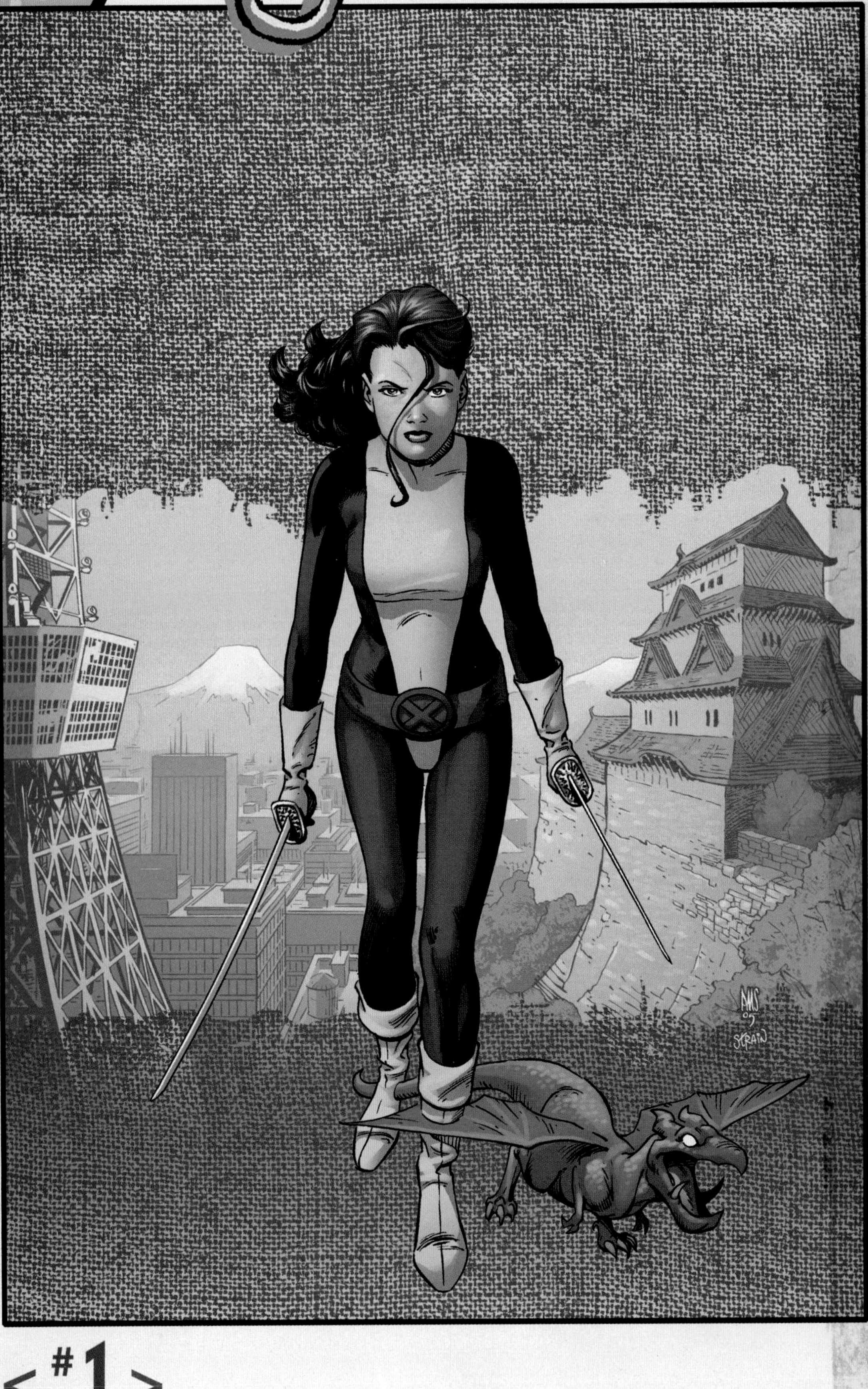

<#1>

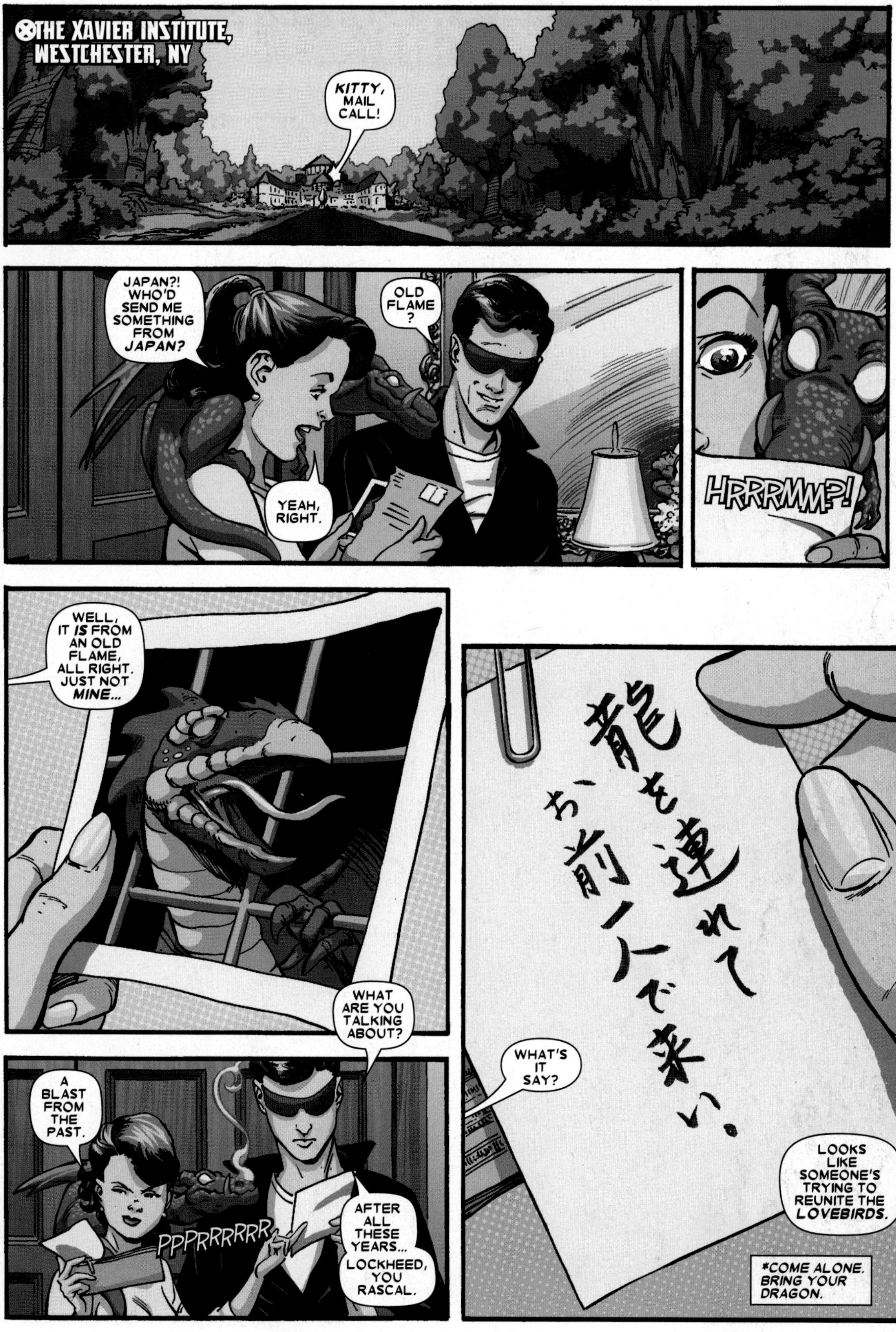
THE XAVIER INSTITUTE, WESTCHESTER, NY
KITTY, MAIL CALL!
JAPAN?! WHO'D SEND ME SOMETHING FROM JAPAN?
OLD FLAME ?
YEAH, RIGHT.
HRRRMMP!
WELL, IT IS FROM AN OLD FLAME, ALL RIGHT. JUST NOT MINE...
WHAT ARE YOU TALKING ABOUT?
龍を連れて
お前一人で来い。
WHAT'S IT SAY?
LOOKS LIKE SOMEONE'S TRYING TO REUNITE THE LOVEBIRDS.
*COME ALONE. BRING YOUR DRAGON.
A BLAST FROM THE PAST.
PPPRRRRRR
AFTER ALL THESE YEARS... LOCKHEED, YOU RASCAL.

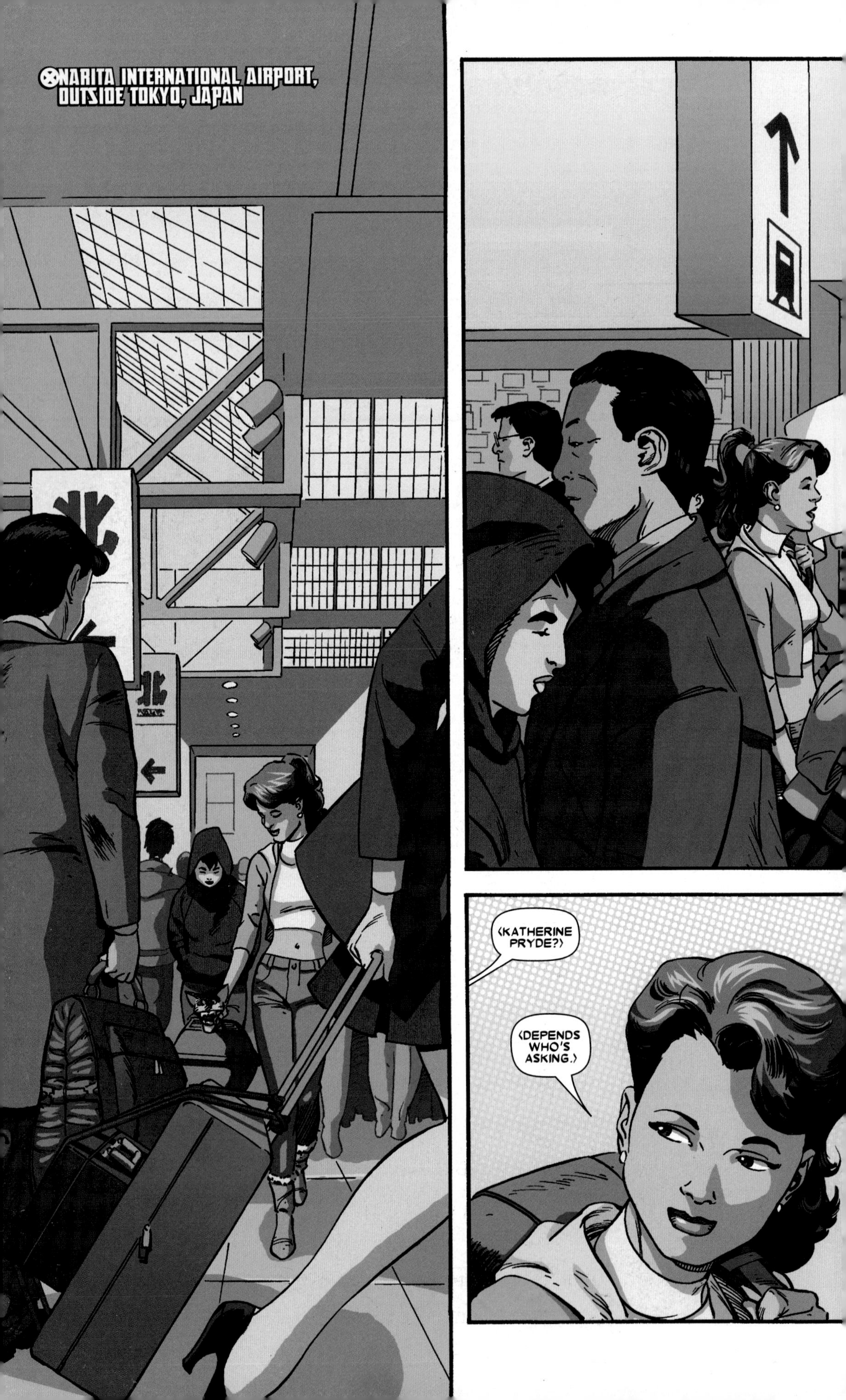
NARITA INTERNATIONAL AIRPORT, OUTSIDE TOKYO, JAPAN
‹KATHERINE PRYDE?›
‹DEPENDS WHO'S ASKING.›

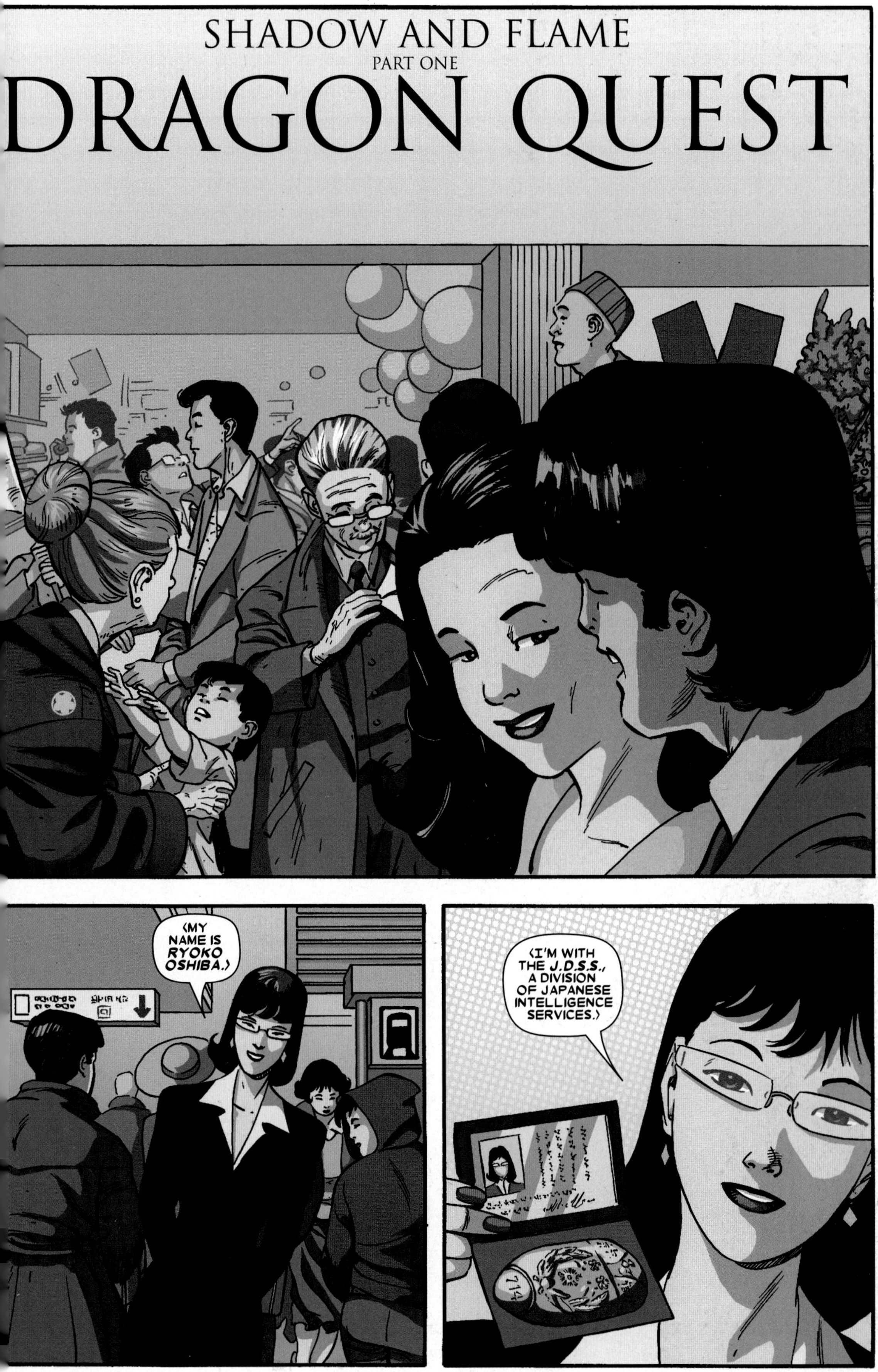
SHADOW AND FLAME
PART ONE
DRAGON QUEST
‹MY NAME IS RYOKO OSHIBA.›
‹I'M WITH THE J.D.S.S., A DIVISION OF JAPANESE INTELLIGENCE SERVICES.›

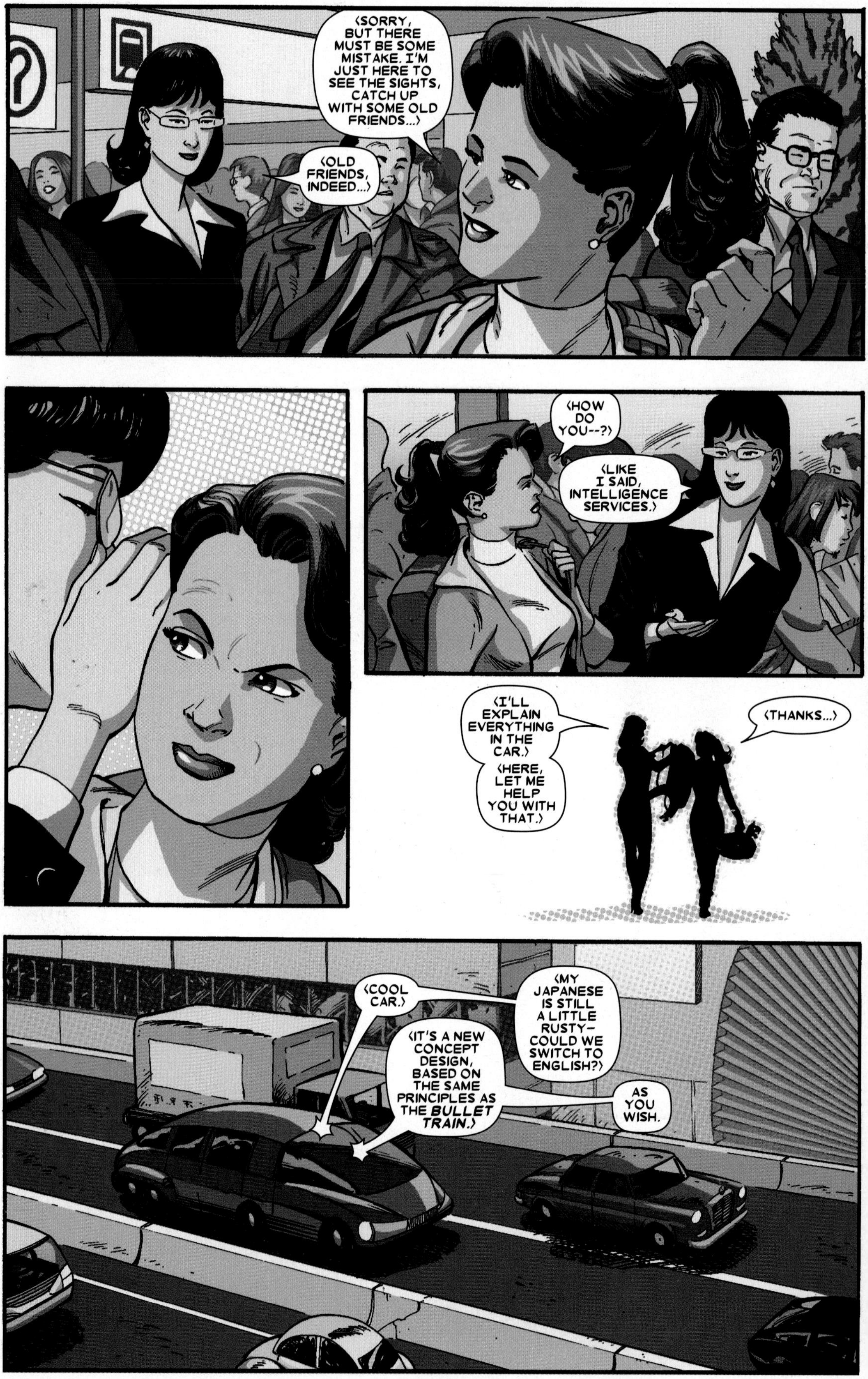

‹SORRY, BUT THERE MUST BE SOME MISTAKE. I'M JUST HERE TO SEE THE SIGHTS, CATCH UP WITH SOME OLD FRIENDS...›
‹OLD FRIENDS, INDEED...›
‹HOW DO YOU--?›
‹LIKE I SAID, INTELLIGENCE SERVICES.›
‹I'LL EXPLAIN EVERYTHING IN THE CAR.›
‹HERE, LET ME HELP YOU WITH THAT.›
‹THANKS...›
‹COOL CAR.›
‹IT'S A NEW CONCEPT DESIGN, BASED ON THE SAME PRINCIPLES AS THE *BULLET TRAIN*.›
‹MY JAPANESE IS STILL A LITTLE RUSTY—COULD WE SWITCH TO ENGLISH?›
AS YOU WISH.

SO-- ABOUT THE DRAGON?

WHERE IS IT?

NO. THE GREEN DRAGON.

ALRIGHT.

YES.

RIGHT THERE IN YOUR LAP, I WOULD HAVE TO ASSUME.

YOU SHOW ME YOURS, I'LL SHOW YOU MINE.

MEEOW

KLIK

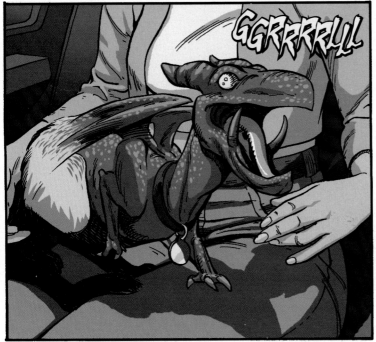

GGRRRRLLL

FASCINATING CREATURES.

YOUR TURN.

SOON. ONCE WE'VE ARRIVED AT OUR DESTINATION.

WHY AM I NOT SURPRISED?

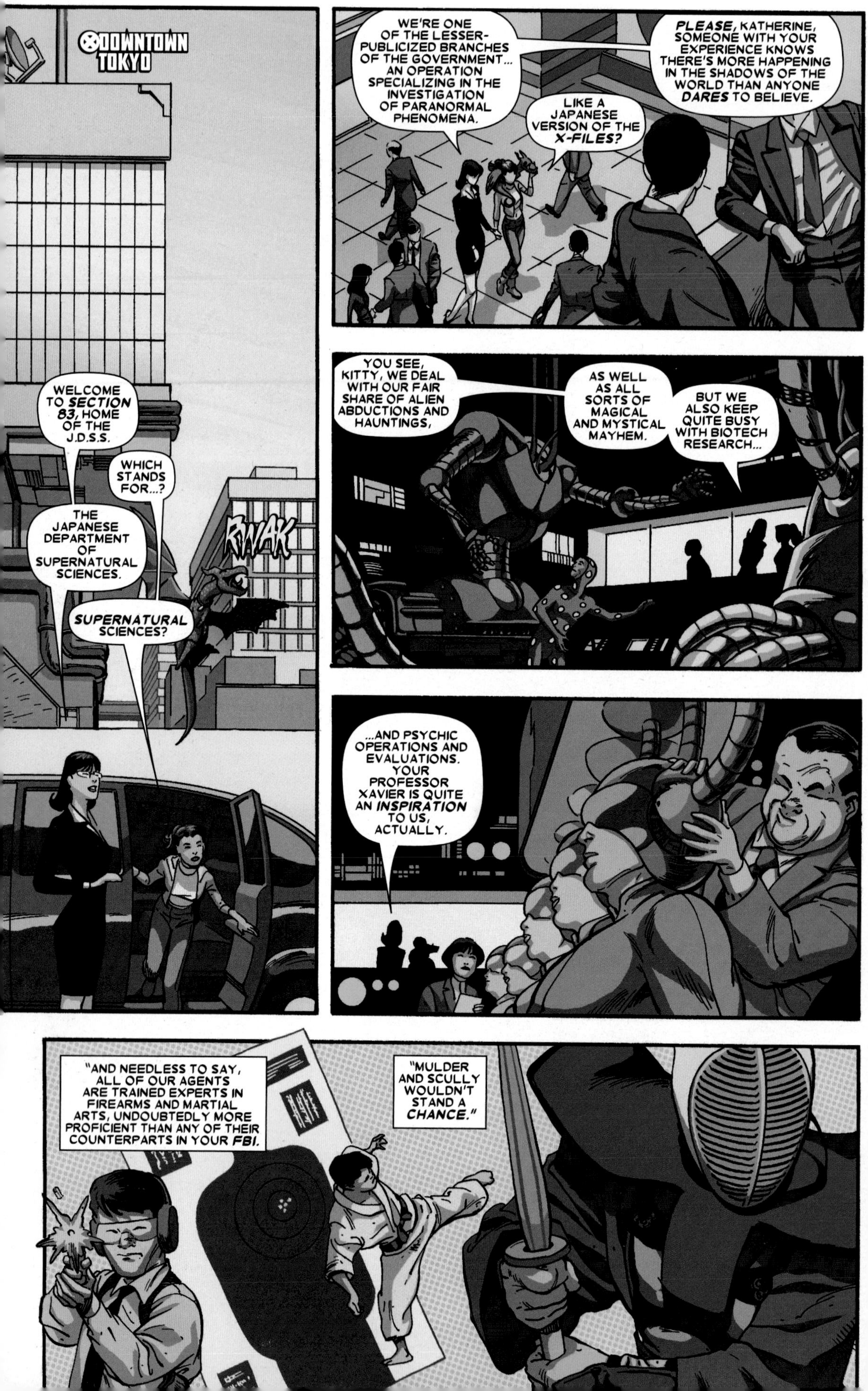
DOWNTOWN TOKYO
WELCOME TO SECTION 83, HOME OF THE J.D.S.S.
WHICH STANDS FOR...?
THE JAPANESE DEPARTMENT OF SUPERNATURAL SCIENCES.
RWAK
SUPERNATURAL SCIENCES?
WE'RE ONE OF THE LESSER-PUBLICIZED BRANCHES OF THE GOVERNMENT... AN OPERATION SPECIALIZING IN THE INVESTIGATION OF PARANORMAL PHENOMENA.
LIKE A JAPANESE VERSION OF THE X-FILES?
PLEASE, KATHERINE, SOMEONE WITH YOUR EXPERIENCE KNOWS THERE'S MORE HAPPENING IN THE SHADOWS OF THE WORLD THAN ANYONE DARES TO BELIEVE.
YOU SEE, KITTY, WE DEAL WITH OUR FAIR SHARE OF ALIEN ABDUCTIONS AND HAUNTINGS,
AS WELL AS ALL SORTS OF MAGICAL AND MYSTICAL MAYHEM.
BUT WE ALSO KEEP QUITE BUSY WITH BIOTECH RESEARCH...
...AND PSYCHIC OPERATIONS AND EVALUATIONS. YOUR PROFESSOR XAVIER IS QUITE AN INSPIRATION TO US, ACTUALLY.
"AND NEEDLESS TO SAY, ALL OF OUR AGENTS ARE TRAINED EXPERTS IN FIREARMS AND MARTIAL ARTS, UNDOUBTEDLY MORE PROFICIENT THAN ANY OF THEIR COUNTERPARTS IN YOUR FBI.
"MULDER AND SCULLY WOULDN'T STAND A CHANCE."

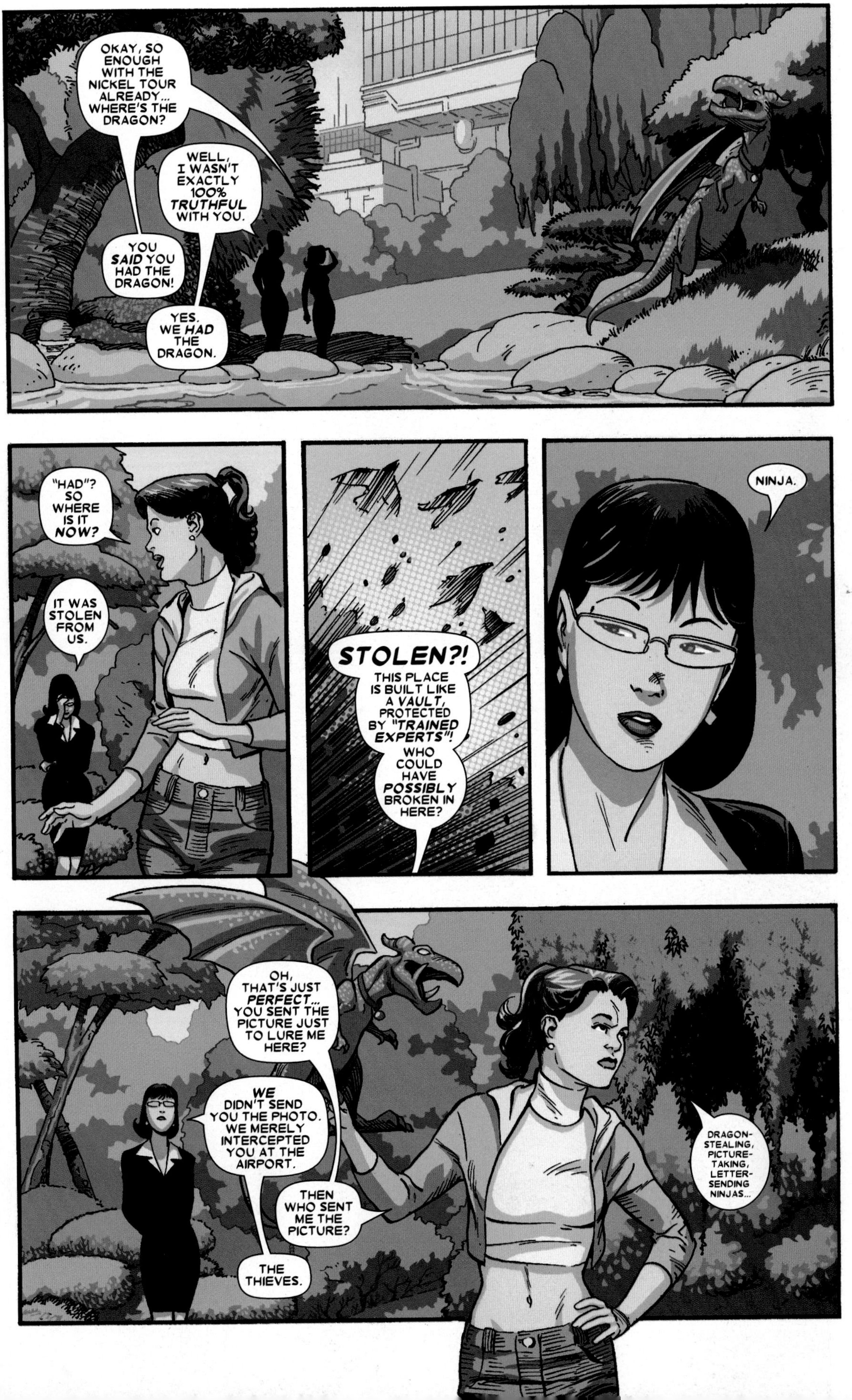

OKAY, SO ENOUGH WITH THE NICKEL TOUR ALREADY... WHERE'S THE DRAGON?
WELL, I WASN'T EXACTLY 100% *TRUTHFUL* WITH YOU.
YOU *SAID* YOU HAD THE DRAGON!
YES. WE *HAD* THE DRAGON.
"HAD"? SO WHERE IS IT *NOW*?
IT WAS STOLEN FROM US.
STOLEN?! THIS PLACE IS BUILT LIKE A *VAULT*, PROTECTED BY *"TRAINED EXPERTS"*! WHO COULD HAVE *POSSIBLY* BROKEN IN HERE?
NINJA.
OH, THAT'S JUST *PERFECT*... YOU SENT THE PICTURE JUST TO LURE ME HERE?
WE DIDN'T SEND YOU THE PHOTO. WE MERELY INTERCEPTED YOU AT THE AIRPORT.
THEN WHO SENT ME THE PICTURE?
THE THIEVES.
DRAGON-STEALING, PICTURE-TAKING, LETTER-SENDING NINJAS...

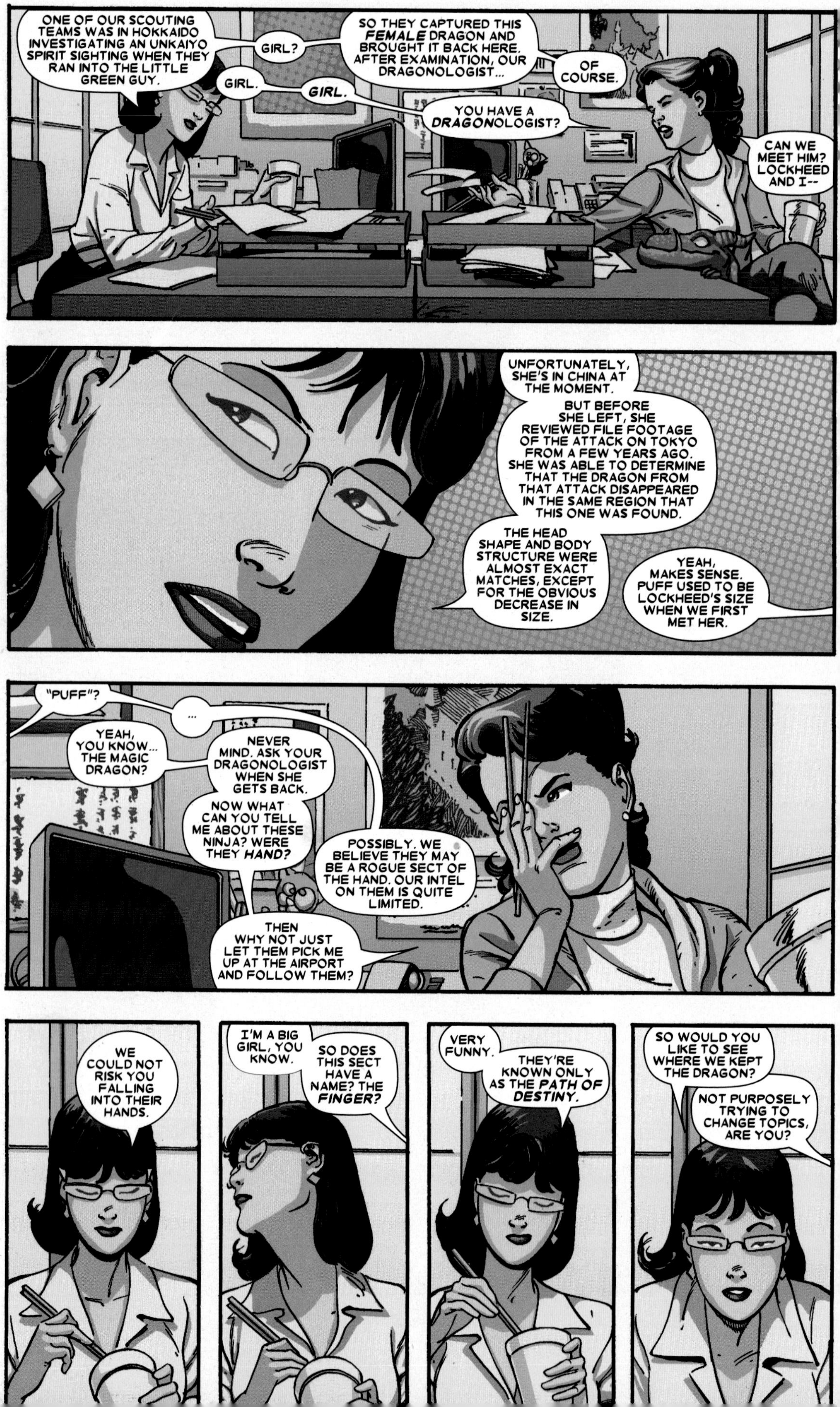
ONE OF OUR SCOUTING TEAMS WAS IN HOKKAIDO INVESTIGATING AN UNKAIYO SPIRIT SIGHTING WHEN THEY RAN INTO THE LITTLE GREEN GUY.
GIRL?
GIRL.
GIRL.
SO THEY CAPTURED THIS FEMALE DRAGON AND BROUGHT IT BACK HERE. AFTER EXAMINATION, OUR DRAGONOLOGIST...
OF COURSE.
YOU HAVE A DRAGONOLOGIST?
CAN WE MEET HIM? LOCKHEED AND I--
UNFORTUNATELY, SHE'S IN CHINA AT THE MOMENT.
BUT BEFORE SHE LEFT, SHE REVIEWED FILE FOOTAGE OF THE ATTACK ON TOKYO FROM A FEW YEARS AGO. SHE WAS ABLE TO DETERMINE THAT THE DRAGON FROM THAT ATTACK DISAPPEARED IN THE SAME REGION THAT THIS ONE WAS FOUND.
THE HEAD SHAPE AND BODY STRUCTURE WERE ALMOST EXACT MATCHES, EXCEPT FOR THE OBVIOUS DECREASE IN SIZE.
YEAH, MAKES SENSE. PUFF USED TO BE LOCKHEED'S SIZE WHEN WE FIRST MET HER.
"PUFF"?
...
YEAH, YOU KNOW... THE MAGIC DRAGON?
NEVER MIND. ASK YOUR DRAGONOLOGIST WHEN SHE GETS BACK.
NOW WHAT CAN YOU TELL ME ABOUT THESE NINJA? WERE THEY HAND?
POSSIBLY. WE BELIEVE THEY MAY BE A ROGUE SECT OF THE HAND. OUR INTEL ON THEM IS QUITE LIMITED.
THEN WHY NOT JUST LET THEM PICK ME UP AT THE AIRPORT AND FOLLOW THEM?
WE COULD NOT RISK YOU FALLING INTO THEIR HANDS.
I'M A BIG GIRL, YOU KNOW.
SO DOES THIS SECT HAVE A NAME? THE FINGER?
VERY FUNNY.
THEY'RE KNOWN ONLY AS THE PATH OF DESTINY.
SO WOULD YOU LIKE TO SEE WHERE WE KEPT THE DRAGON?
NOT PURPOSELY TRYING TO CHANGE TOPICS, ARE YOU?

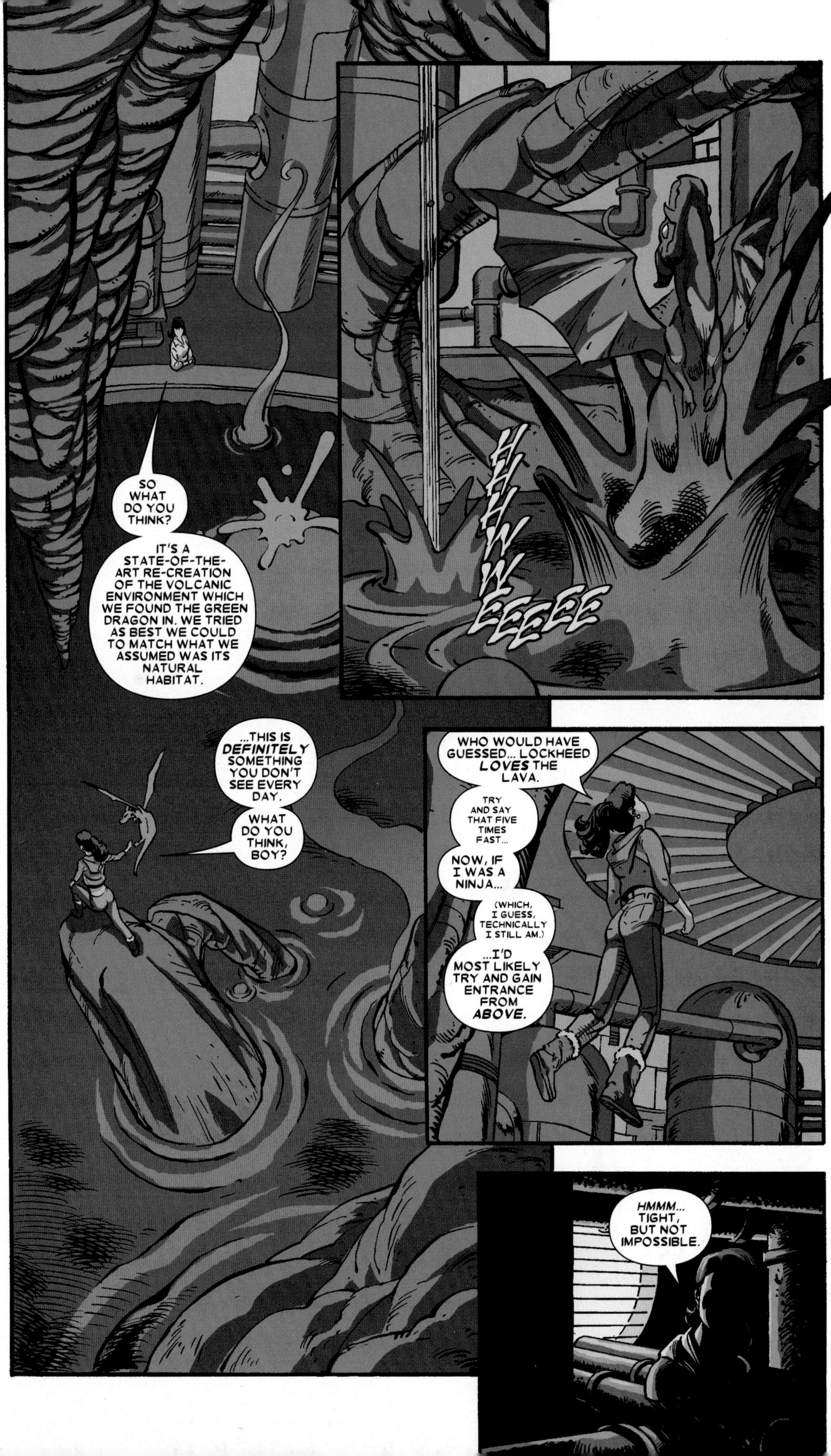

SO WHAT DO YOU THINK?
IT'S A STATE-OF-THE-ART RE-CREATION OF THE VOLCANIC ENVIRONMENT WHICH WE FOUND THE GREEN DRAGON IN. WE TRIED AS BEST WE COULD TO MATCH WHAT WE ASSUMED WAS ITS NATURAL HABITAT.
HHHWWEEEEE
...THIS IS DEFINITELY SOMETHING YOU DON'T SEE EVERY DAY.
WHAT DO YOU THINK, BOY?
WHO WOULD HAVE GUESSED... LOCKHEED LOVES THE LAVA.
TRY AND SAY THAT FIVE TIMES FAST...
NOW, IF I WAS A NINJA...
(WHICH, I GUESS, TECHNICALLY I STILL AM.)
...I'D MOST LIKELY TRY AND GAIN ENTRANCE FROM ABOVE.
HMMM... TIGHT, BUT NOT IMPOSSIBLE.

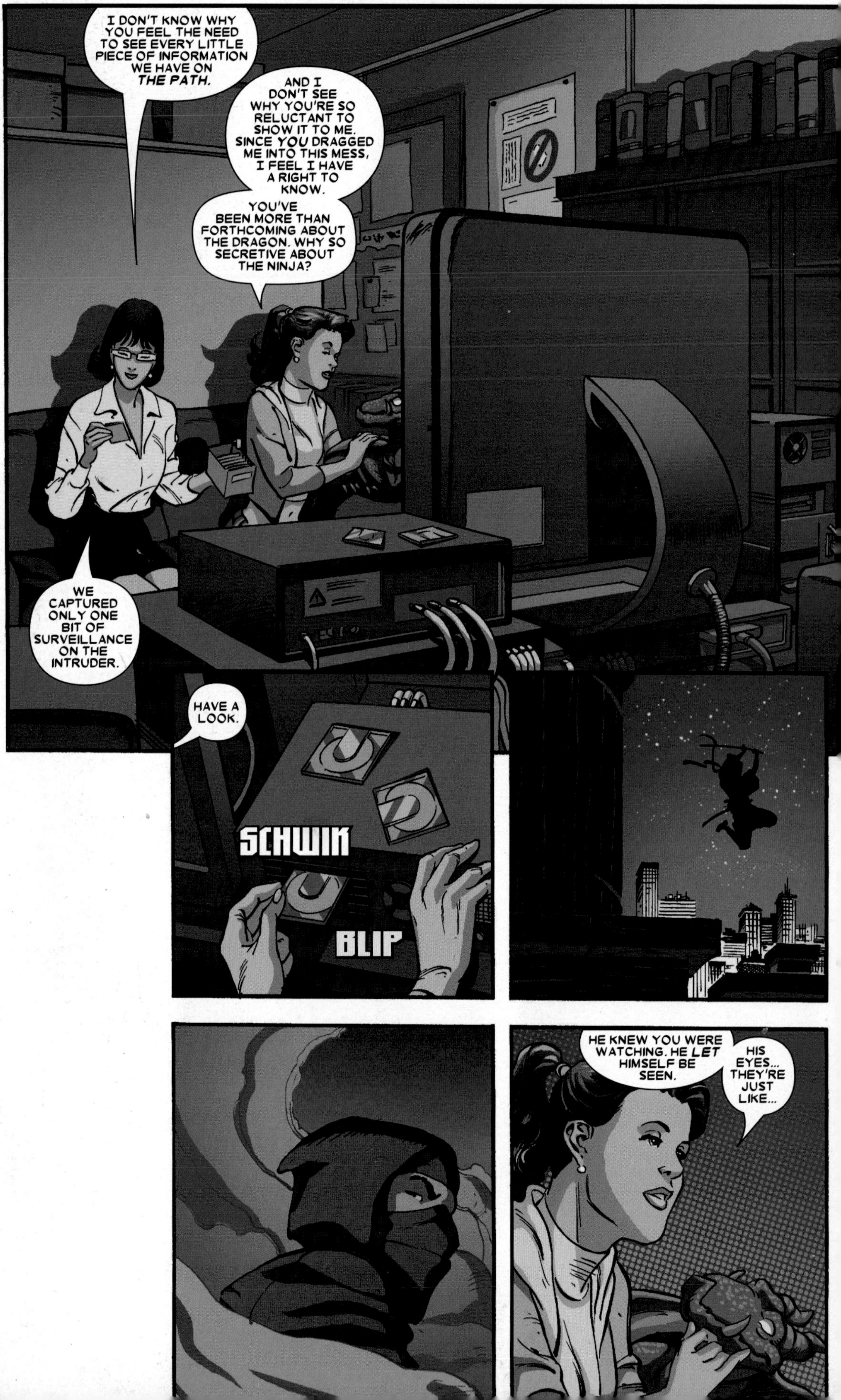
I DON'T KNOW WHY YOU FEEL THE NEED TO SEE EVERY LITTLE PIECE OF INFORMATION WE HAVE ON *THE PATH.*
AND I DON'T SEE WHY YOU'RE SO RELUCTANT TO SHOW IT TO ME. SINCE *YOU* DRAGGED ME INTO THIS MESS, I FEEL I HAVE A RIGHT TO KNOW.
YOU'VE BEEN MORE THAN FORTHCOMING ABOUT THE DRAGON. WHY SO SECRETIVE ABOUT THE NINJA?
WE CAPTURED ONLY ONE BIT OF SURVEILLANCE ON THE INTRUDER.
HAVE A LOOK.
SCHWIK
BLIP
HE KNEW YOU WERE WATCHING. HE *LET* HIMSELF BE SEEN.
HIS EYES... THEY'RE JUST LIKE...

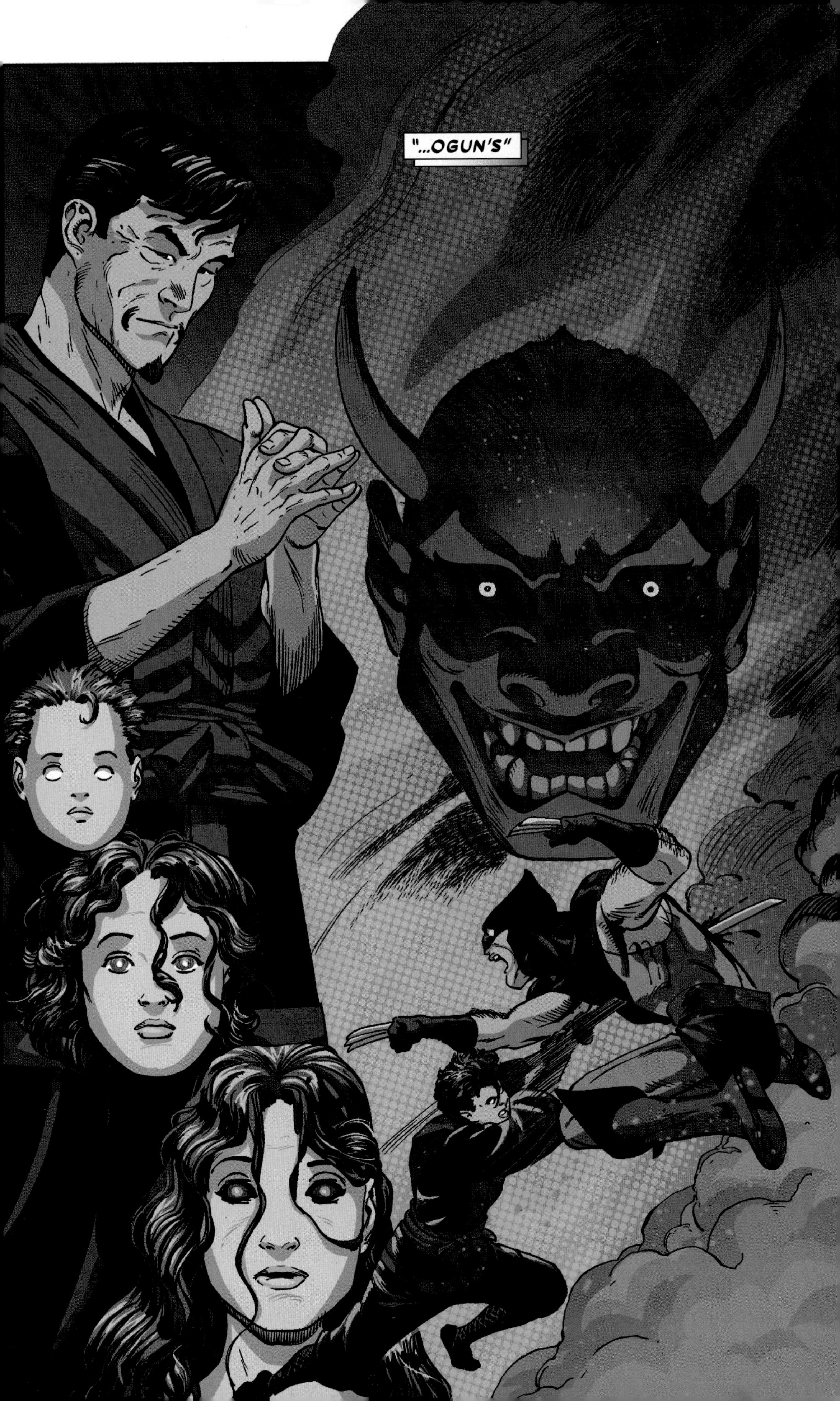
"...OGUN'S"

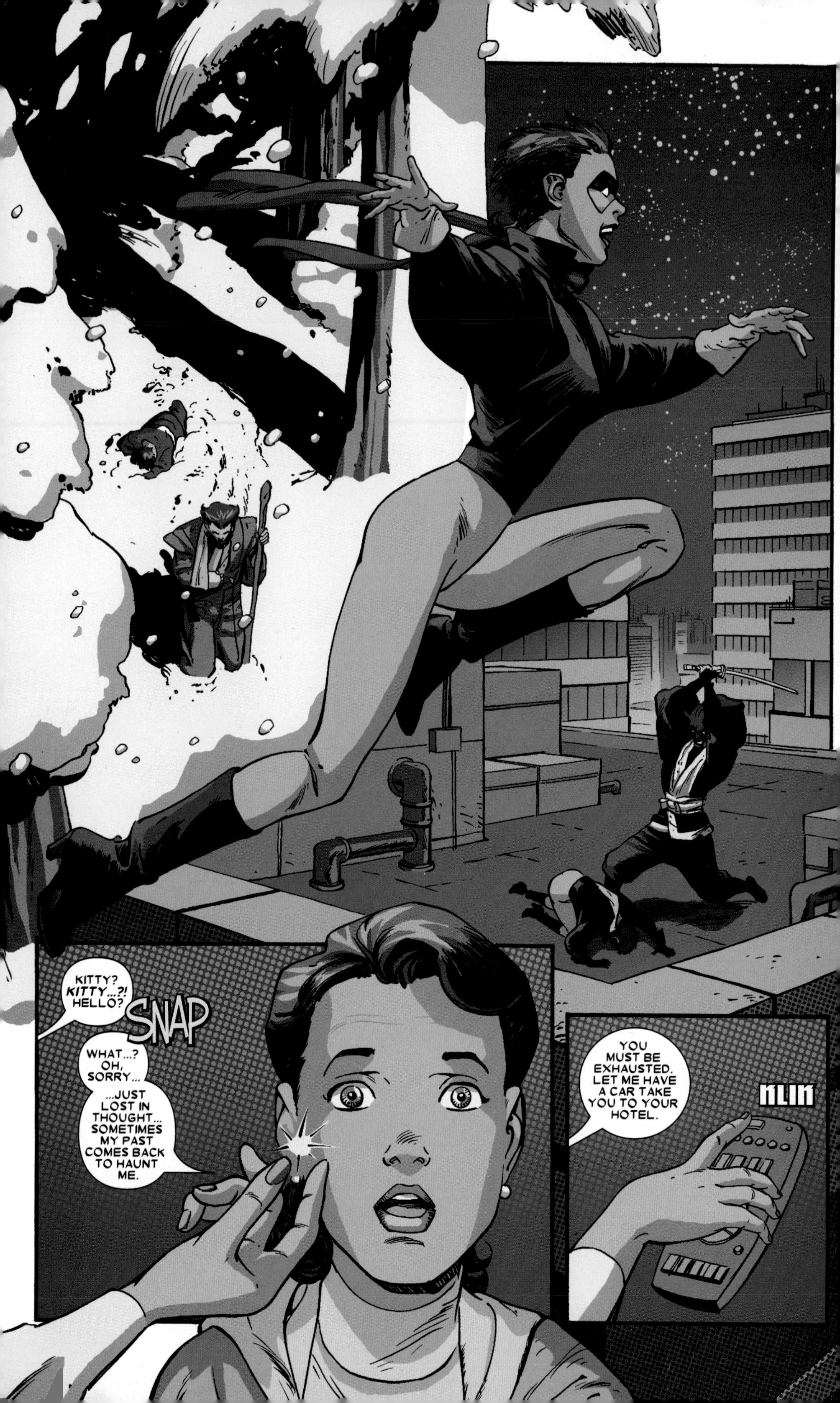

KITTY? KITTY...?! HELLO?
SNAP
WHAT...? OH, SORRY...
...JUST LOST IN THOUGHT... SOMETIMES MY PAST COMES BACK TO HAUNT ME.
YOU MUST BE EXHAUSTED. LET ME HAVE A CAR TAKE YOU TO YOUR HOTEL.
KLIK

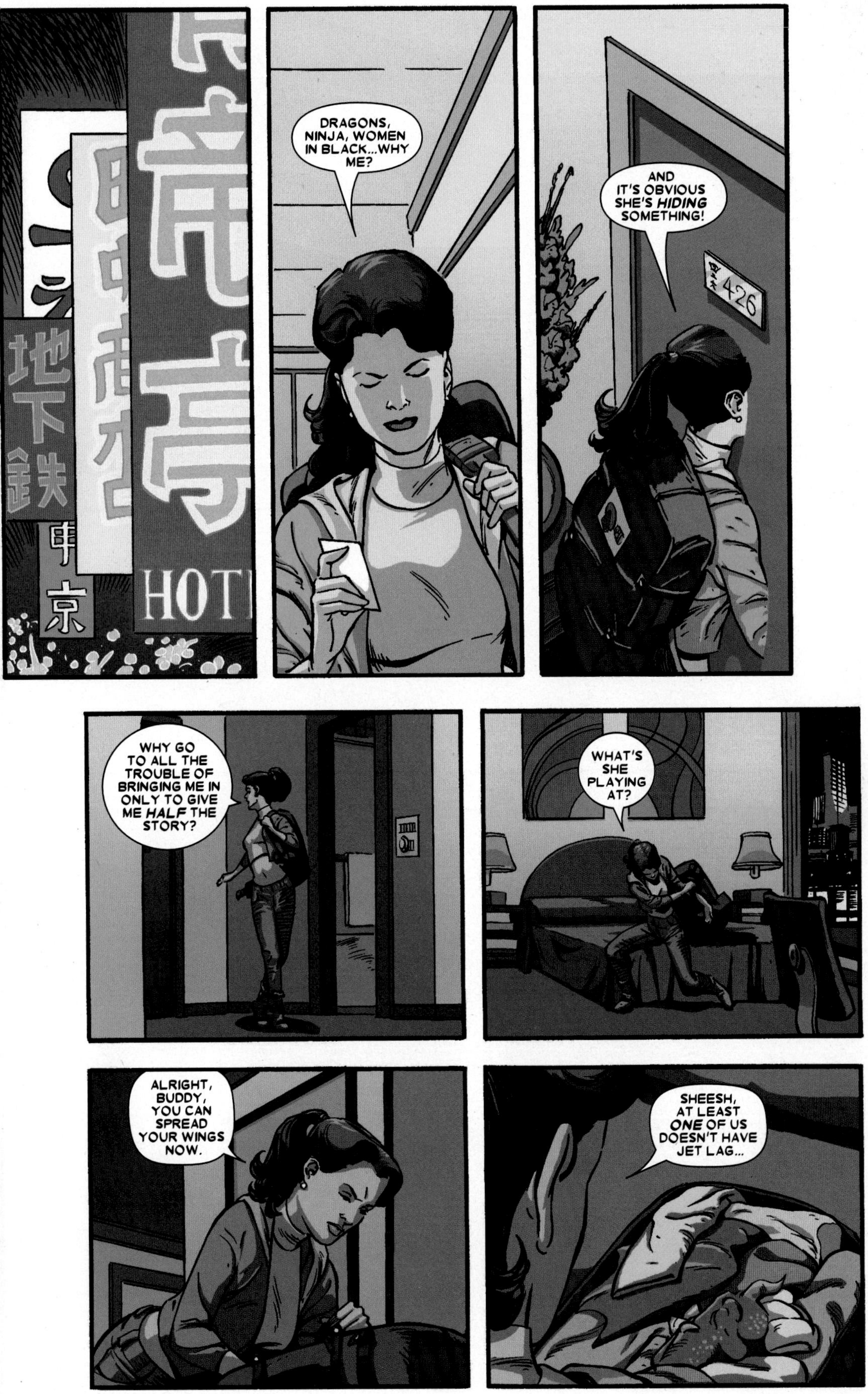
地下鉄
DRAGONS, NINJA, WOMEN IN BLACK...WHY ME?
AND IT'S OBVIOUS SHE'S *HIDING* SOMETHING!
426
WHY GO TO ALL THE TROUBLE OF BRINGING ME IN ONLY TO GIVE ME *HALF* THE STORY?
WHAT'S SHE PLAYING AT?
ALRIGHT, BUDDY, YOU CAN SPREAD YOUR WINGS NOW.
SHEESH, AT LEAST *ONE* OF US DOESN'T HAVE JET LAG...

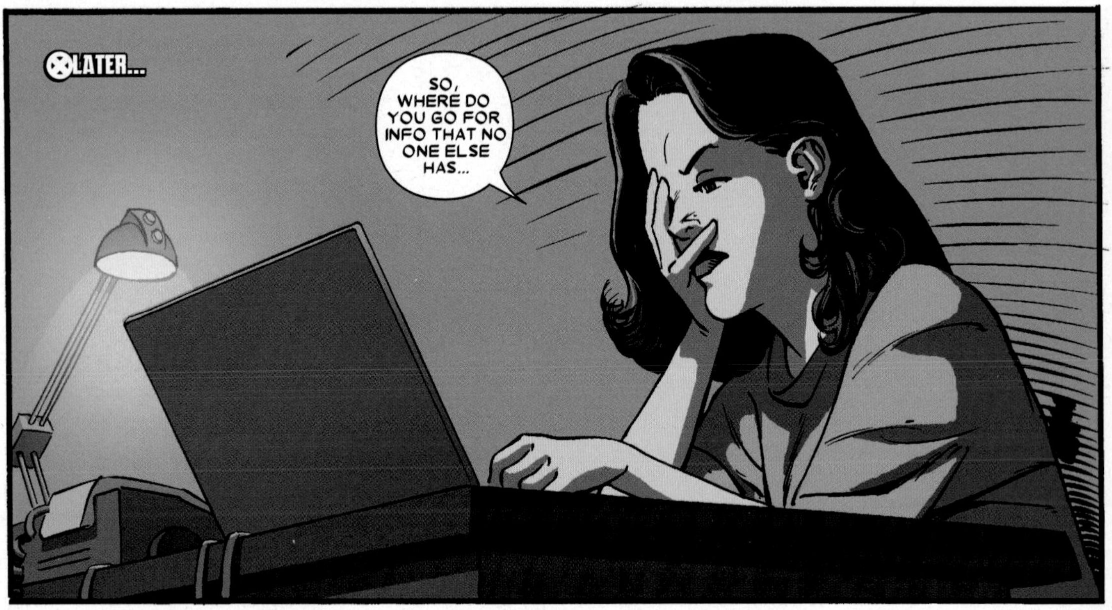
LATER...
SO, WHERE DO YOU GO FOR INFO THAT NO ONE ELSE HAS...

To: snikt1@xaviers.com
From: nekochan@jmail.com
Subject: Path of Destiny?

Hey, Logan-

I'm here in Tokyo. Made it in one piece. It's been a while since I've been back and it's a little weird, to be honest. The memories are hard to keep down. I wish you were here but understand you wanting to sit this one out having just gotten back. If I get the time, I'll try and head down to Kyoto to see Amiko and this Mana woman.

Anyway, I came here looking for a dragon and now find myself mixed up with ninja. Long story, I'll explain later…Given your "history" with The Hand, I was wondering if you ever heard anything about a splinter group called the Path of Destiny? Seems they've got the green dragon now. Any info would help. Thanks!

I'm gonna give Yukio a call, too. Maybe she knows something.

Love ya,
Kitty

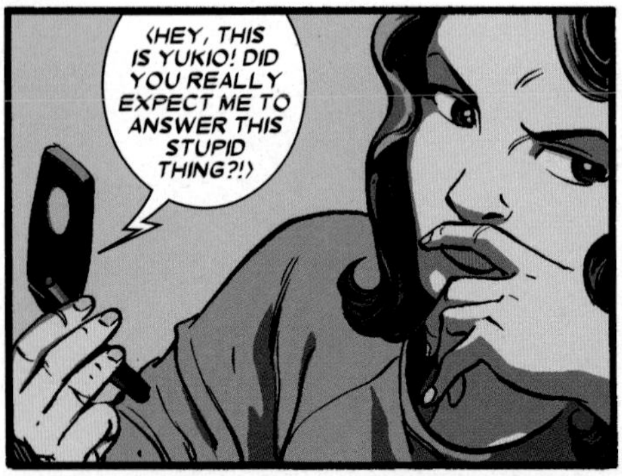
‹HEY, THIS IS YUKIO! DID YOU REALLY EXPECT ME TO ANSWER THIS STUPID THING?!›

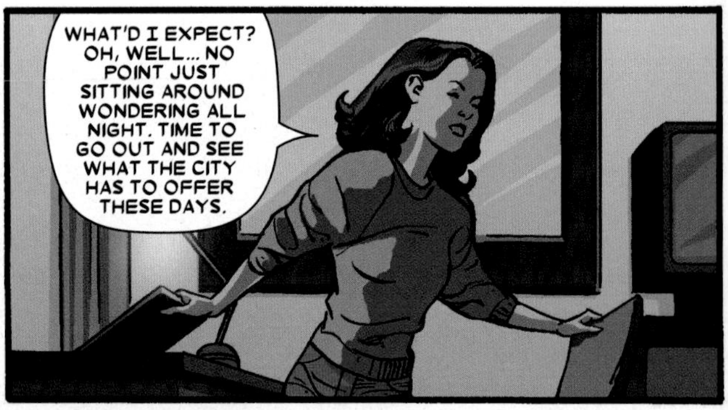
WHAT'D I EXPECT? OH, WELL... NO POINT JUST SITTING AROUND WONDERING ALL NIGHT. TIME TO GO OUT AND SEE WHAT THE CITY HAS TO OFFER THESE DAYS.

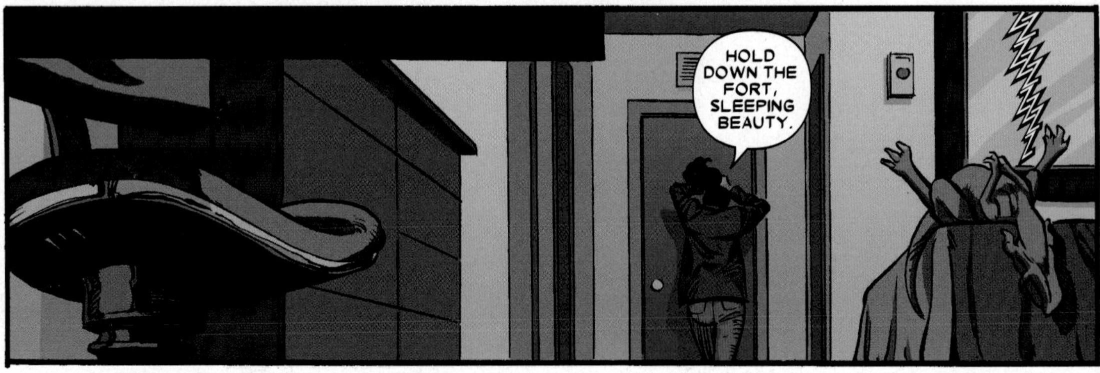
HOLD DOWN THE FORT, SLEEPING BEAUTY.

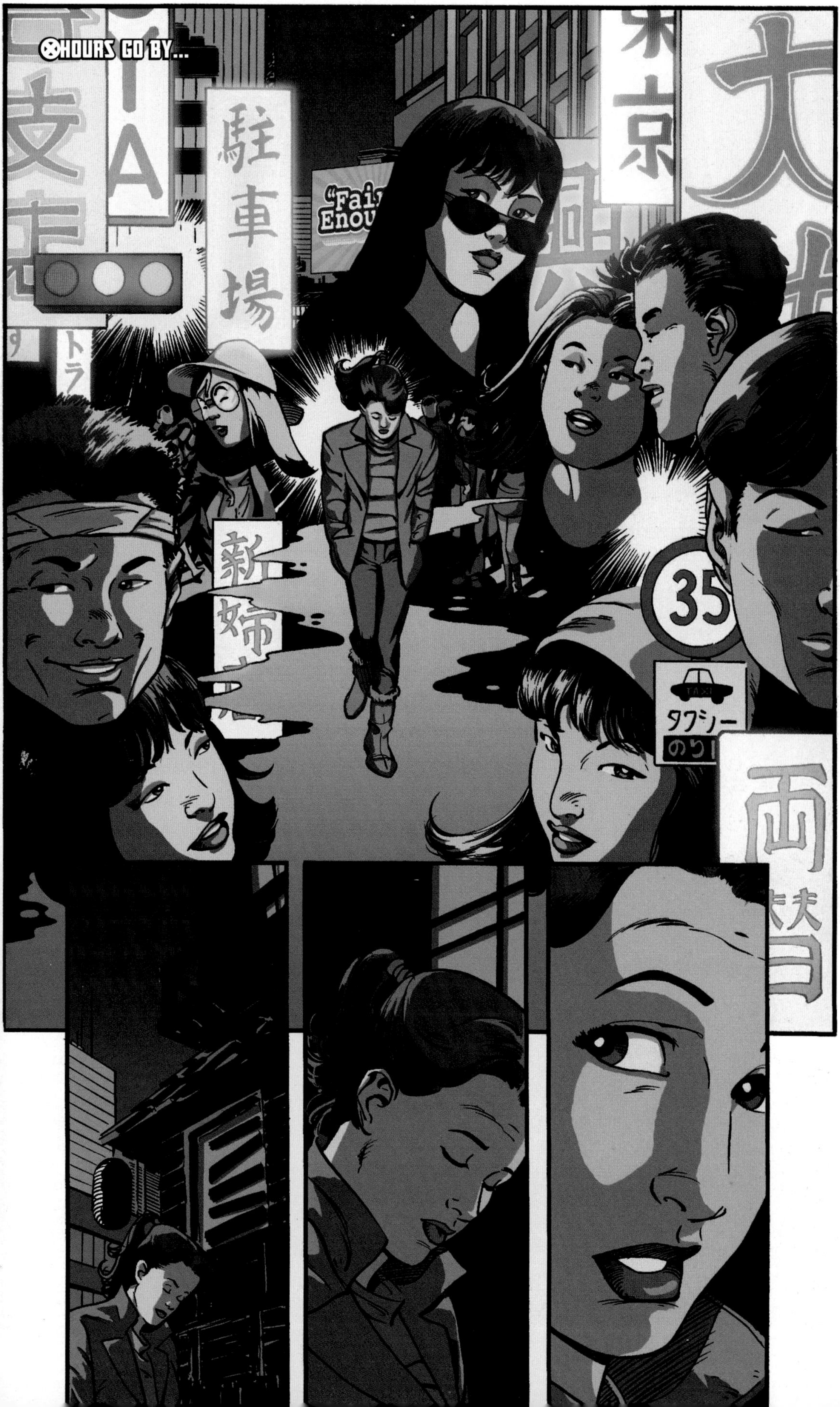
HOURS GO BY...
駐車場
東京
35
TAXI
タクシー

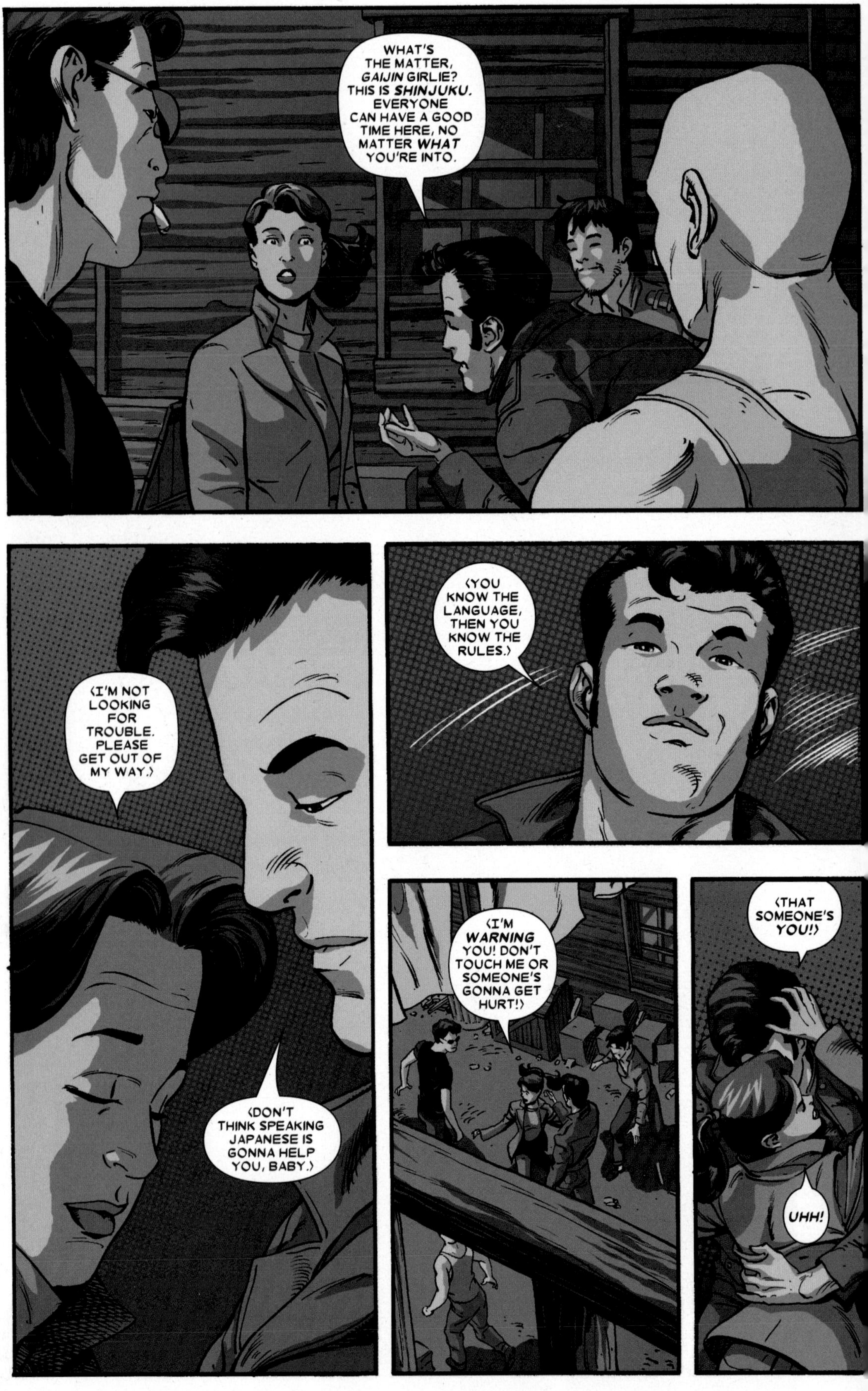
WHAT'S THE MATTER, GAIJIN GIRLIE? THIS IS SHINJUKU. EVERYONE CAN HAVE A GOOD TIME HERE, NO MATTER WHAT YOU'RE INTO.
‹I'M NOT LOOKING FOR TROUBLE. PLEASE GET OUT OF MY WAY.›
‹DON'T THINK SPEAKING JAPANESE IS GONNA HELP YOU, BABY.›
‹YOU KNOW THE LANGUAGE, THEN YOU KNOW THE RULES.›
‹I'M WARNING YOU! DON'T TOUCH ME OR SOMEONE'S GONNA GET HURT!›
‹THAT SOMEONE'S YOU!›
UHH!

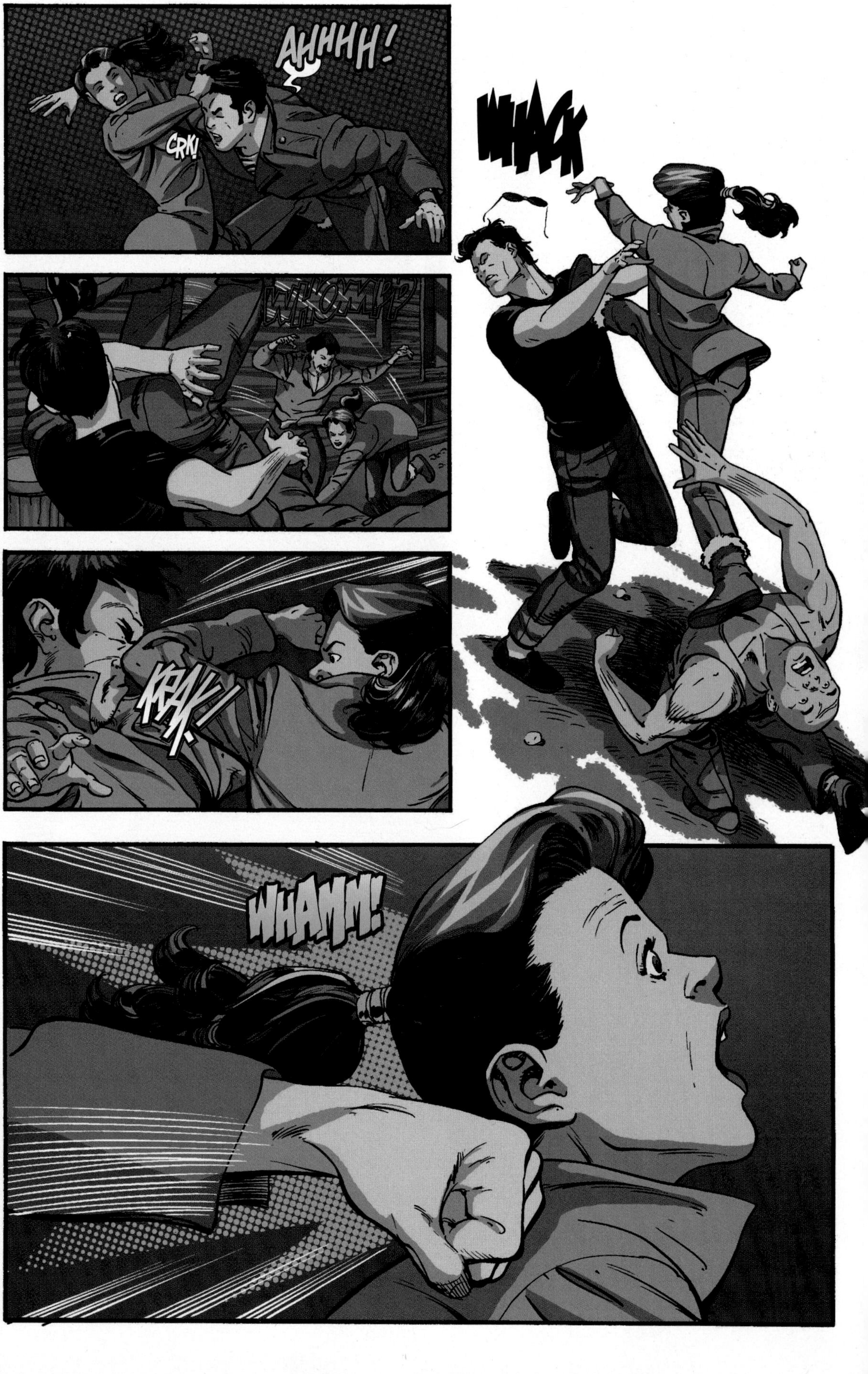
AHHHH!
CRK!
WHOMPP
KRAK!
WHACK
WHAMM!

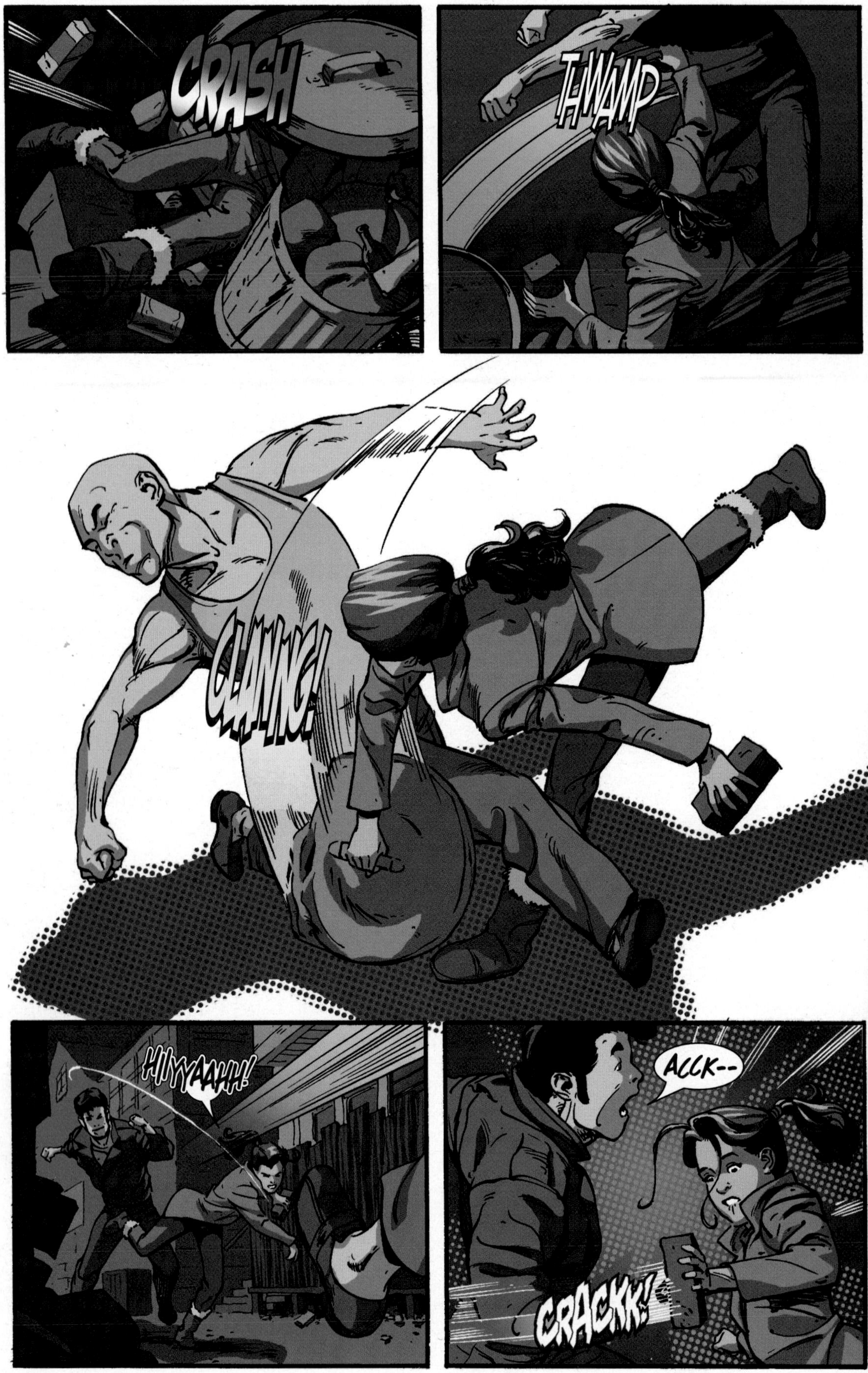
CRASH
THWAMP
CLANNG!
HIIYYAAHH!
ACCK--
CRACKK!

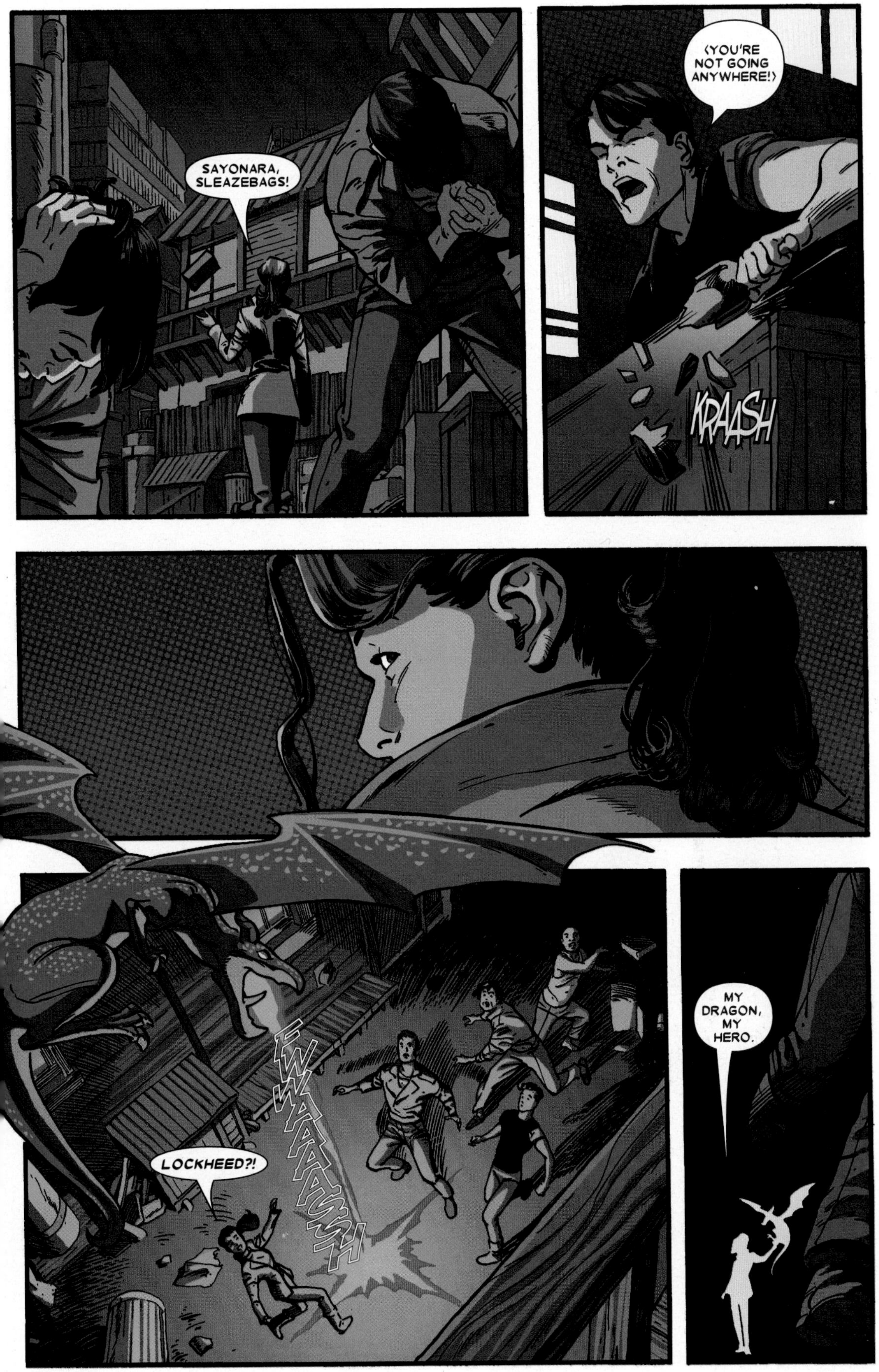
SAYONARA, SLEAZEBAGS!
‹YOU'RE NOT GOING ANYWHERE!›
KRAASH
LOCKHEED?!
FWAAAAASH
MY DRAGON, MY HERO.

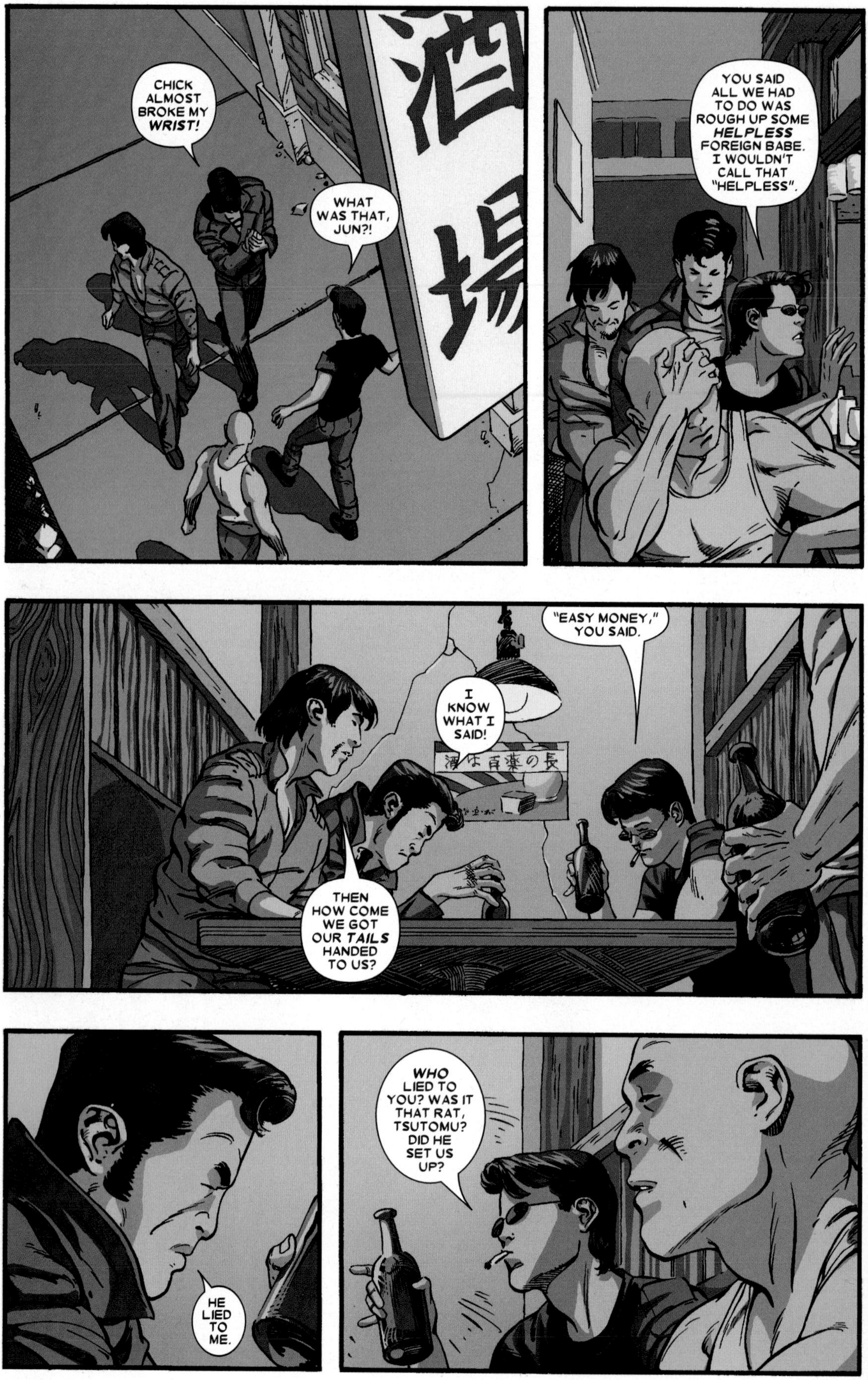
CHICK ALMOST BROKE MY *WRIST!*
WHAT WAS THAT, JUN?!
YOU SAID ALL WE HAD TO DO WAS ROUGH UP SOME ***HELPLESS*** FOREIGN BABE. I WOULDN'T CALL THAT "HELPLESS".
"EASY MONEY," YOU SAID.
I KNOW WHAT I SAID!
酒は百薬の長
THEN HOW COME WE GOT OUR *TAILS* HANDED TO US?
HE LIED TO ME.
WHO LIED TO YOU? WAS IT THAT RAT, TSUTOMU? DID HE SET US UP?

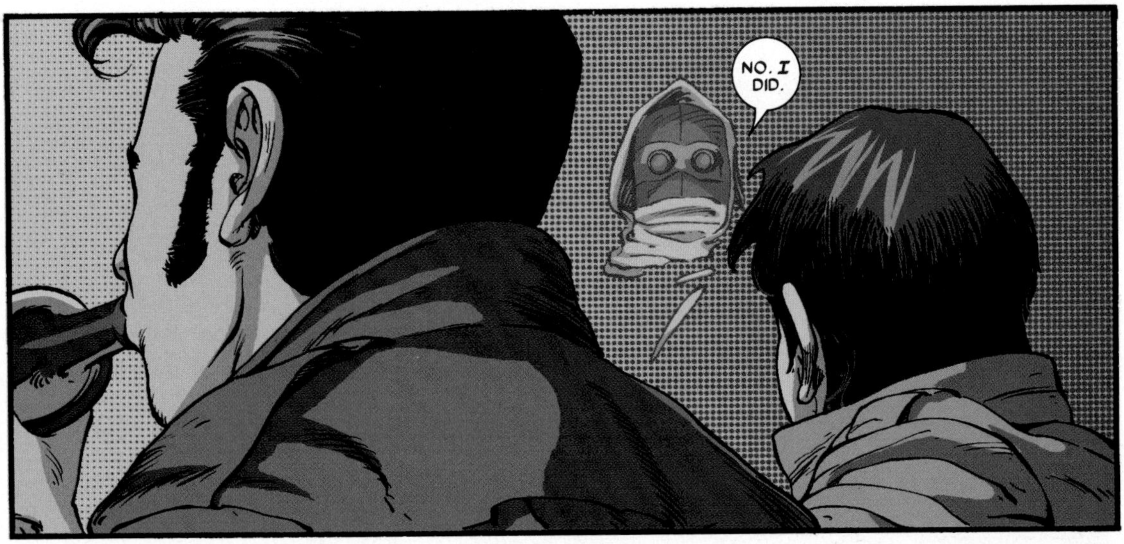
NO. I DID.

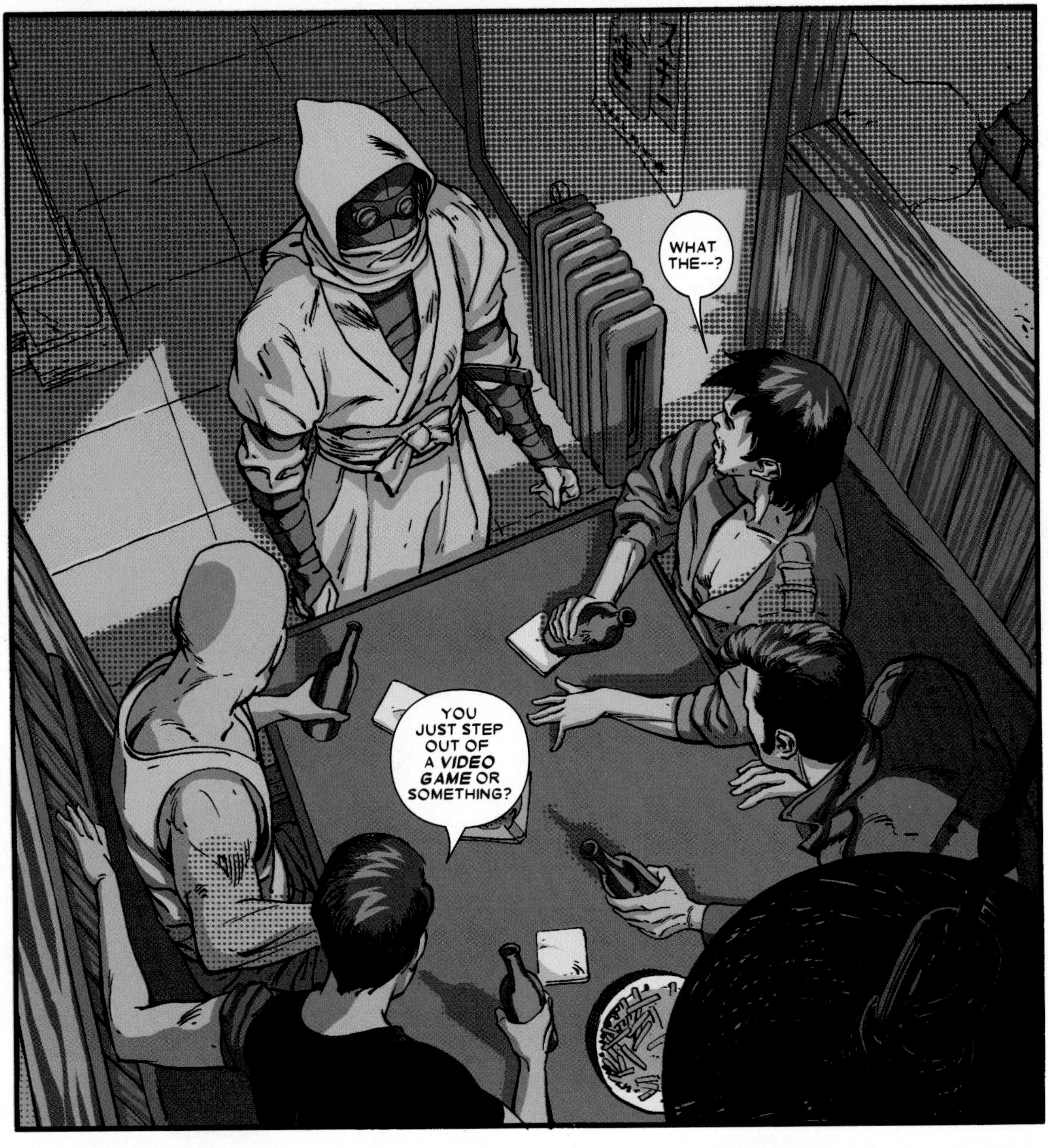
WHAT THE--?
YOU JUST STEP OUT OF A VIDEO GAME OR SOMETHING?

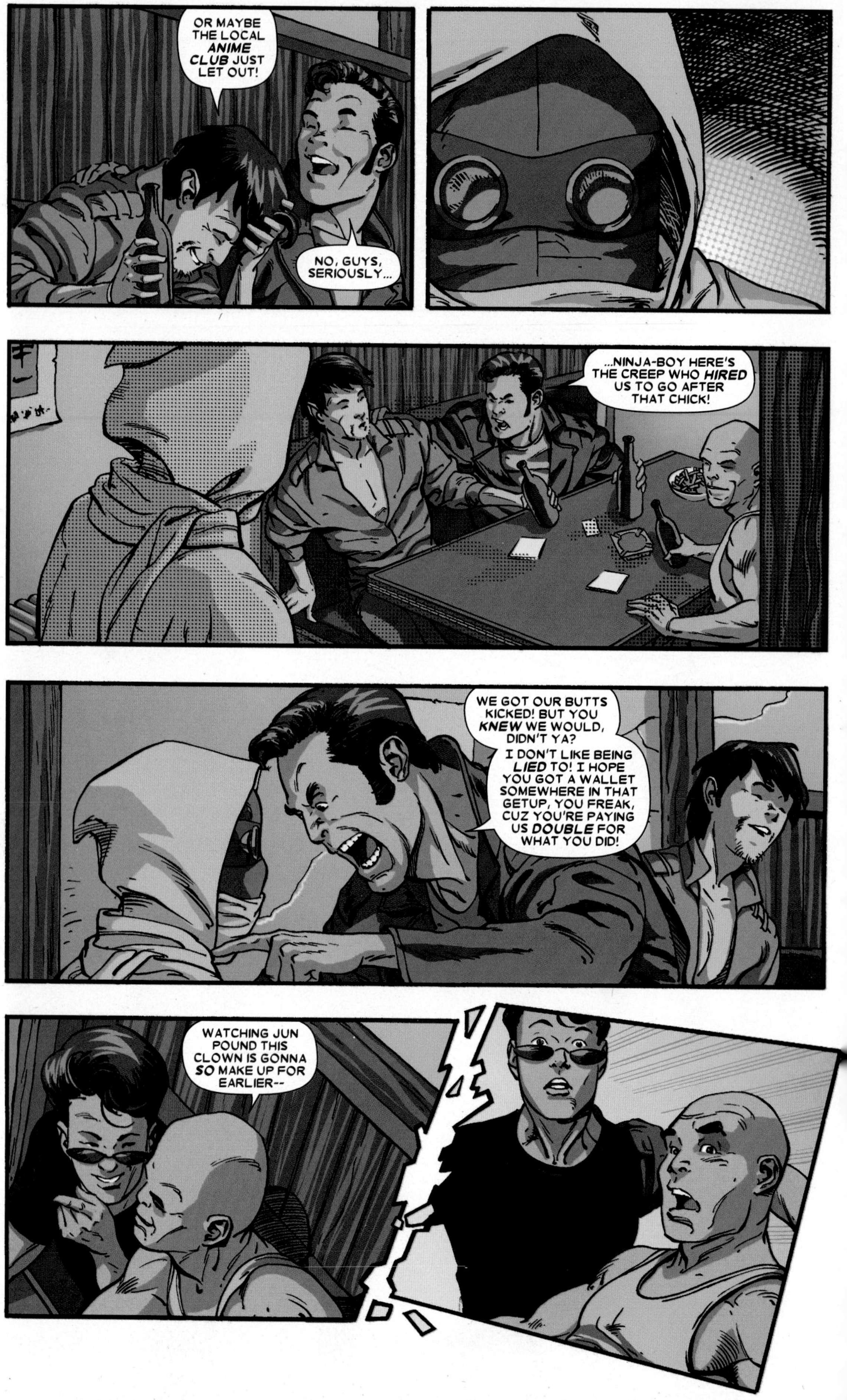
OR MAYBE THE LOCAL ANIME CLUB JUST LET OUT!
NO, GUYS, SERIOUSLY...
...NINJA-BOY HERE'S THE CREEP WHO HIRED US TO GO AFTER THAT CHICK!
WE GOT OUR BUTTS KICKED! BUT YOU KNEW WE WOULD, DIDN'T YA?
I DON'T LIKE BEING LIED TO! I HOPE YOU GOT A WALLET SOMEWHERE IN THAT GETUP, YOU FREAK, CUZ YOU'RE PAYING US DOUBLE FOR WHAT YOU DID!
WATCHING JUN POUND THIS CLOWN IS GONNA SO MAKE UP FOR EARLIER--

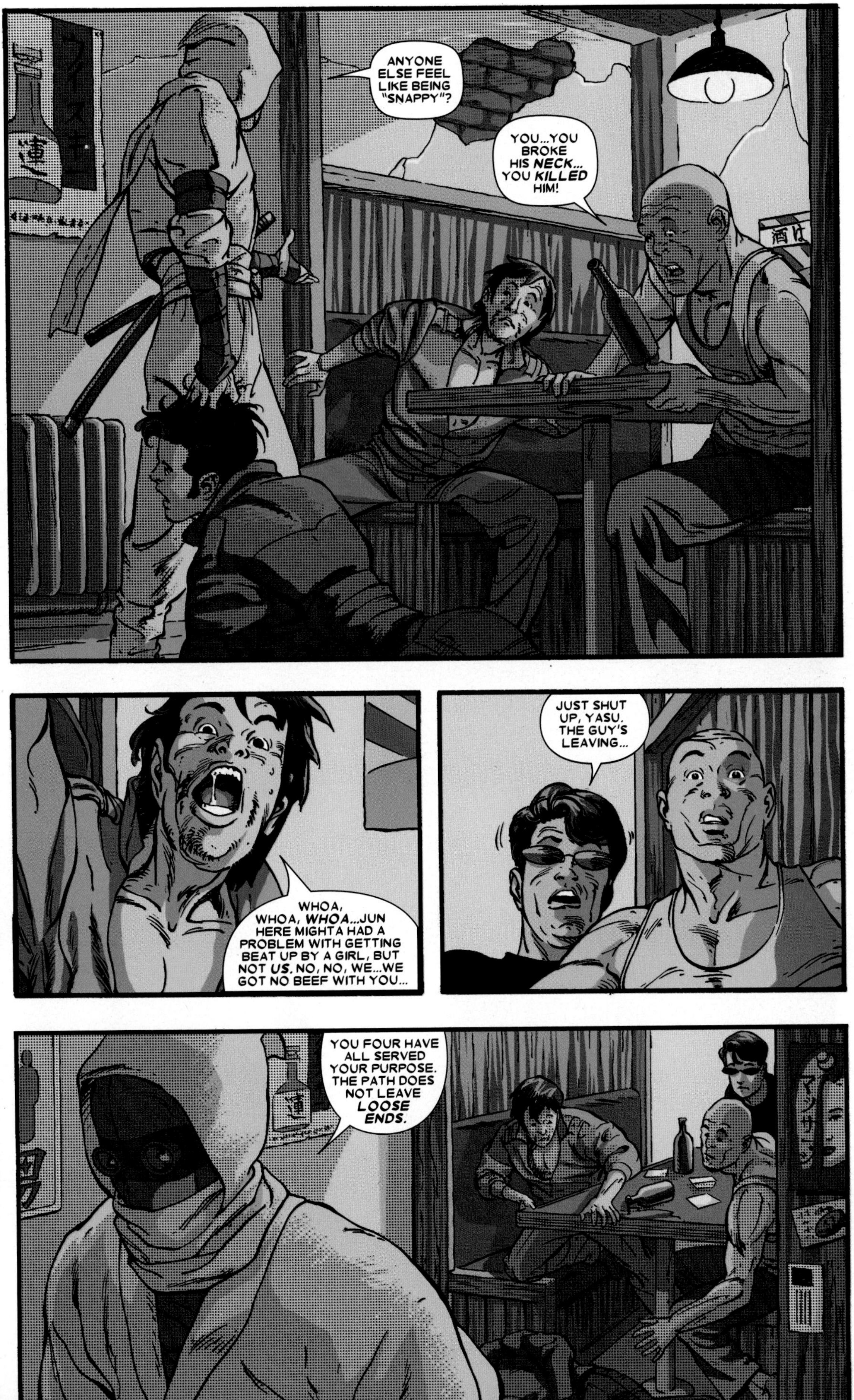

ANYONE ELSE FEEL LIKE BEING "SNAPPY"?
YOU...YOU BROKE HIS NECK... YOU KILLED HIM!
WHOA, WHOA, WHOA...JUN HERE MIGHTA HAD A PROBLEM WITH GETTING BEAT UP BY A GIRL, BUT NOT US. NO, NO, WE...WE GOT NO BEEF WITH YOU...
JUST SHUT UP, YASU. THE GUY'S LEAVING...
YOU FOUR HAVE ALL SERVED YOUR PURPOSE. THE PATH DOES NOT LEAVE LOOSE ENDS.

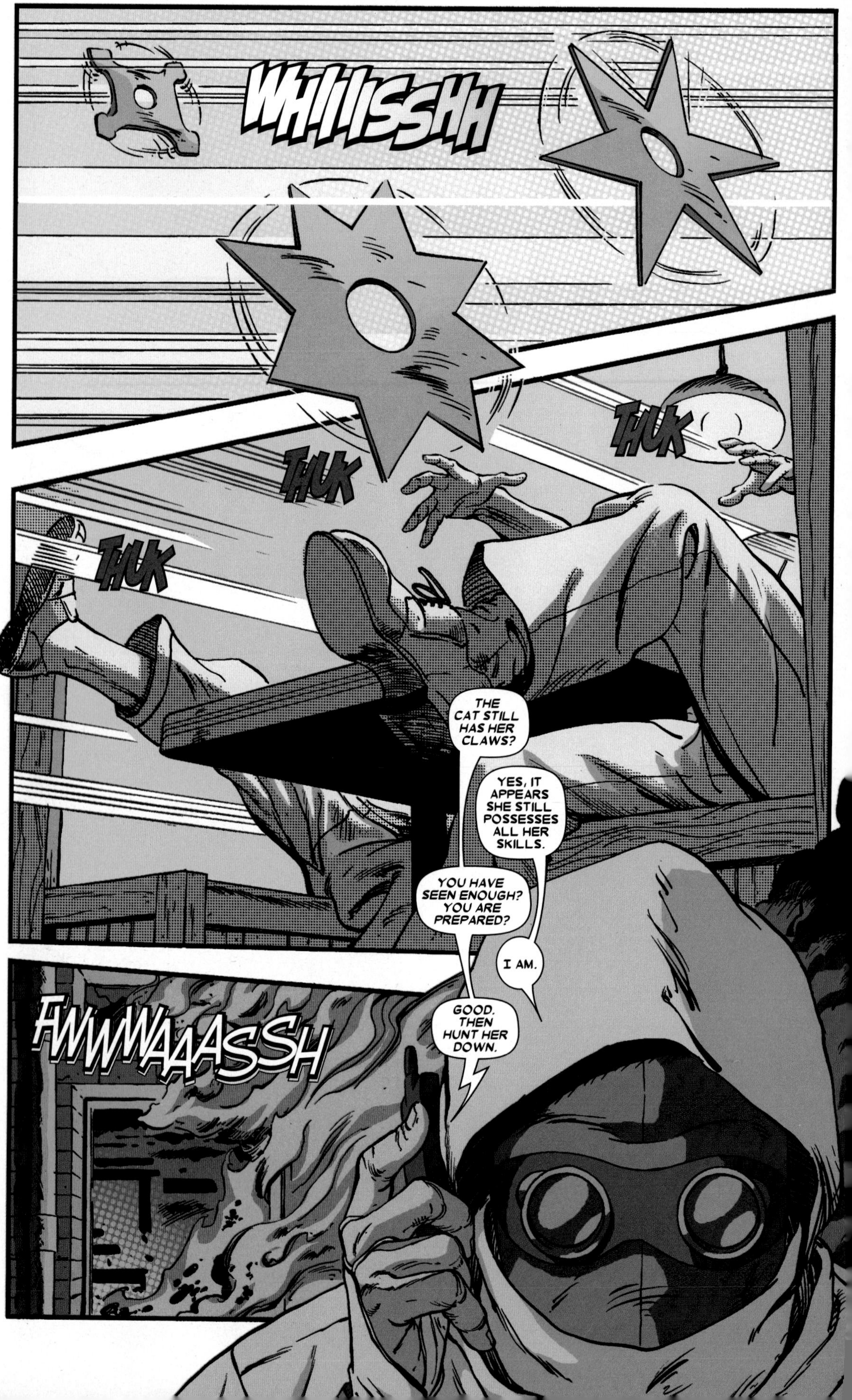
WHIIISSHH
THUK
THUK
THUK
THE CAT STILL HAS HER CLAWS?
YES, IT APPEARS SHE STILL POSSESSES ALL HER SKILLS.
YOU HAVE SEEN ENOUGH? YOU ARE PREPARED?
I AM.
GOOD. THEN HUNT HER DOWN.
FWWWAAASSH

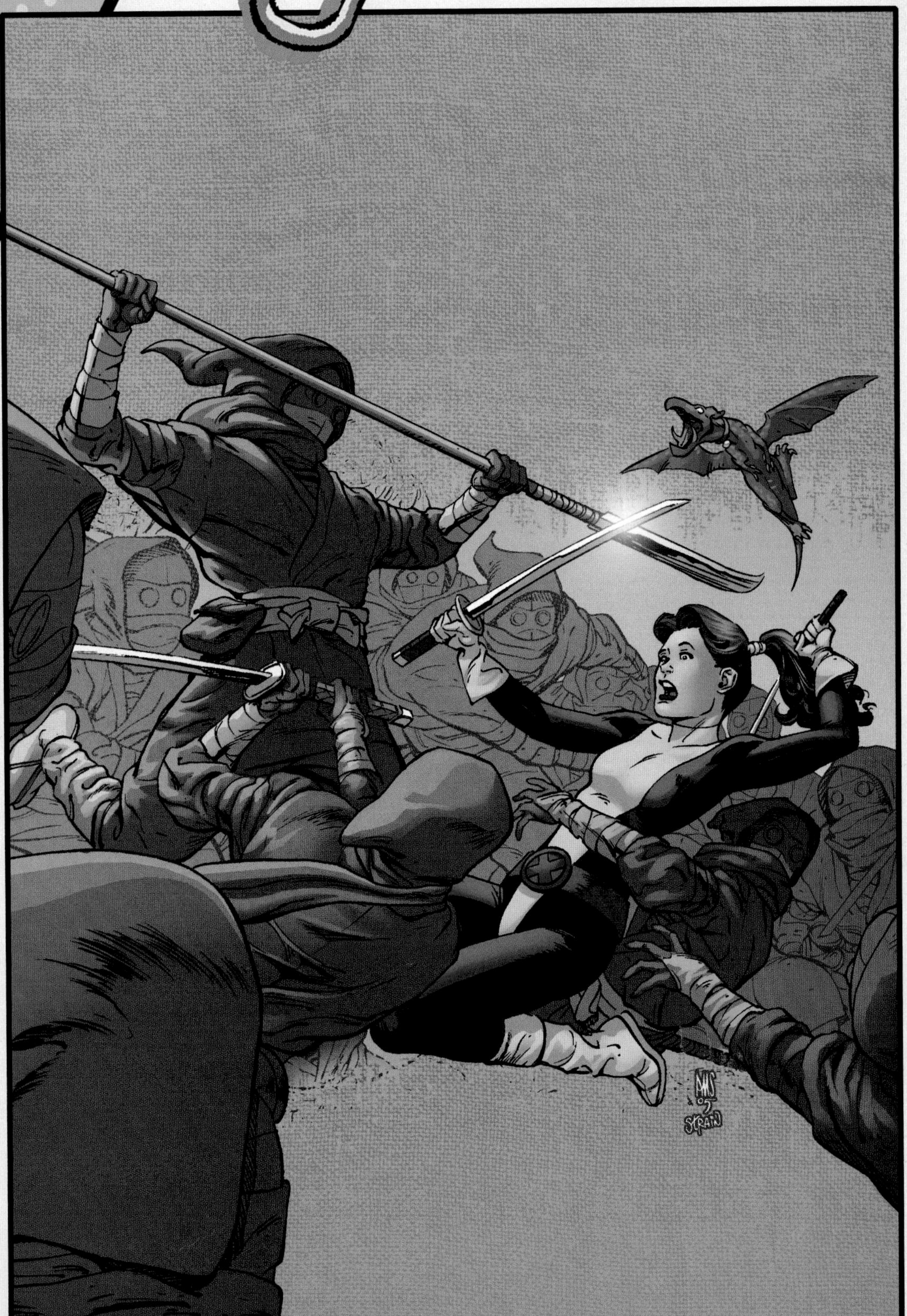

< #2 >

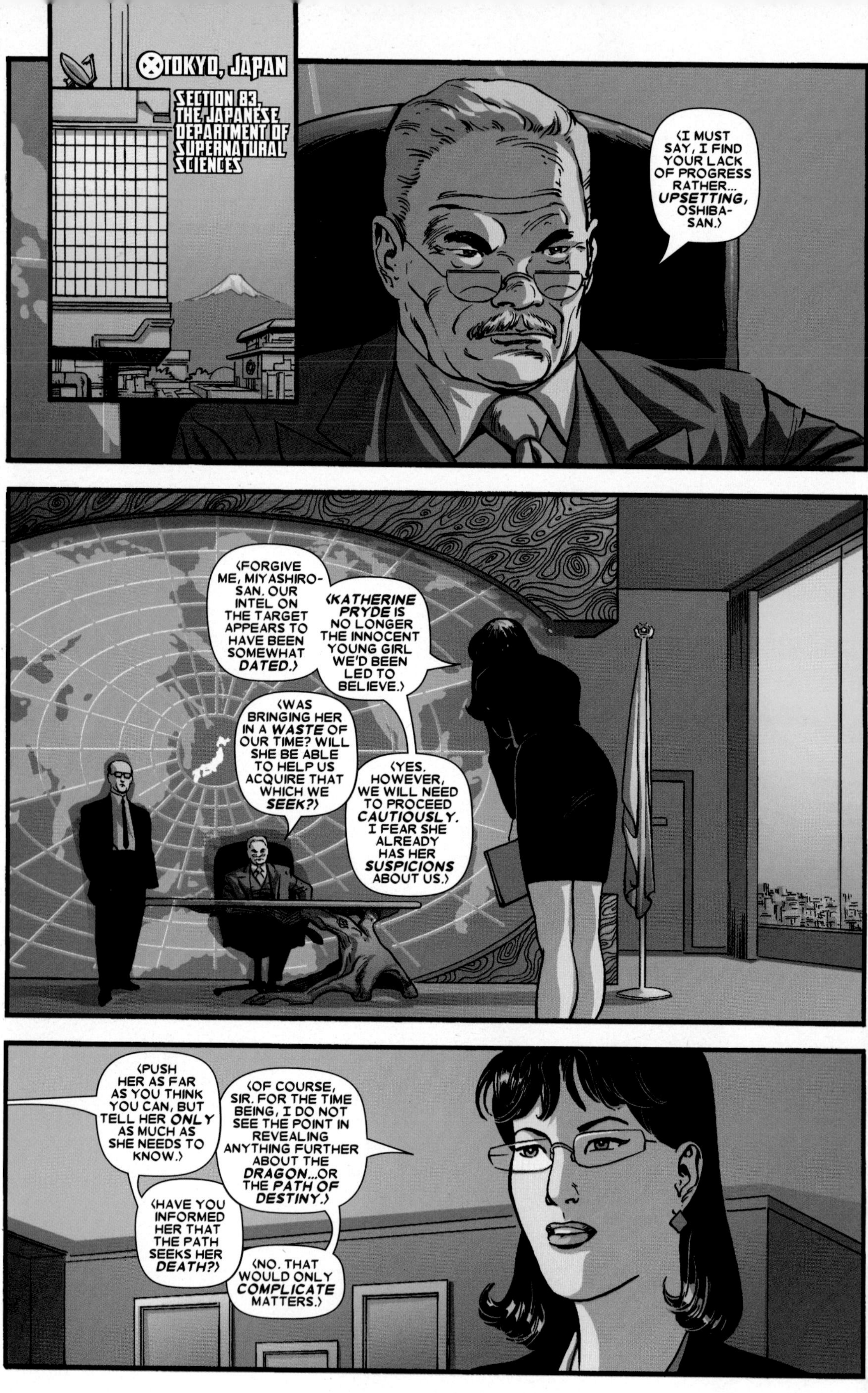
TOKYO, JAPAN
SECTION 83, THE JAPANESE DEPARTMENT OF SUPERNATURAL SCIENCES
‹I MUST SAY, I FIND YOUR LACK OF PROGRESS RATHER... UPSETTING, OSHIBA-SAN.›
‹FORGIVE ME, MIYASHIRO-SAN. OUR INTEL ON THE TARGET APPEARS TO HAVE BEEN SOMEWHAT DATED.›
‹KATHERINE PRYDE IS NO LONGER THE INNOCENT YOUNG GIRL WE'D BEEN LED TO BELIEVE.›
‹WAS BRINGING HER IN A WASTE OF OUR TIME? WILL SHE BE ABLE TO HELP US ACQUIRE THAT WHICH WE SEEK?›
‹YES. HOWEVER, WE WILL NEED TO PROCEED CAUTIOUSLY. I FEAR SHE ALREADY HAS HER SUSPICIONS ABOUT US.›
‹PUSH HER AS FAR AS YOU THINK YOU CAN, BUT TELL HER ONLY AS MUCH AS SHE NEEDS TO KNOW.›
‹OF COURSE, SIR. FOR THE TIME BEING, I DO NOT SEE THE POINT IN REVEALING ANYTHING FURTHER ABOUT THE DRAGON...OR THE PATH OF DESTINY.›
‹HAVE YOU INFORMED HER THAT THE PATH SEEKS HER DEATH?›
‹NO. THAT WOULD ONLY COMPLICATE MATTERS.›

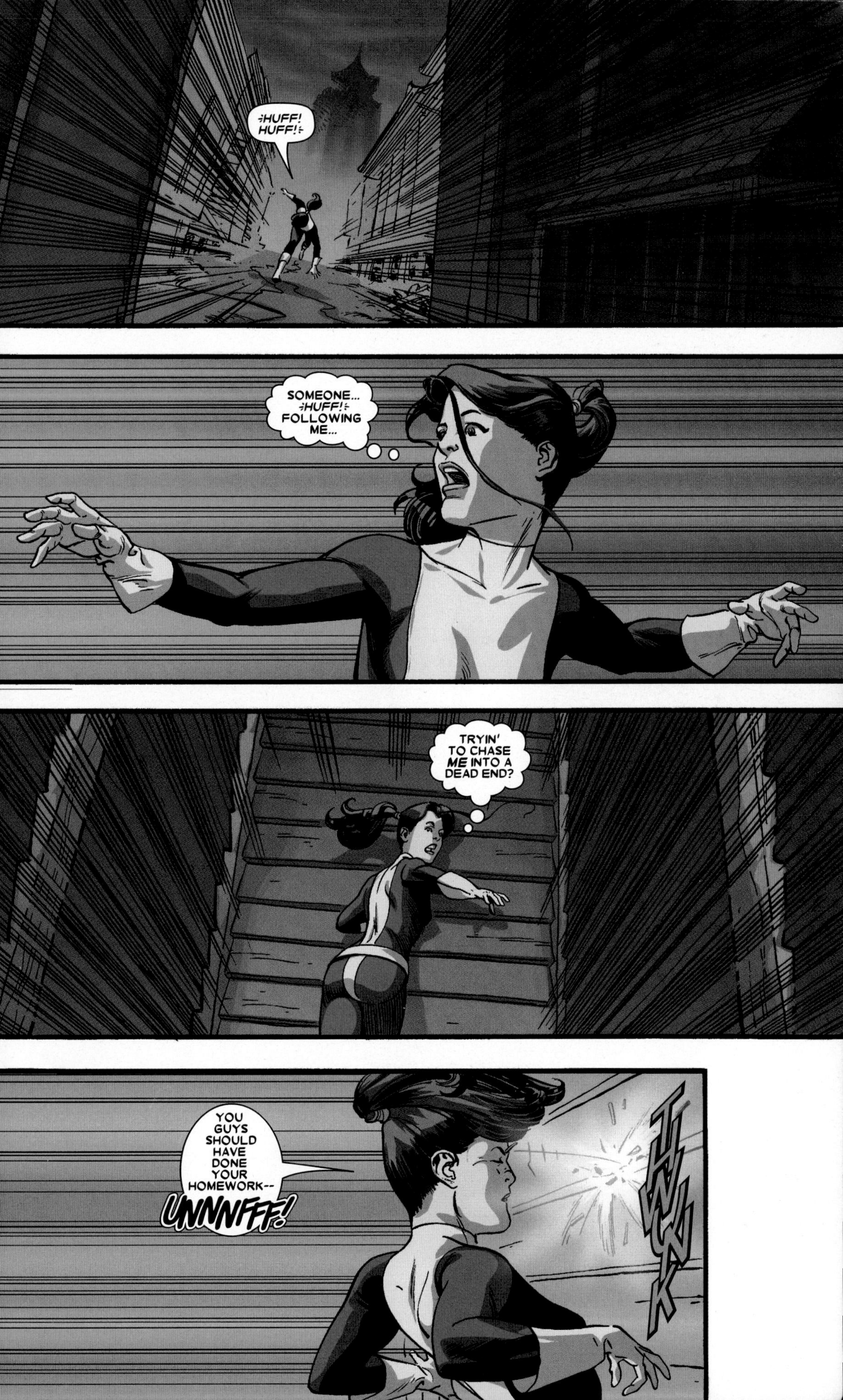

HUFF! HUFF!
SOMEONE... HUFF! FOLLOWING ME...
TRYIN' TO CHASE ME INTO A DEAD END?
YOU GUYS SHOULD HAVE DONE YOUR HOMEWORK-- UNNNFFF!
THUNK

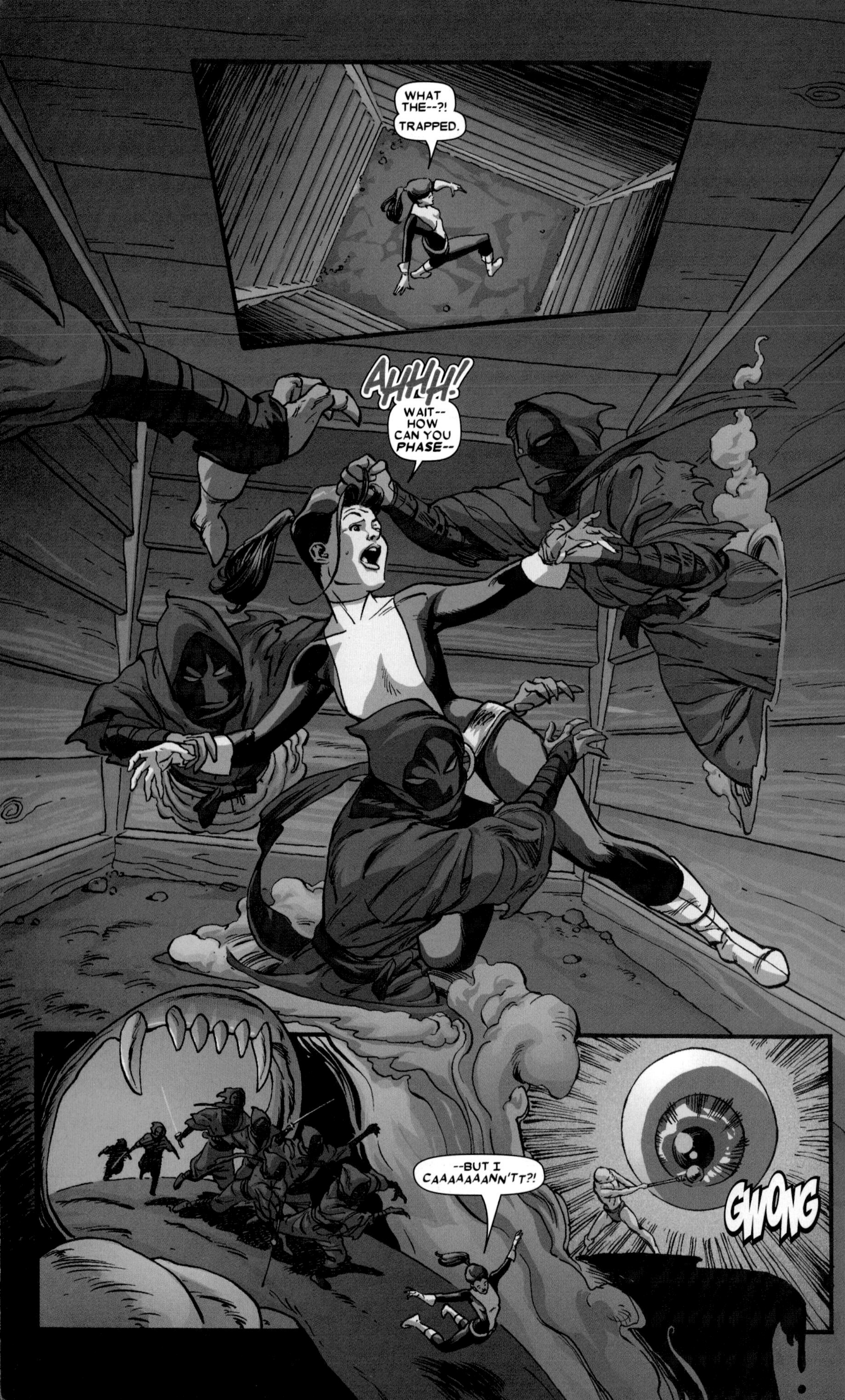
WHAT THE--?!
TRAPPED.
AHHH!
WAIT-- HOW CAN YOU PHASE--
--BUT I CAAAAAAANN'TT?!
GWONG

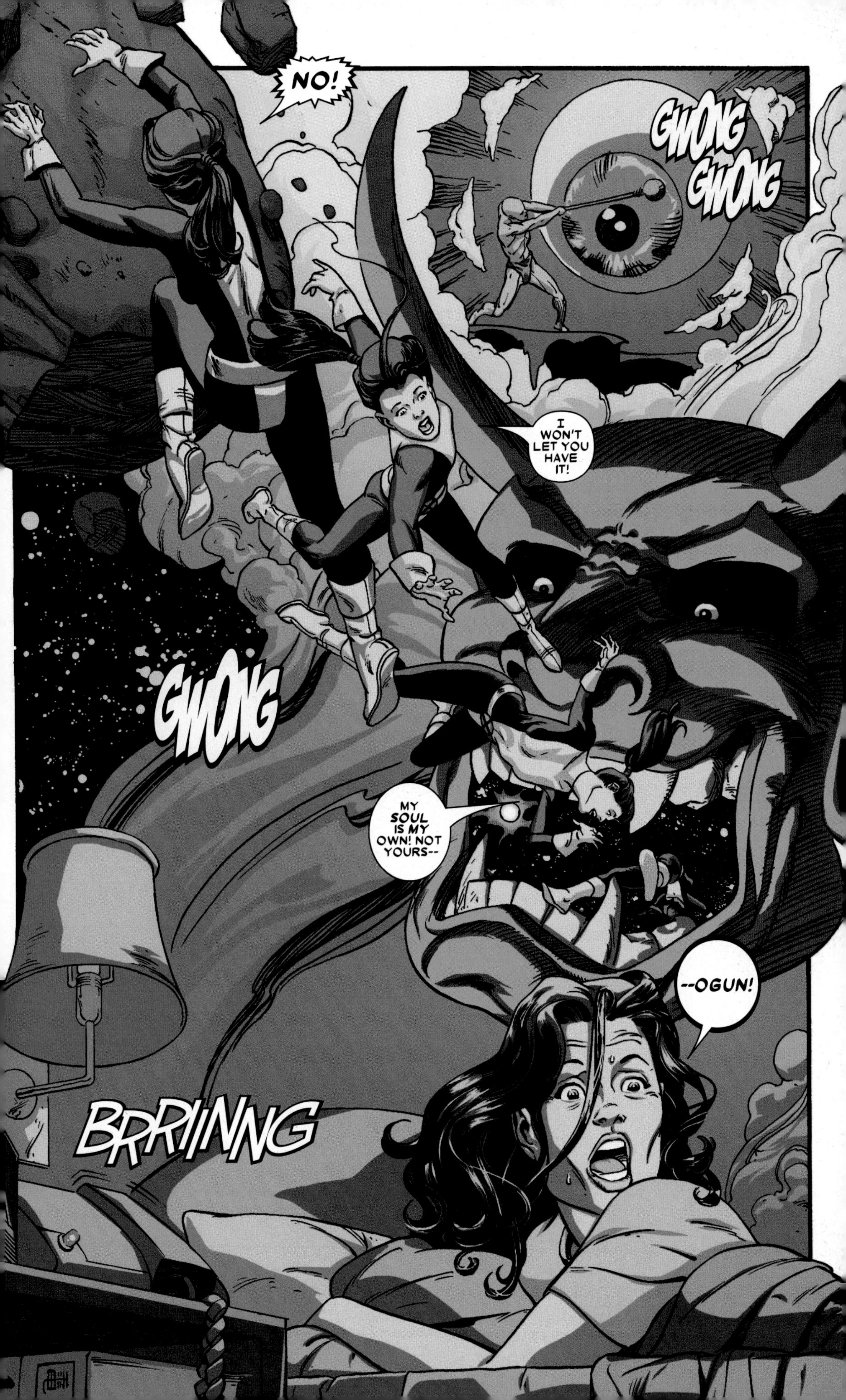
NO!
GWONG GWONG
I WON'T LET YOU HAVE IT!
GWONG
MY SOUL IS MY OWN! NOT YOURS--
--OGUN!
BRRIINNG

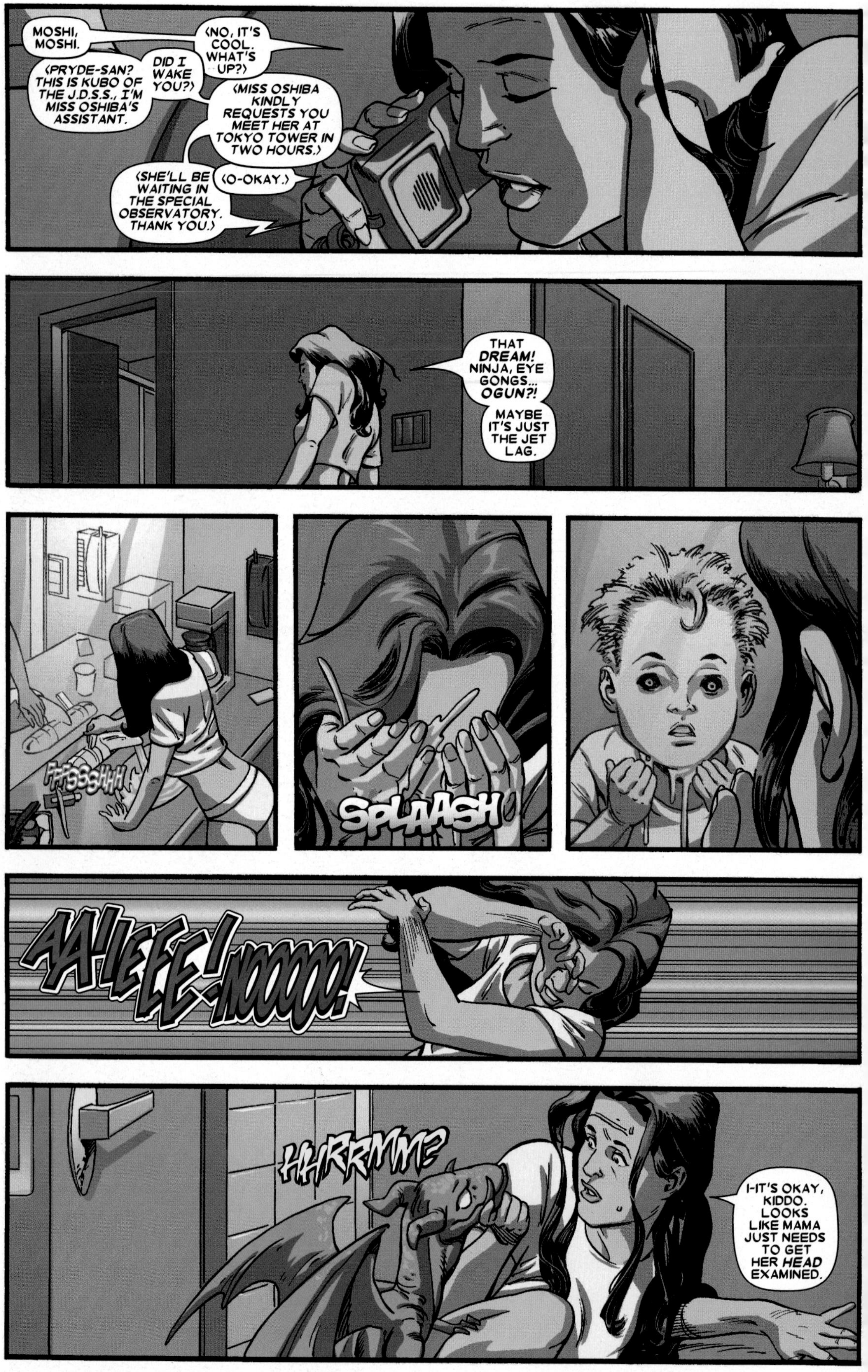

MOSHI, MOSHI.
‹PRYDE-SAN? THIS IS KUBO OF THE J.D.S.S., I'M MISS OSHIBA'S ASSISTANT.
DID I WAKE YOU?›
‹NO, IT'S COOL. WHAT'S UP?›
‹MISS OSHIBA KINDLY REQUESTS YOU MEET HER AT TOKYO TOWER IN TWO HOURS.›
‹O-OKAY.›
‹SHE'LL BE WAITING IN THE SPECIAL OBSERVATORY. THANK YOU.›
THAT DREAM! NINJA, EYE GONGS... OGUN?!
MAYBE IT'S JUST THE JET LAG.
PFFSSSHHH
SPLAASH
AAIIEEE! -NOOOOO!
HHRRMM?
I-IT'S OKAY, KIDDO. LOOKS LIKE MAMA JUST NEEDS TO GET HER HEAD EXAMINED.

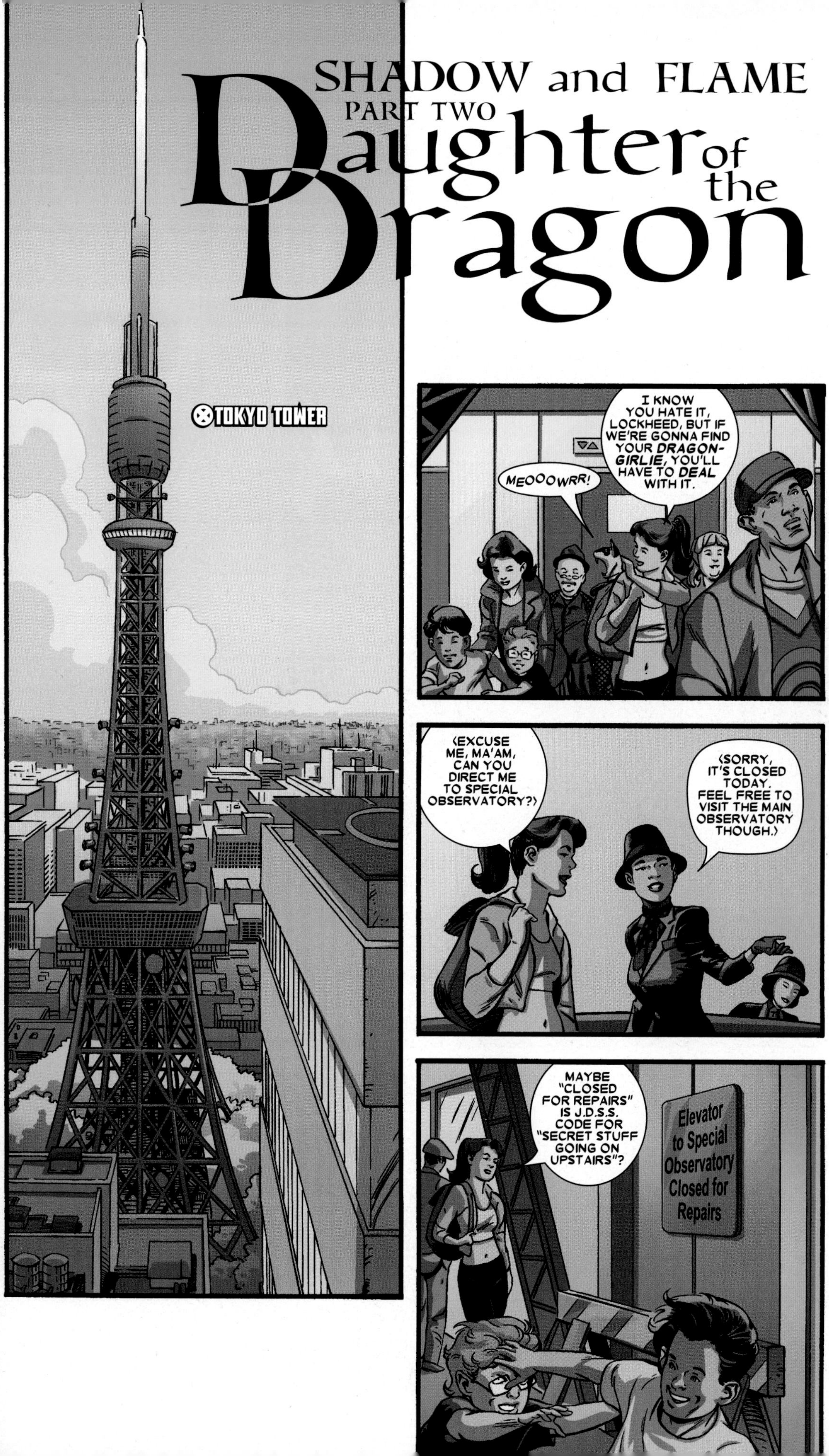
SHADOW and FLAME
PART TWO
Daughter of the Dragon
TOKYO TOWER
I KNOW YOU HATE IT, LOCKHEED, BUT IF WE'RE GONNA FIND YOUR DRAGON-GIRLIE, YOU'LL HAVE TO DEAL WITH IT.
MEOOOWRR!
‹EXCUSE ME, MA'AM, CAN YOU DIRECT ME TO SPECIAL OBSERVATORY?›
‹SORRY, IT'S CLOSED TODAY. FEEL FREE TO VISIT THE MAIN OBSERVATORY THOUGH.›
MAYBE "CLOSED FOR REPAIRS" IS J.D.S.S. CODE FOR "SECRET STUFF GOING ON UPSTAIRS"?
Elevator to Special Observatory Closed for Repairs

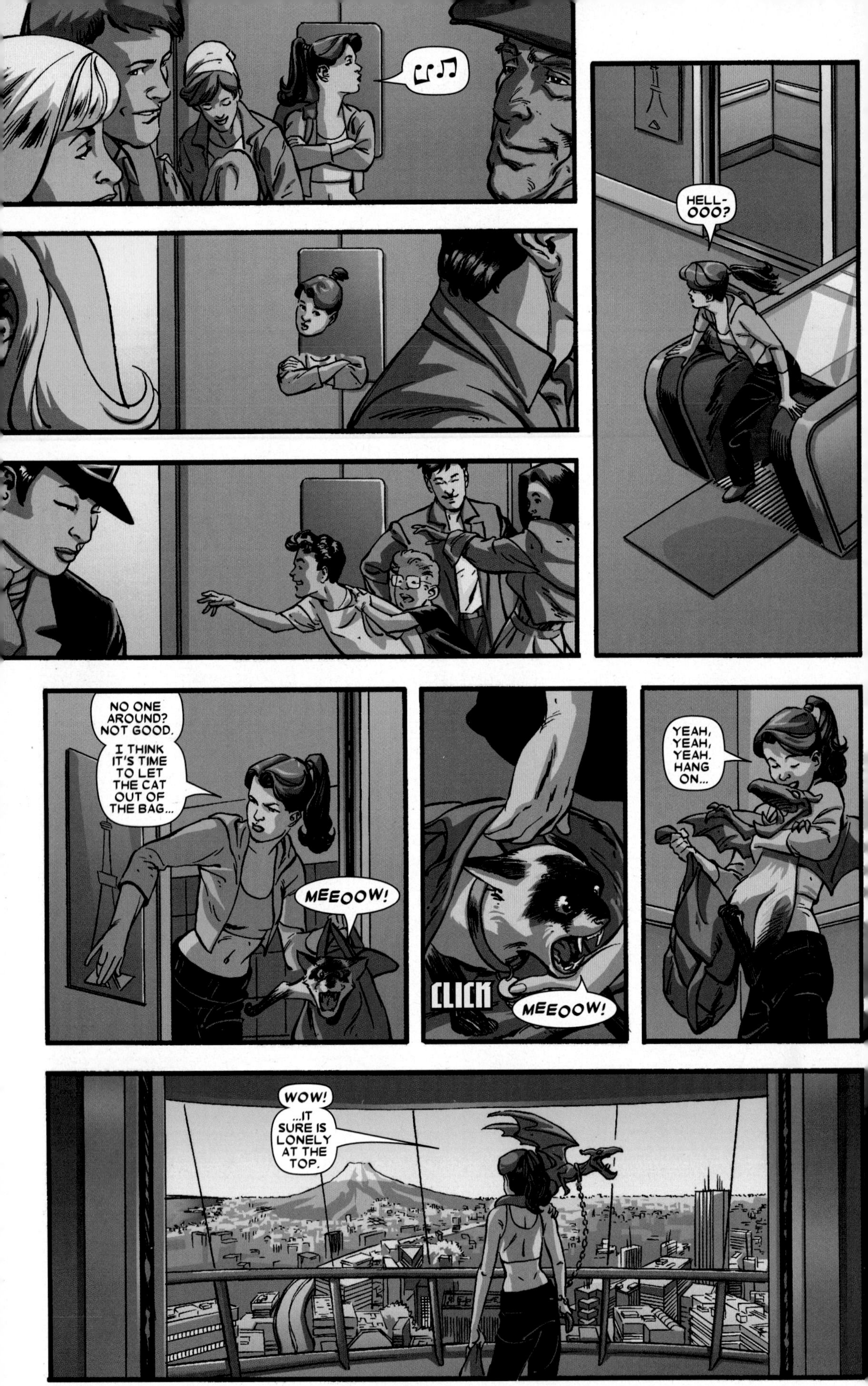
HELL-OOO?
NO ONE AROUND? NOT GOOD.
I THINK IT'S TIME TO LET THE CAT OUT OF THE BAG...
MEEOOW!
CLICK
MEEOOW!
YEAH, YEAH, YEAH. HANG ON...
WOW!
...IT SURE IS LONELY AT THE TOP.

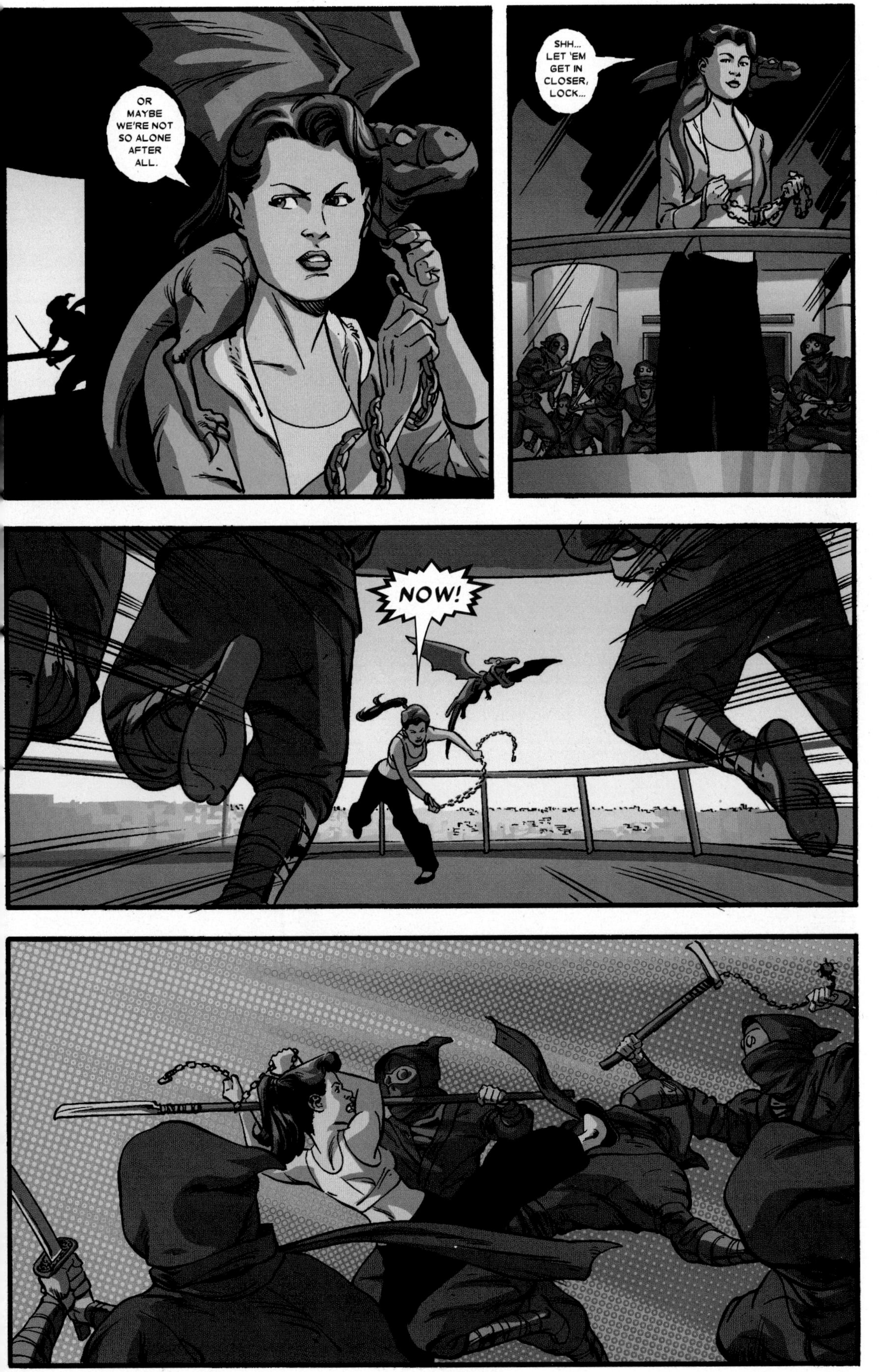
OR MAYBE WE'RE NOT SO ALONE AFTER ALL.
SHH... LET 'EM GET IN CLOSER, LOCK...
NOW!

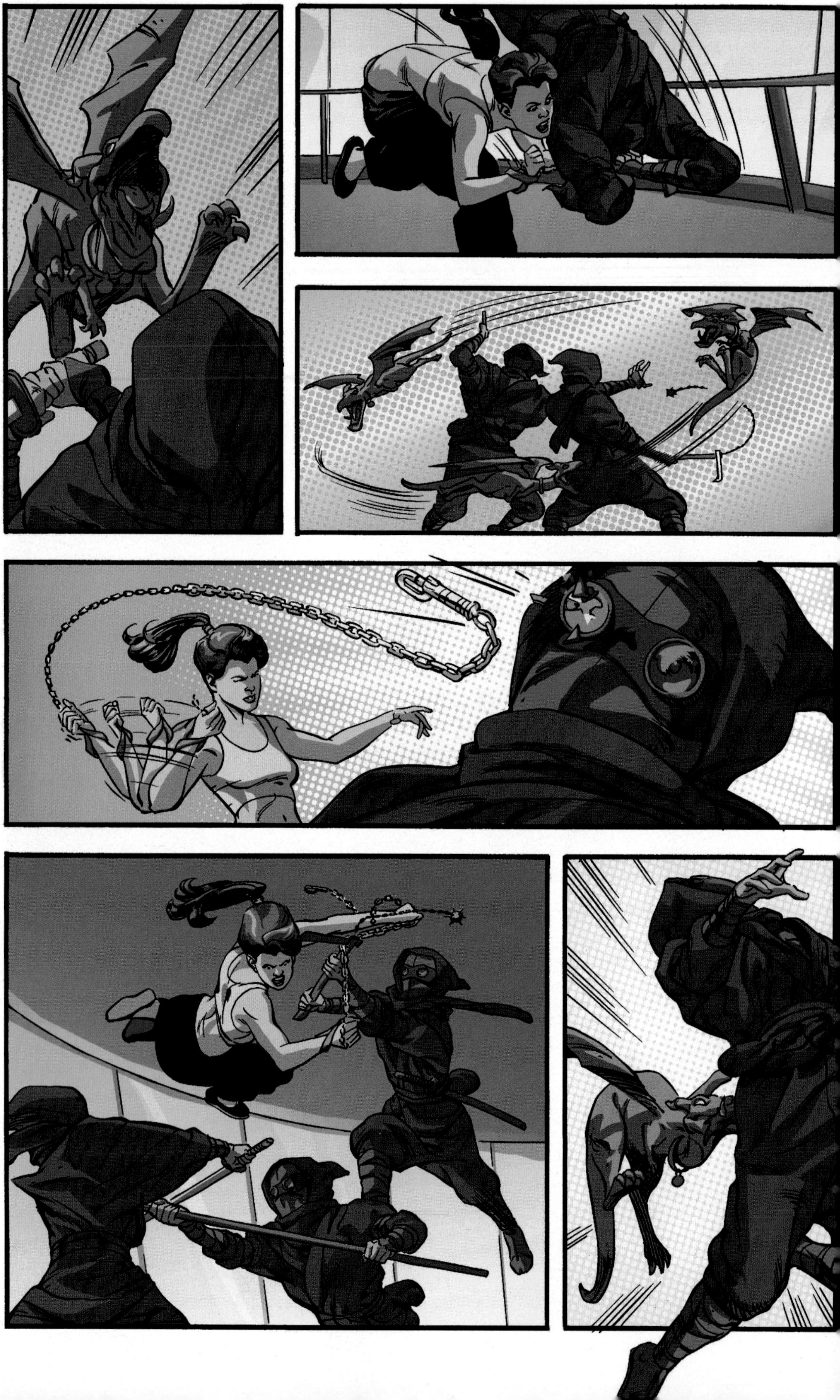

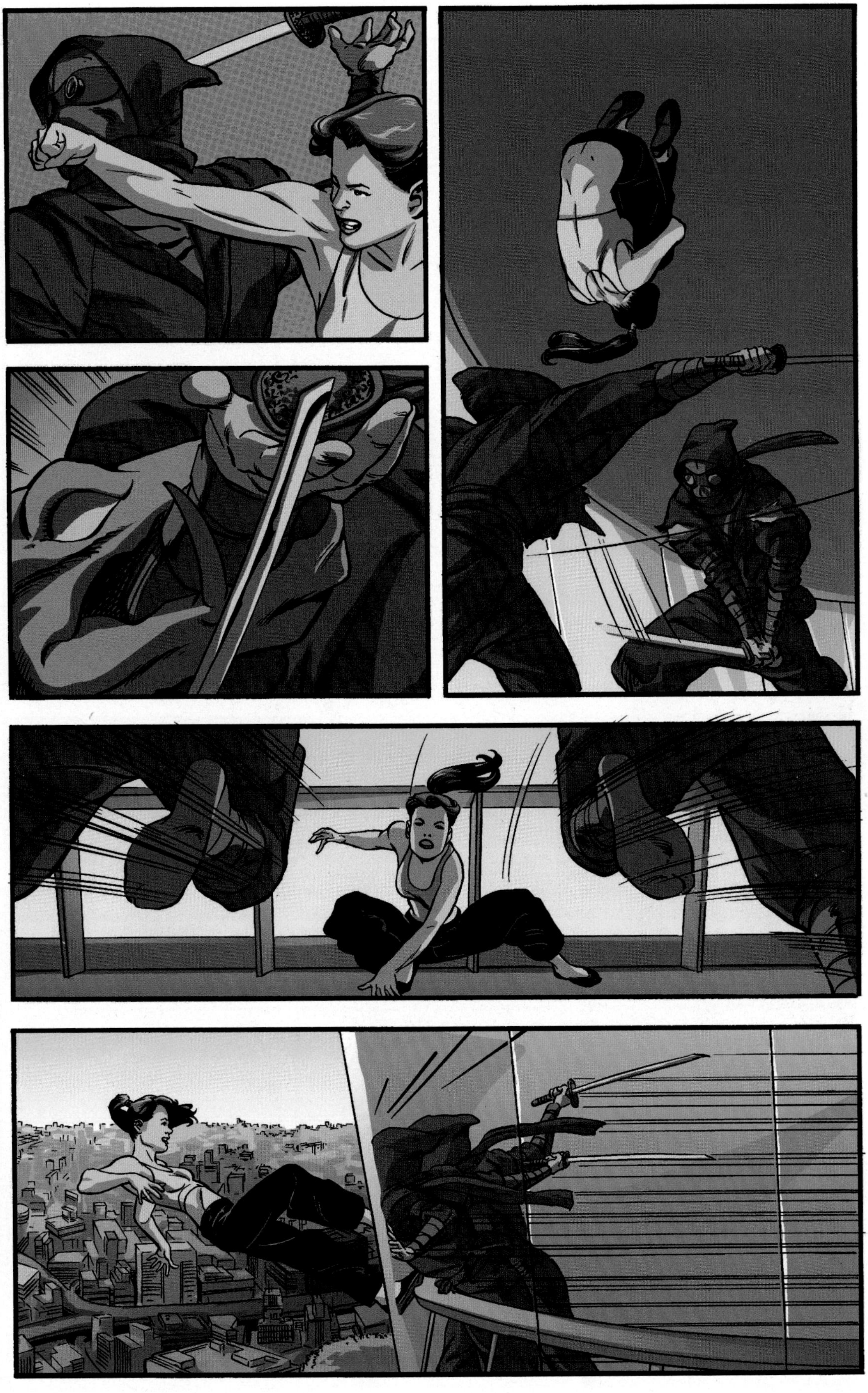

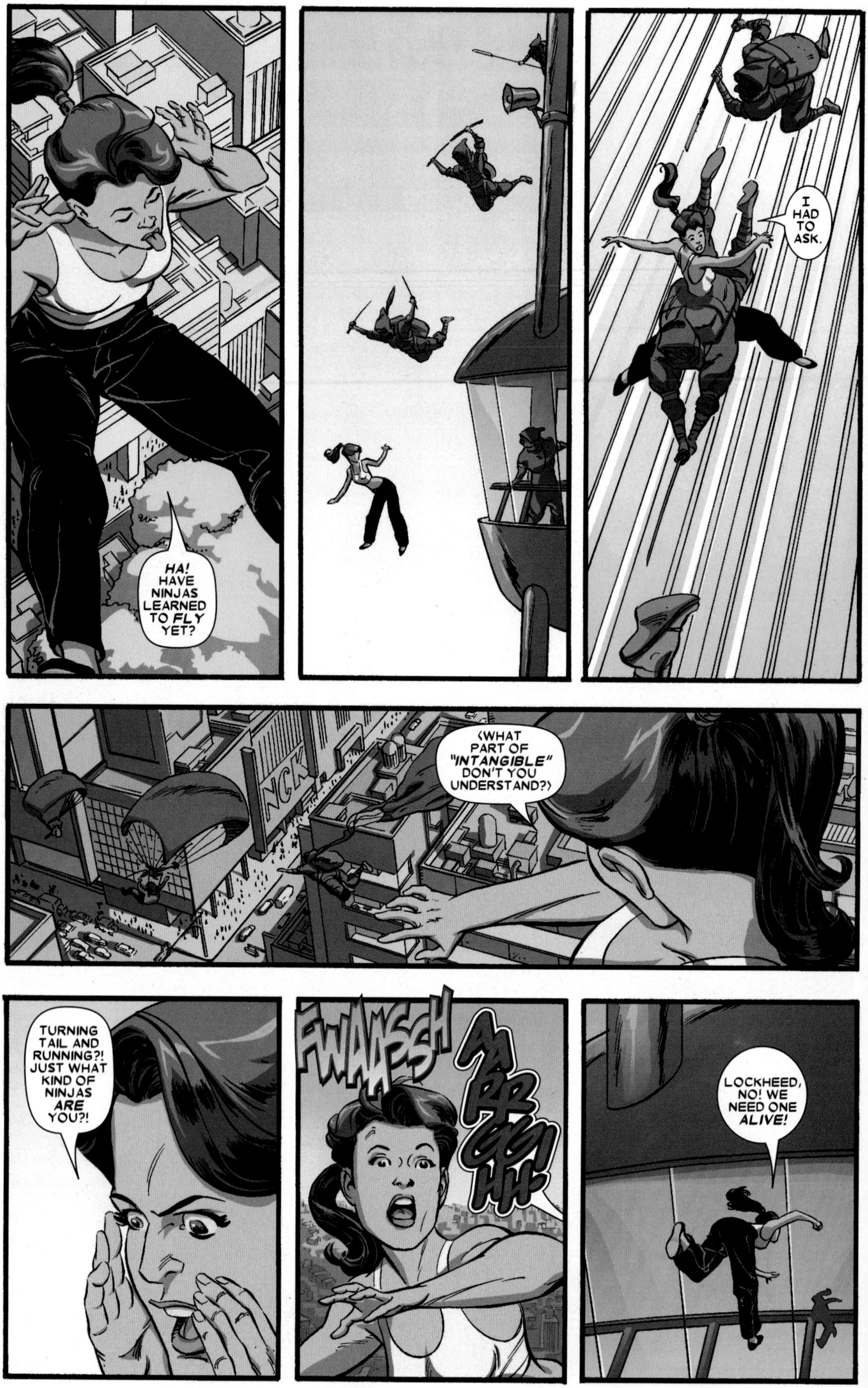
HA! HAVE NINJAS LEARNED TO FLY YET?
I HAD TO ASK.
‹WHAT PART OF "INTANGIBLE" DON'T YOU UNDERSTAND?›
NCK
TURNING TAIL AND RUNNING?! JUST WHAT KIND OF NINJAS ARE YOU?!
FWAASSH
AARRGGHH
LOCKHEED, NO! WE NEED ONE ALIVE!

FWAAASSH

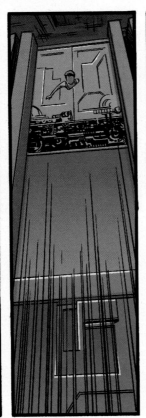

THEY HAD THEIR ESCAPE ROUTES ALL PLANNED OUT.

‹YOU BETTER START TALKING, YOU HAND BOZO!›

‹HAND? WE HAVE *NOTHING* TO DO WITH THOSE MERCENARY DOGS!›

‹THEN WHO ARE YOU?›

‹WE LIVE ONLY TO FOLLOW *THE PATH*.›

‹NOT GOOD ENOUGH!›

SWISS

SLAASH

‹IT'S A WONDER TO BEHOLD YOUR SKILLS FIRSTHAND. YOU TRULY ARE EVERY BIT THE *MASTER* WE HAVE BEEN LED TO BELIEVE.›

SNAP!

‹I ENTER THE NEXT REALM KNOWING I HAD THE HONOR OF DYING BEFORE THE *DAUGHTER OF DEMON*.›

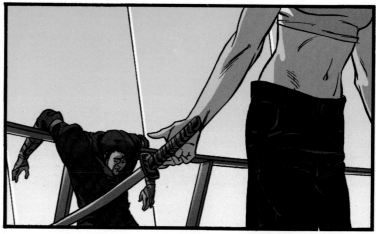

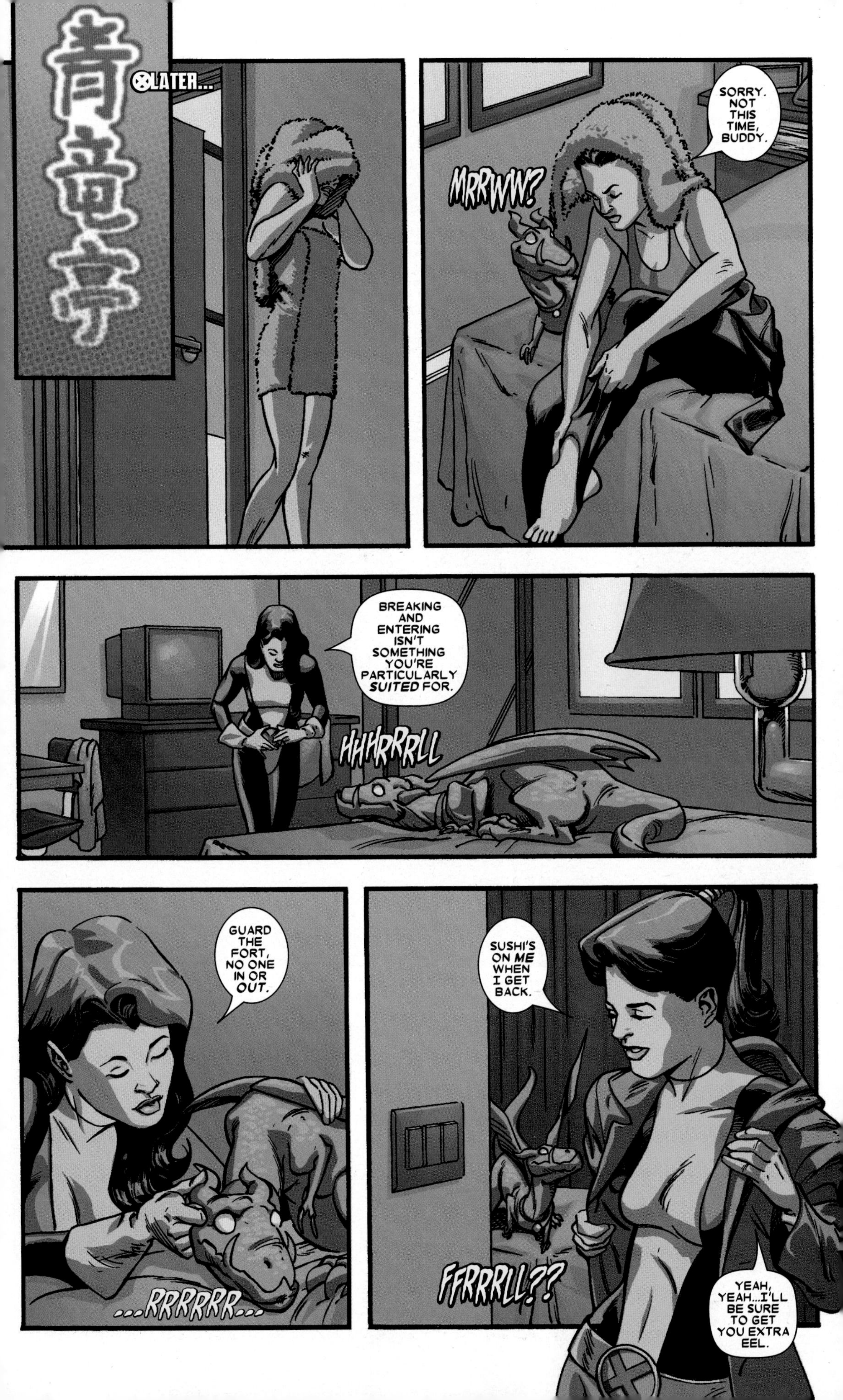
青竜亭
LATER...
SORRY. NOT THIS TIME, BUDDY.
MRRWW?
BREAKING AND ENTERING ISN'T SOMETHING YOU'RE PARTICULARLY *SUITED* FOR.
HHHRRRLL
GUARD THE FORT, NO ONE IN OR *OUT*.
...RRRRRR...
SUSHI'S ON *ME* WHEN I GET BACK.
FFRRRLL??
YEAH, YEAH...I'LL BE SURE TO GET YOU EXTRA EEL.

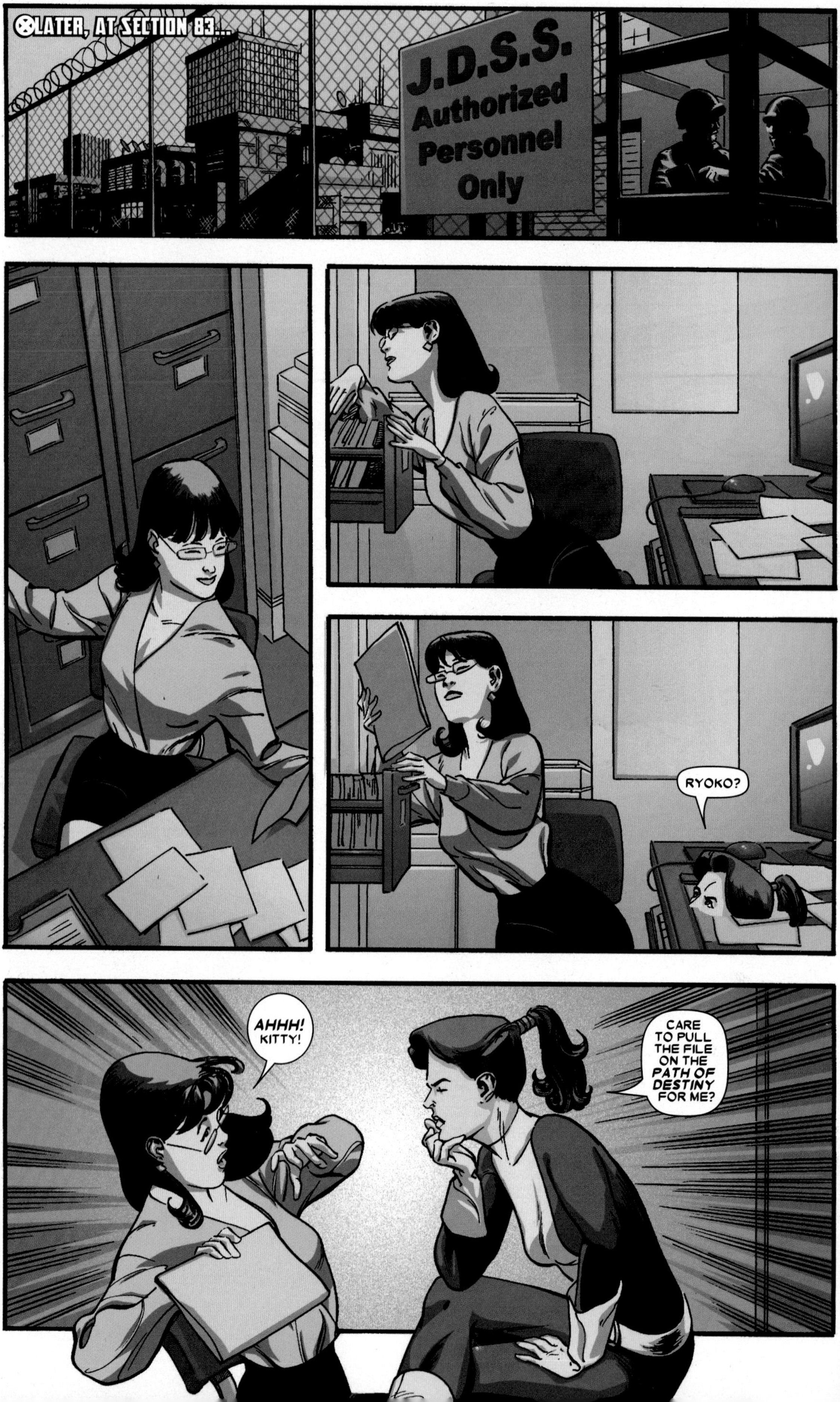
LATER, AT SECTION 83...
J.D.S.S. Authorized Personnel Only
RYOKO?
AHHH! KITTY!
CARE TO PULL THE FILE ON THE PATH OF DESTINY FOR ME?

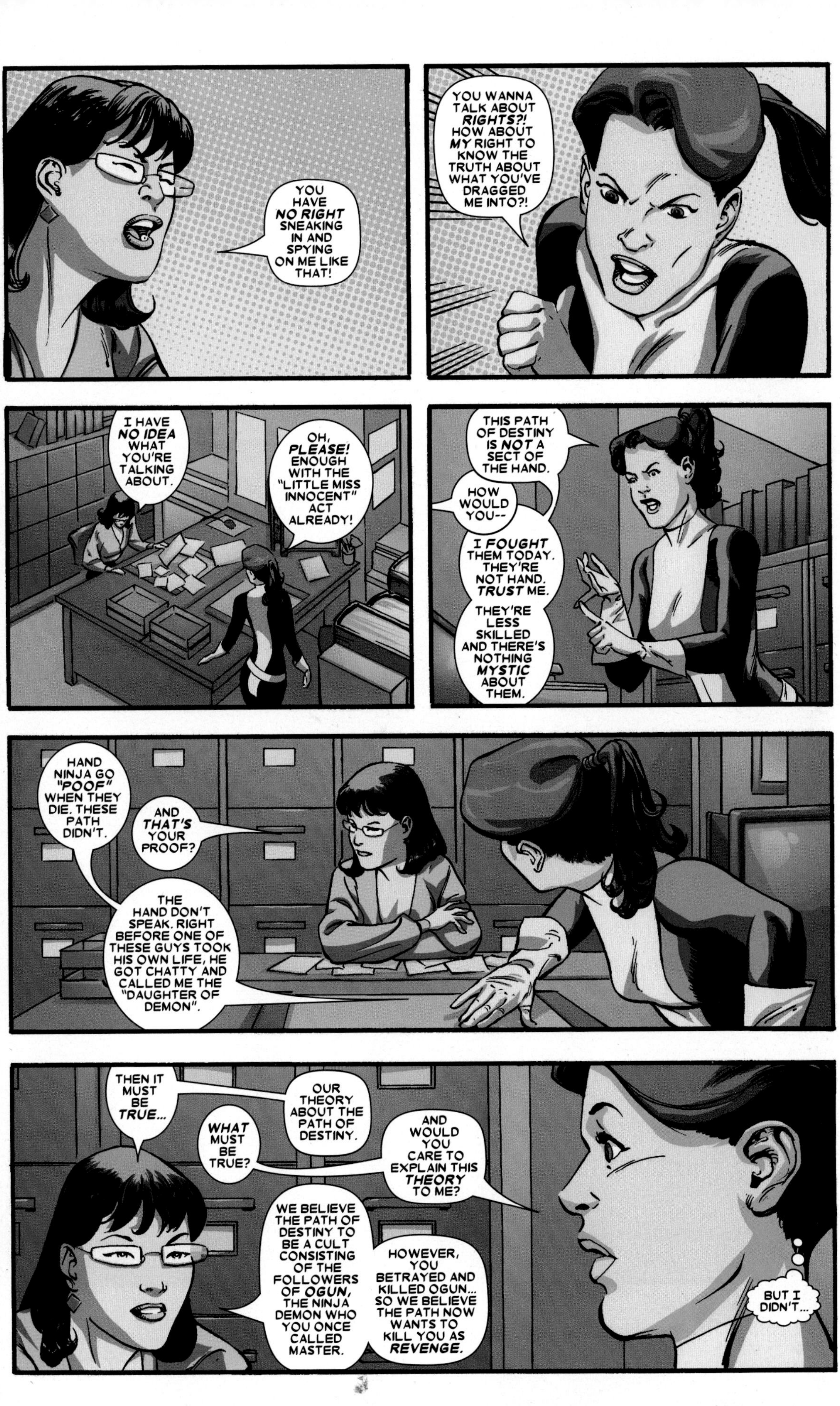

YOU HAVE NO RIGHT SNEAKING IN AND SPYING ON ME LIKE THAT!
YOU WANNA TALK ABOUT RIGHTS?! HOW ABOUT MY RIGHT TO KNOW THE TRUTH ABOUT WHAT YOU'VE DRAGGED ME INTO?!
I HAVE NO IDEA WHAT YOU'RE TALKING ABOUT.
OH, PLEASE! ENOUGH WITH THE "LITTLE MISS INNOCENT" ACT ALREADY!
THIS PATH OF DESTINY IS NOT A SECT OF THE HAND.
HOW WOULD YOU--
I FOUGHT THEM TODAY. THEY'RE NOT HAND. TRUST ME.
THEY'RE LESS SKILLED AND THERE'S NOTHING MYSTIC ABOUT THEM.
HAND NINJA GO "POOF" WHEN THEY DIE. THESE PATH DIDN'T.
AND THAT'S YOUR PROOF?
THE HAND DON'T SPEAK. RIGHT BEFORE ONE OF THESE GUYS TOOK HIS OWN LIFE, HE GOT CHATTY AND CALLED ME THE "DAUGHTER OF DEMON".
THEN IT MUST BE TRUE...
WHAT MUST BE TRUE?
OUR THEORY ABOUT THE PATH OF DESTINY.
AND WOULD YOU CARE TO EXPLAIN THIS THEORY TO ME?
WE BELIEVE THE PATH OF DESTINY TO BE A CULT CONSISTING OF THE FOLLOWERS OF OGUN, THE NINJA DEMON WHO YOU ONCE CALLED MASTER.
HOWEVER, YOU BETRAYED AND KILLED OGUN... SO WE BELIEVE THE PATH NOW WANTS TO KILL YOU AS REVENGE.
BUT I DIDN'T...

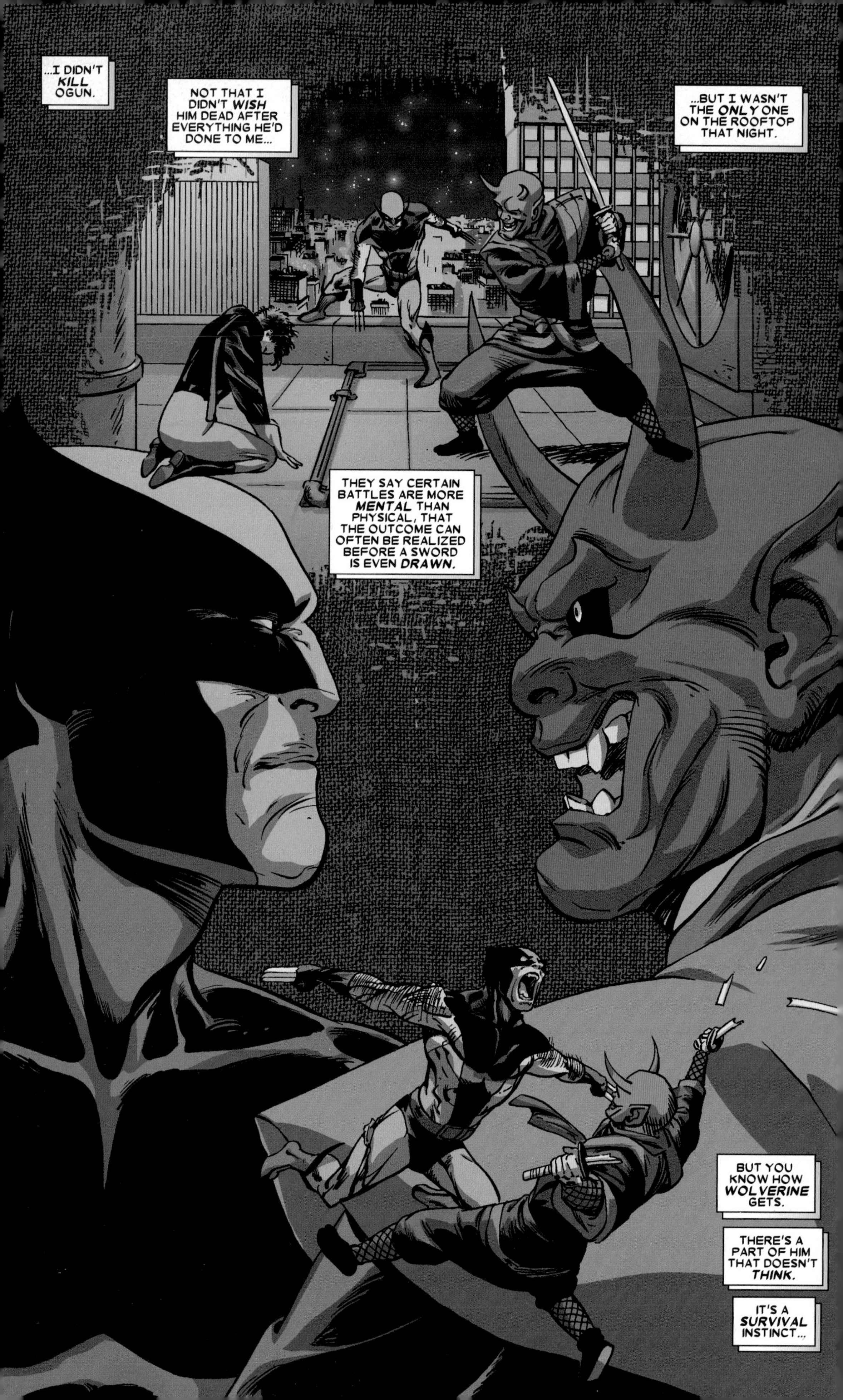

...I DIDN'T KILL OGUN.
NOT THAT I DIDN'T WISH HIM DEAD AFTER EVERYTHING HE'D DONE TO ME...
...BUT I WASN'T THE ONLY ONE ON THE ROOFTOP THAT NIGHT.
THEY SAY CERTAIN BATTLES ARE MORE MENTAL THAN PHYSICAL, THAT THE OUTCOME CAN OFTEN BE REALIZED BEFORE A SWORD IS EVEN DRAWN.
BUT YOU KNOW HOW WOLVERINE GETS.
THERE'S A PART OF HIM THAT DOESN'T THINK.
IT'S A SURVIVAL INSTINCT...

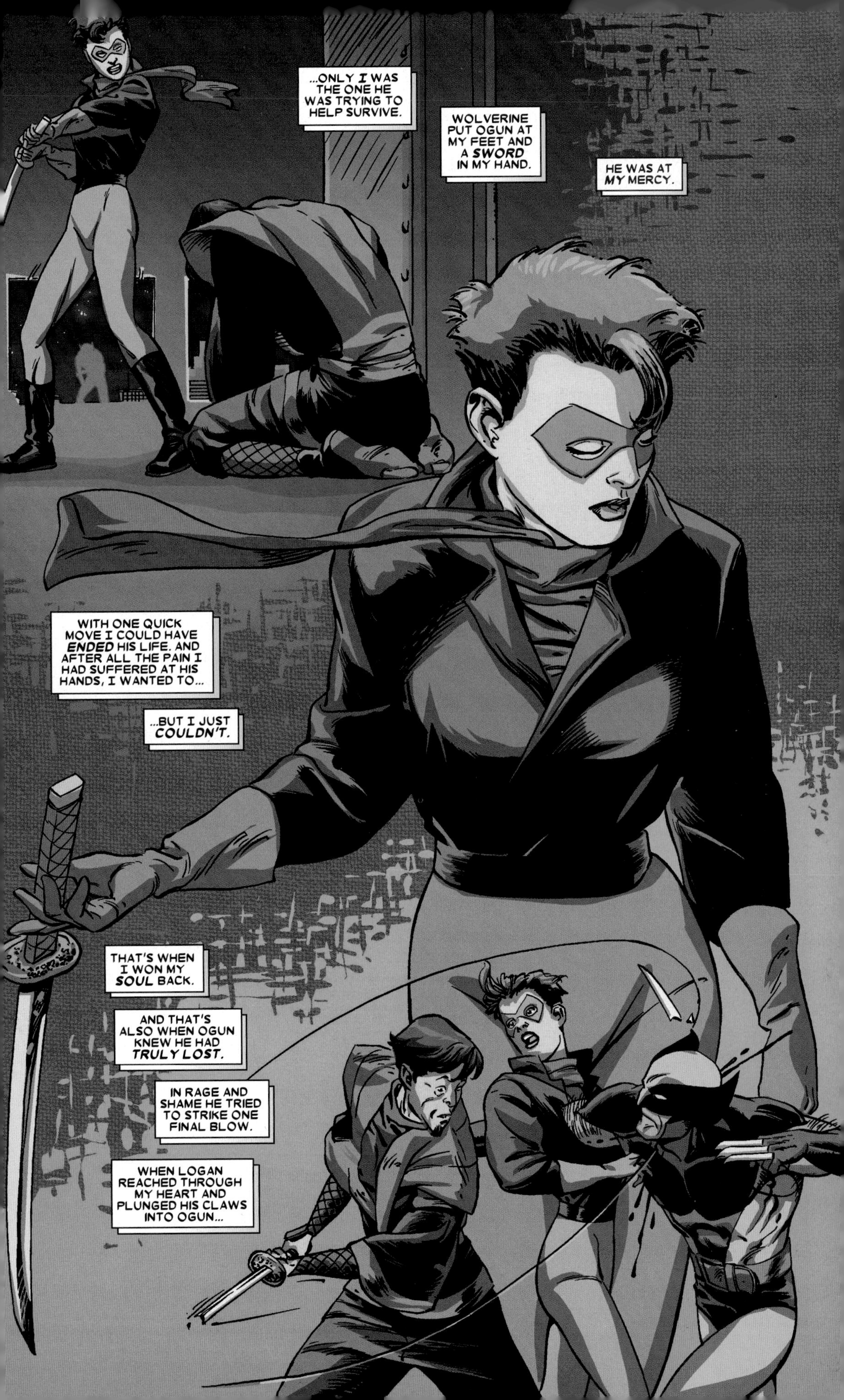
...ONLY *I* WAS THE ONE HE WAS TRYING TO HELP SURVIVE.
WOLVERINE PUT OGUN AT MY FEET AND A *SWORD* IN MY HAND.
HE WAS AT *MY* MERCY.
WITH ONE QUICK MOVE I COULD HAVE *ENDED* HIS LIFE. AND AFTER ALL THE PAIN I HAD SUFFERED AT HIS HANDS, I WANTED TO...
...BUT I JUST *COULDN'T.*
THAT'S WHEN I WON MY *SOUL* BACK.
AND THAT'S ALSO WHEN OGUN KNEW HE HAD *TRULY LOST.*
IN RAGE AND SHAME HE TRIED TO STRIKE ONE FINAL BLOW.
WHEN LOGAN REACHED THROUGH MY HEART AND PLUNGED HIS CLAWS INTO OGUN...

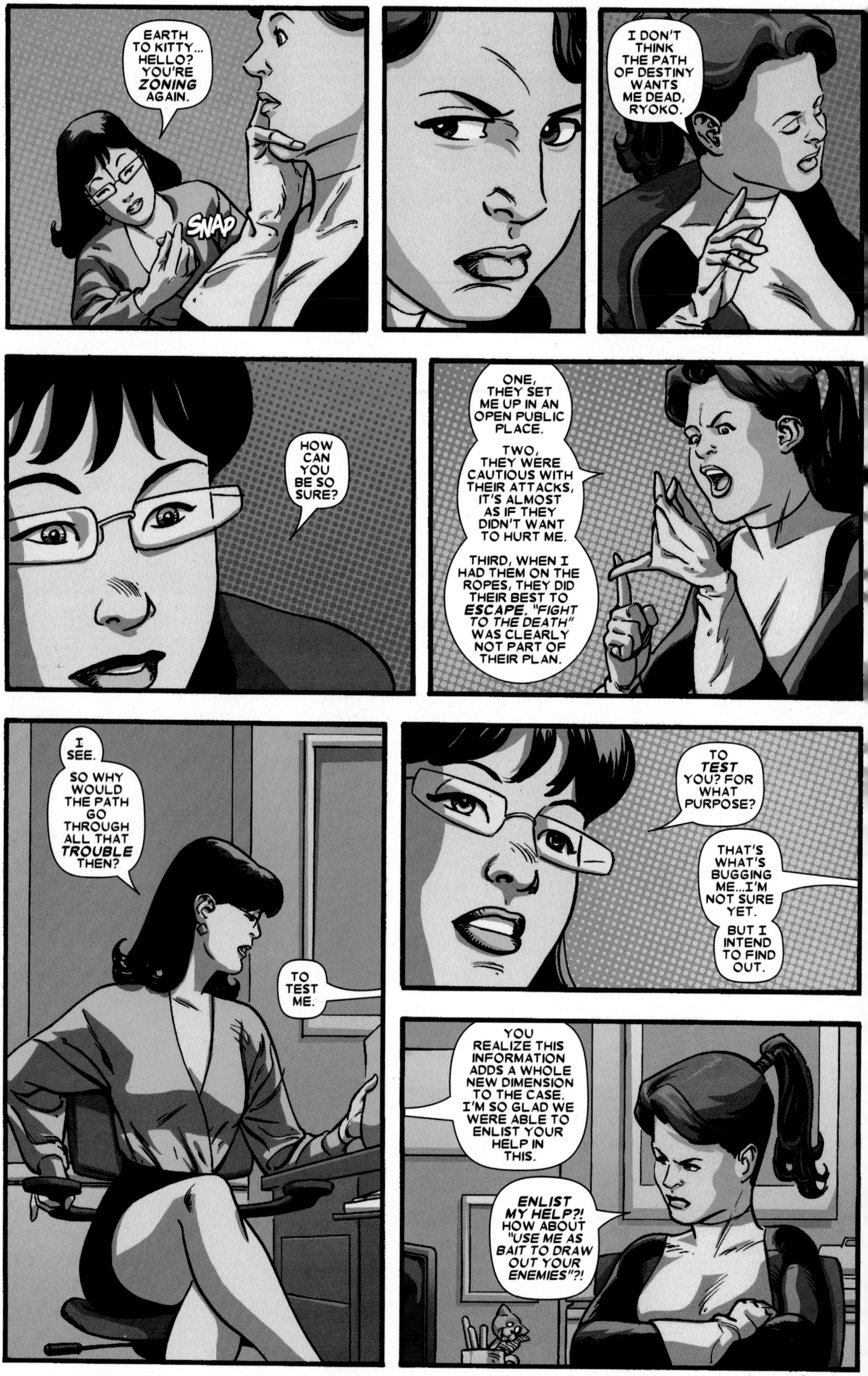
EARTH TO KITTY... HELLO? YOU'RE ZONING AGAIN.
SNAP
I DON'T THINK THE PATH OF DESTINY WANTS ME DEAD, RYOKO.
HOW CAN YOU BE SO SURE?
ONE, THEY SET ME UP IN AN OPEN PUBLIC PLACE.
TWO, THEY WERE CAUTIOUS WITH THEIR ATTACKS, IT'S ALMOST AS IF THEY DIDN'T WANT TO HURT ME.
THIRD, WHEN I HAD THEM ON THE ROPES, THEY DID THEIR BEST TO ESCAPE. "FIGHT TO THE DEATH" WAS CLEARLY NOT PART OF THEIR PLAN.
I SEE.
SO WHY WOULD THE PATH GO THROUGH ALL THAT TROUBLE THEN?
TO TEST ME.
TO TEST YOU? FOR WHAT PURPOSE?
THAT'S WHAT'S BUGGING ME...I'M NOT SURE YET.
BUT I INTEND TO FIND OUT.
YOU REALIZE THIS INFORMATION ADDS A WHOLE NEW DIMENSION TO THE CASE. I'M SO GLAD WE WERE ABLE TO ENLIST YOUR HELP IN THIS.
ENLIST MY HELP?! HOW ABOUT "USE ME AS BAIT TO DRAW OUT YOUR ENEMIES"?!

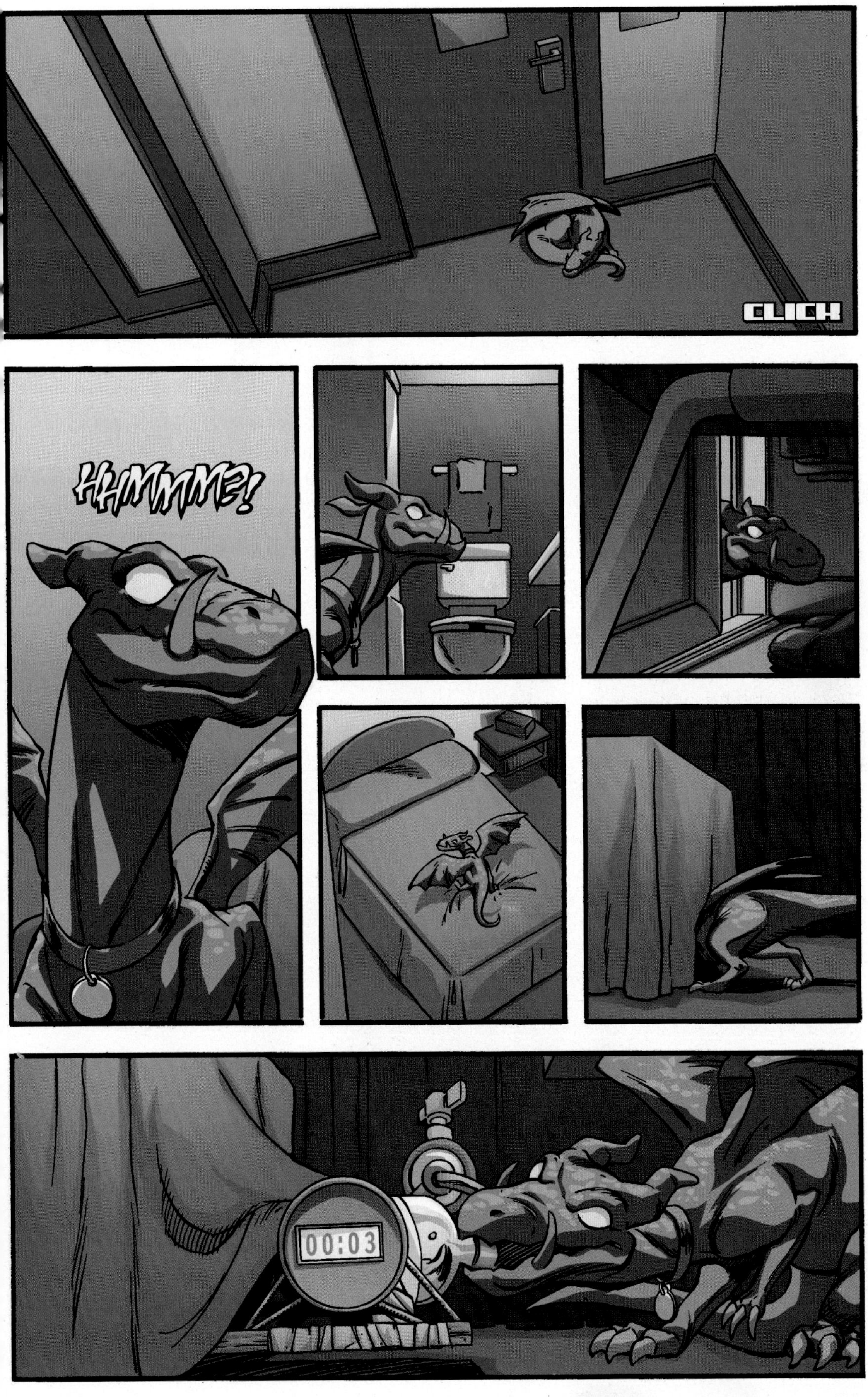
CLICK
HHMMM?!
00:03

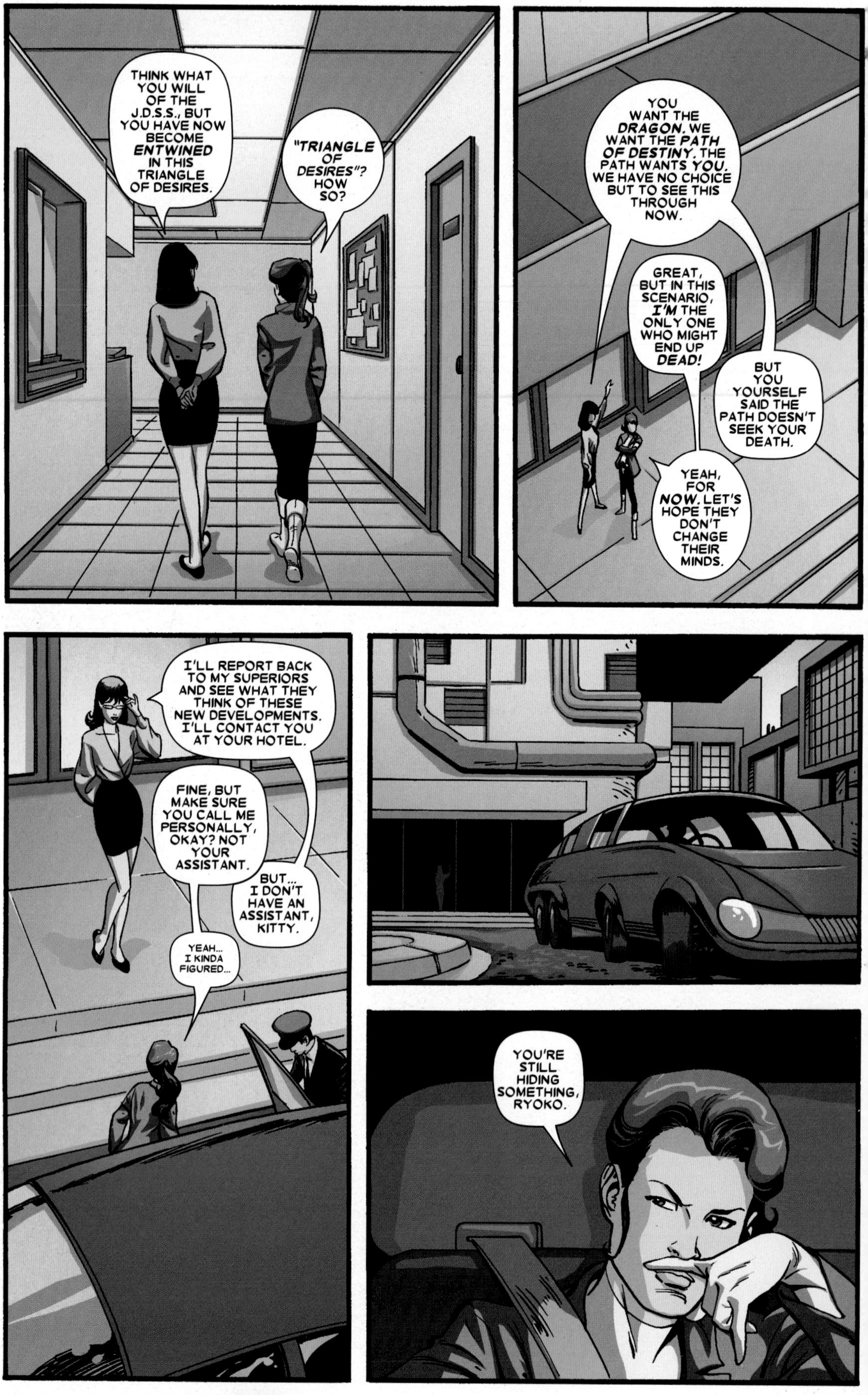
THINK WHAT YOU WILL OF THE J.D.S.S., BUT YOU HAVE NOW BECOME ENTWINED IN THIS TRIANGLE OF DESIRES.
"TRIANGLE OF DESIRES"? HOW SO?
YOU WANT THE DRAGON. WE WANT THE PATH OF DESTINY. THE PATH WANTS YOU. WE HAVE NO CHOICE BUT TO SEE THIS THROUGH NOW.
GREAT, BUT IN THIS SCENARIO, I'M THE ONLY ONE WHO MIGHT END UP DEAD!
BUT YOU YOURSELF SAID THE PATH DOESN'T SEEK YOUR DEATH.
YEAH, FOR NOW. LET'S HOPE THEY DON'T CHANGE THEIR MINDS.
I'LL REPORT BACK TO MY SUPERIORS AND SEE WHAT THEY THINK OF THESE NEW DEVELOPMENTS. I'LL CONTACT YOU AT YOUR HOTEL.
FINE, BUT MAKE SURE YOU CALL ME PERSONALLY, OKAY? NOT YOUR ASSISTANT.
BUT... I DON'T HAVE AN ASSISTANT, KITTY.
YEAH... I KINDA FIGURED...
YOU'RE STILL HIDING SOMETHING, RYOKO.

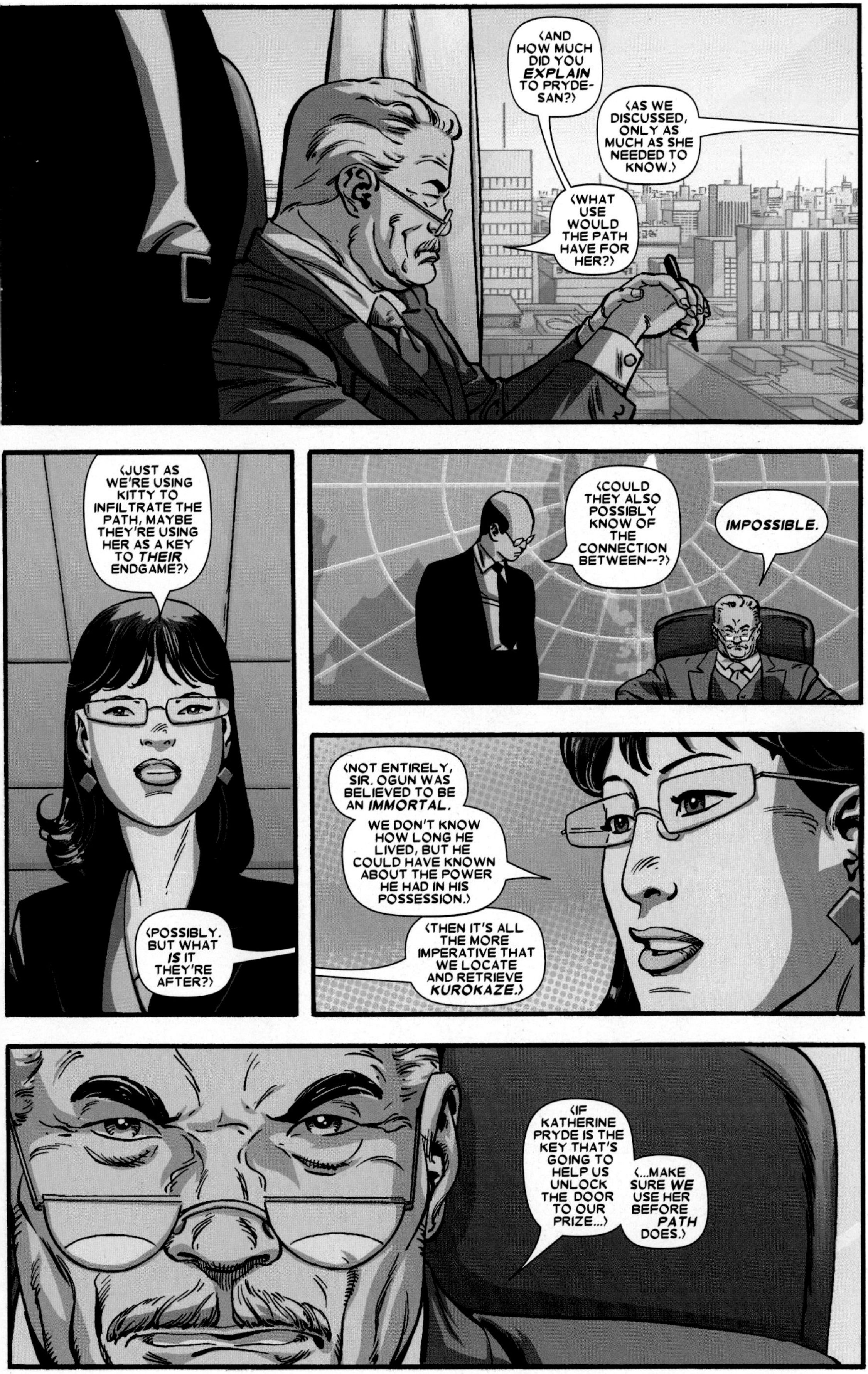

‹AND HOW MUCH DID YOU EXPLAIN TO PRYDE-SAN?›
‹AS WE DISCUSSED, ONLY AS MUCH AS SHE NEEDED TO KNOW.›
‹WHAT USE WOULD THE PATH HAVE FOR HER?›
‹JUST AS WE'RE USING KITTY TO INFILTRATE THE PATH, MAYBE THEY'RE USING HER AS A KEY TO THEIR ENDGAME?›
‹COULD THEY ALSO POSSIBLY KNOW OF THE CONNECTION BETWEEN--?›
IMPOSSIBLE.
‹POSSIBLY. BUT WHAT IS IT THEY'RE AFTER?›
‹NOT ENTIRELY, SIR. OGUN WAS BELIEVED TO BE AN IMMORTAL.
WE DON'T KNOW HOW LONG HE LIVED, BUT HE COULD HAVE KNOWN ABOUT THE POWER HE HAD IN HIS POSSESSION.›
‹THEN IT'S ALL THE MORE IMPERATIVE THAT WE LOCATE AND RETRIEVE KUROKAZE.›
‹IF KATHERINE PRYDE IS THE KEY THAT'S GOING TO HELP US UNLOCK THE DOOR TO OUR PRIZE...›
‹...MAKE SURE WE USE HER BEFORE PATH DOES.›

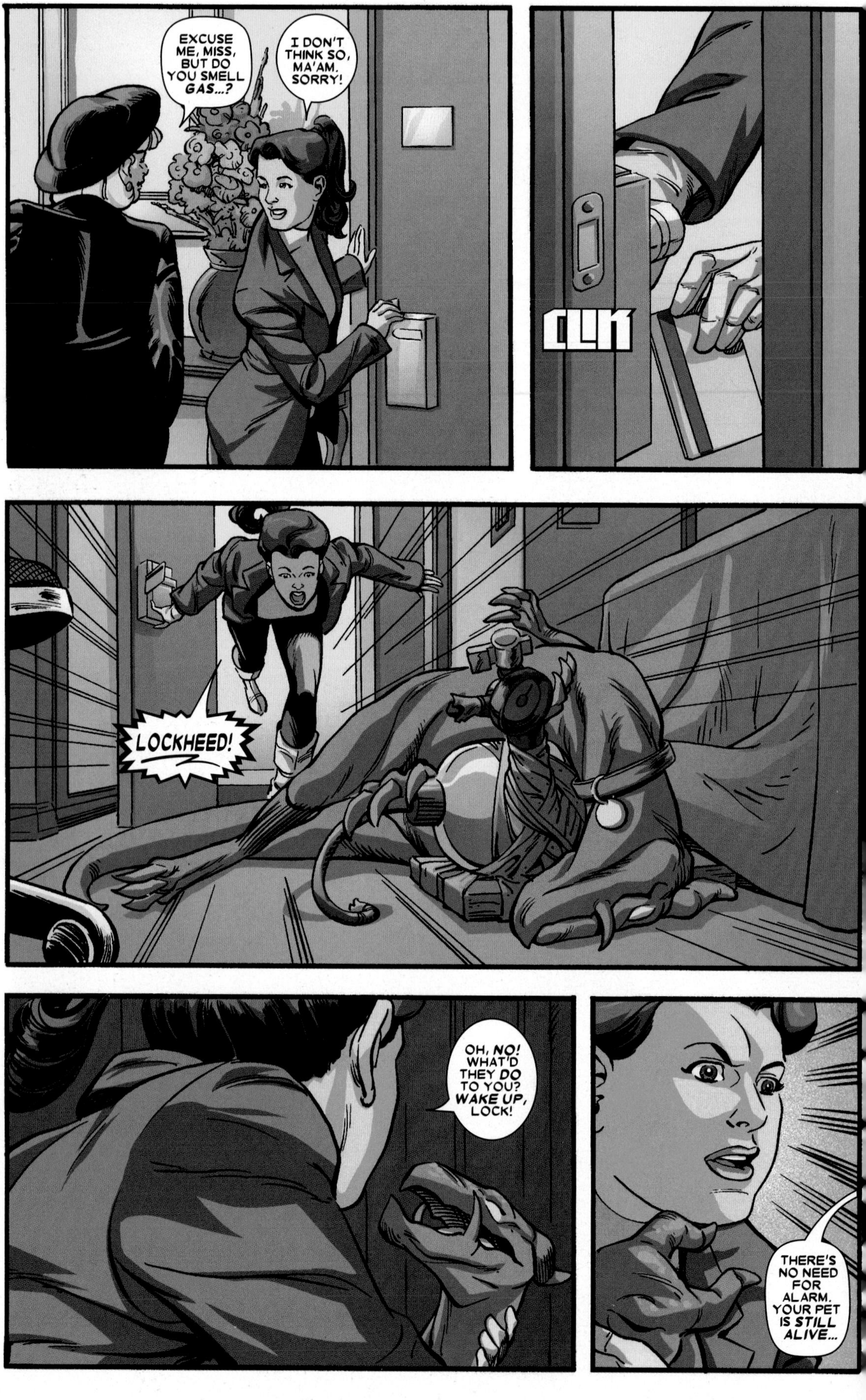
EXCUSE ME, MISS, BUT DO YOU SMELL GAS...?
I DON'T THINK SO, MA'AM. SORRY!
CLIK
LOCKHEED!
OH, NO! WHAT'D THEY DO TO YOU? WAKE UP, LOCK!
THERE'S NO NEED FOR ALARM. YOUR PET IS STILL ALIVE...

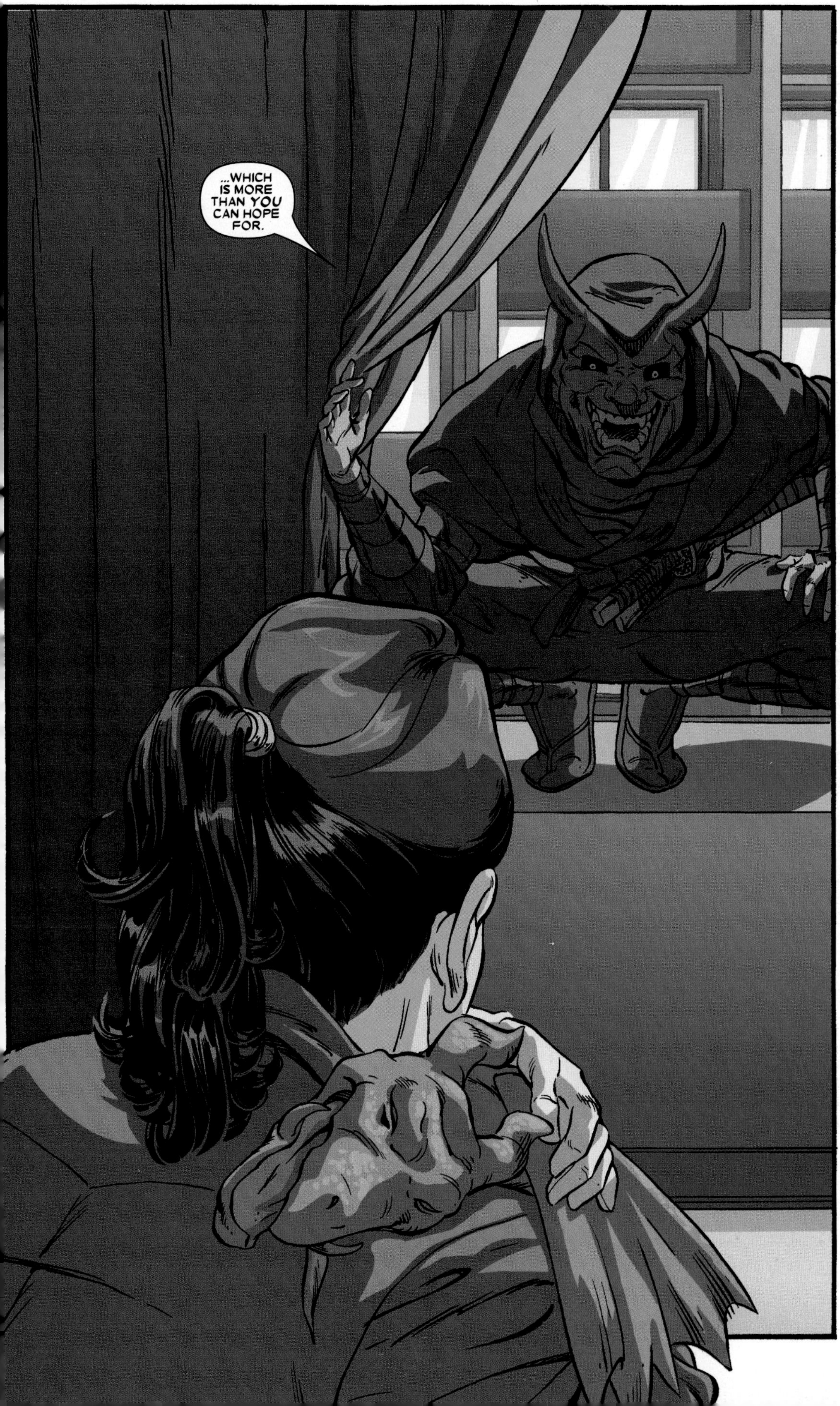
...WHICH IS MORE THAN YOU CAN HOPE FOR.

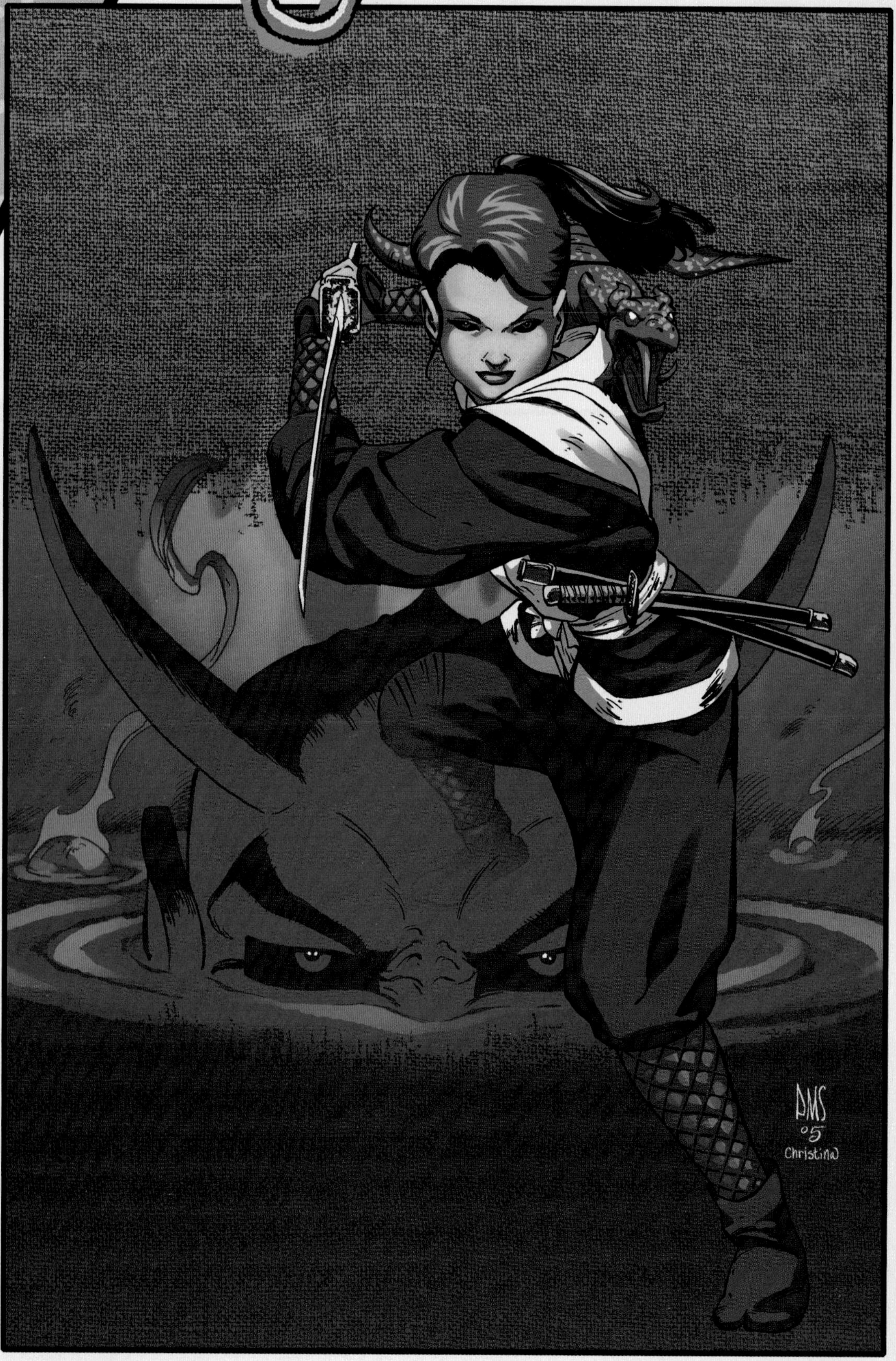
DMS
'05
Christina

< #3 >

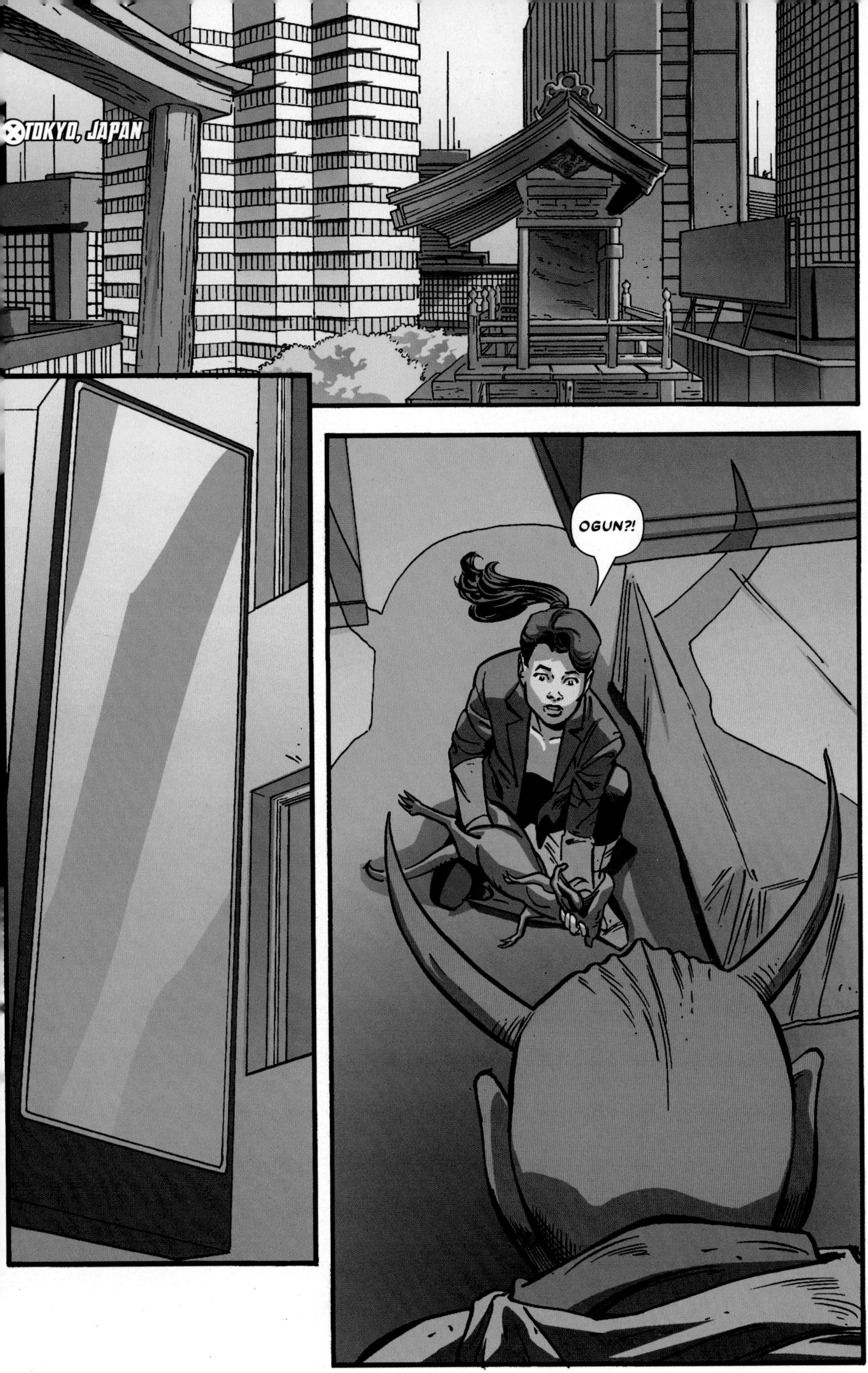
TOKYO, JAPAN
OGUN?!

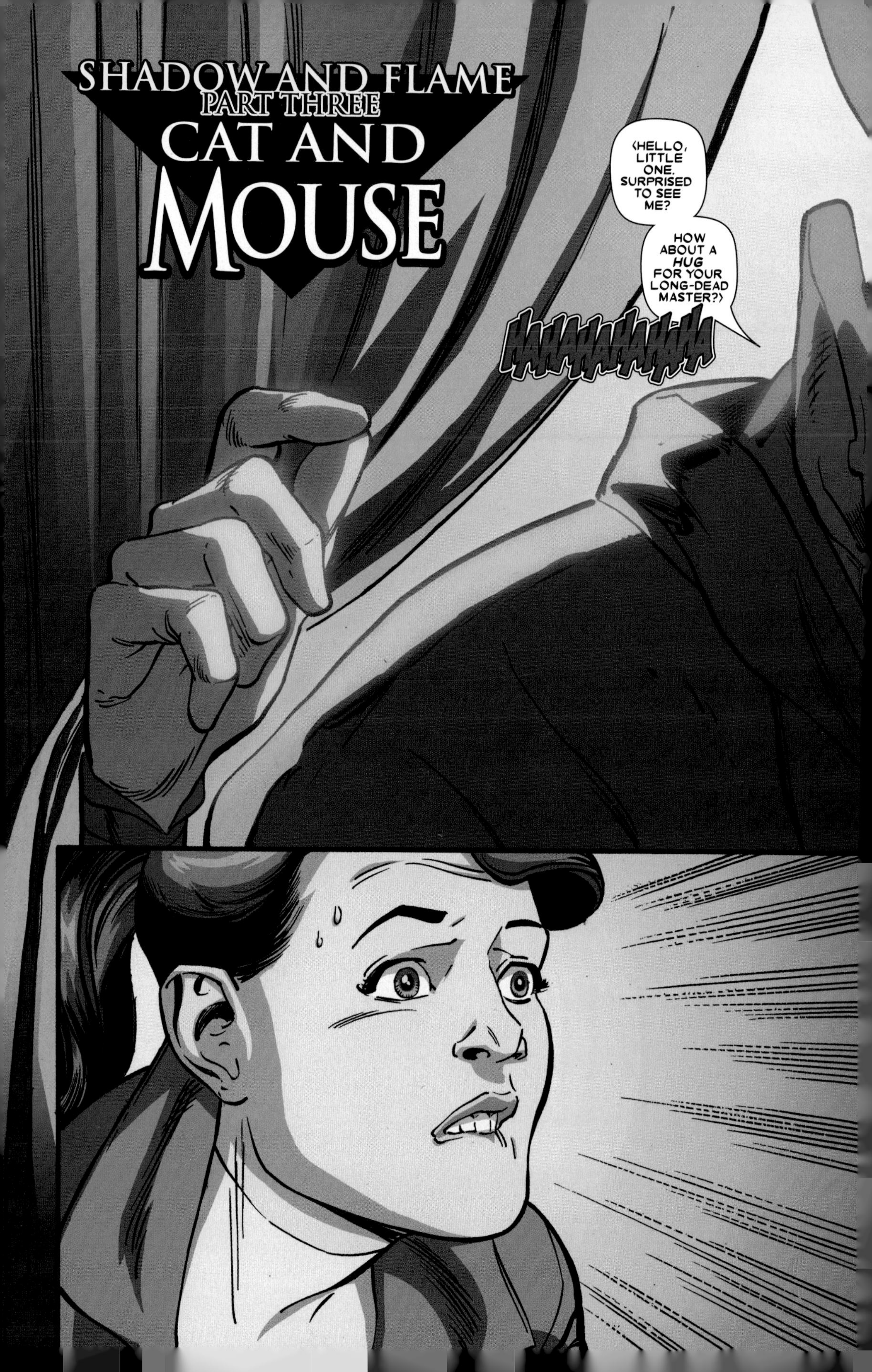
SHADOW AND FLAME
PART THREE
CAT AND MOUSE
‹HELLO, LITTLE ONE. SURPRISED TO SEE ME?
HOW ABOUT A HUG FOR YOUR LONG-DEAD MASTER?›
HAHAHAHAHAHAHA

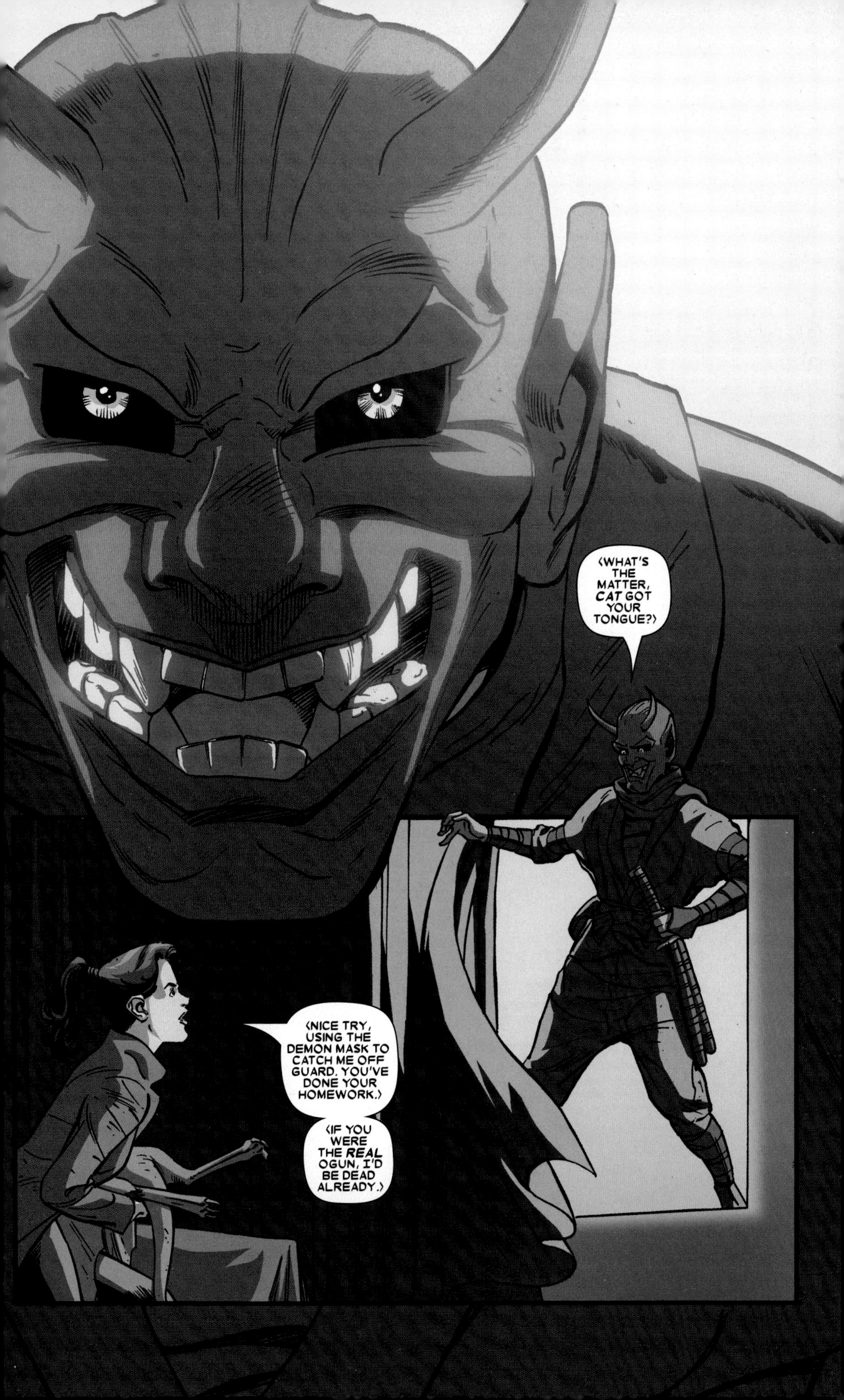
‹WHAT'S THE MATTER, CAT GOT YOUR TONGUE?›
‹NICE TRY, USING THE DEMON MASK TO CATCH ME OFF GUARD. YOU'VE DONE YOUR HOMEWORK.›
‹IF YOU WERE THE REAL OGUN, I'D BE DEAD ALREADY.›

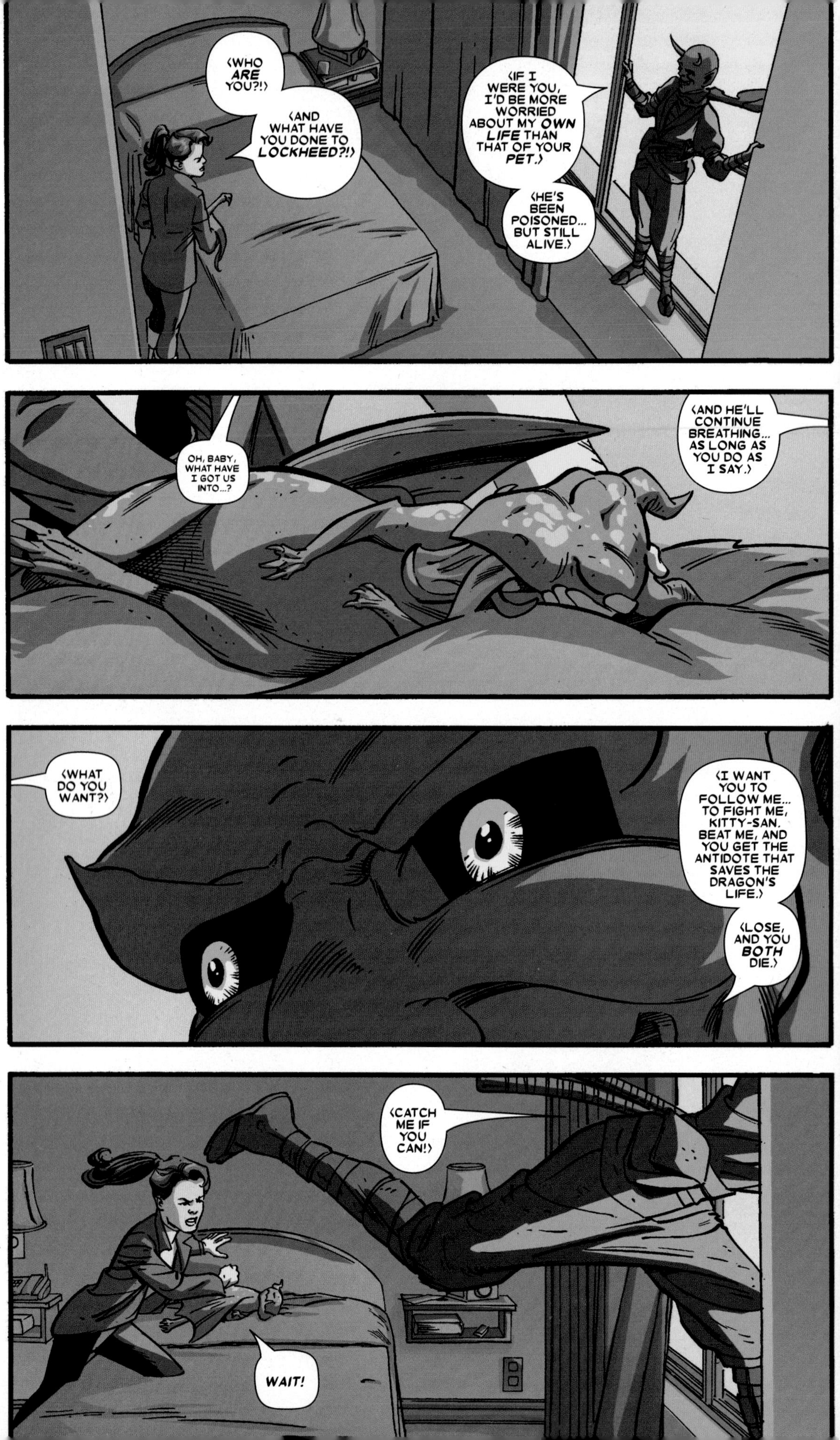
‹WHO ARE YOU?!›
‹AND WHAT HAVE YOU DONE TO LOCKHEED?!›
‹IF I WERE YOU, I'D BE MORE WORRIED ABOUT MY OWN LIFE THAN THAT OF YOUR PET.›
‹HE'S BEEN POISONED... BUT STILL ALIVE.›
OH, BABY, WHAT HAVE I GOT US INTO...?
‹AND HE'LL CONTINUE BREATHING... AS LONG AS YOU DO AS I SAY.›
‹WHAT DO YOU WANT?›
‹I WANT YOU TO FOLLOW ME... TO FIGHT ME, KITTY-SAN. BEAT ME, AND YOU GET THE ANTIDOTE THAT SAVES THE DRAGON'S LIFE.›
‹LOSE, AND YOU BOTH DIE.›
‹CATCH ME IF YOU CAN!›
WAIT!

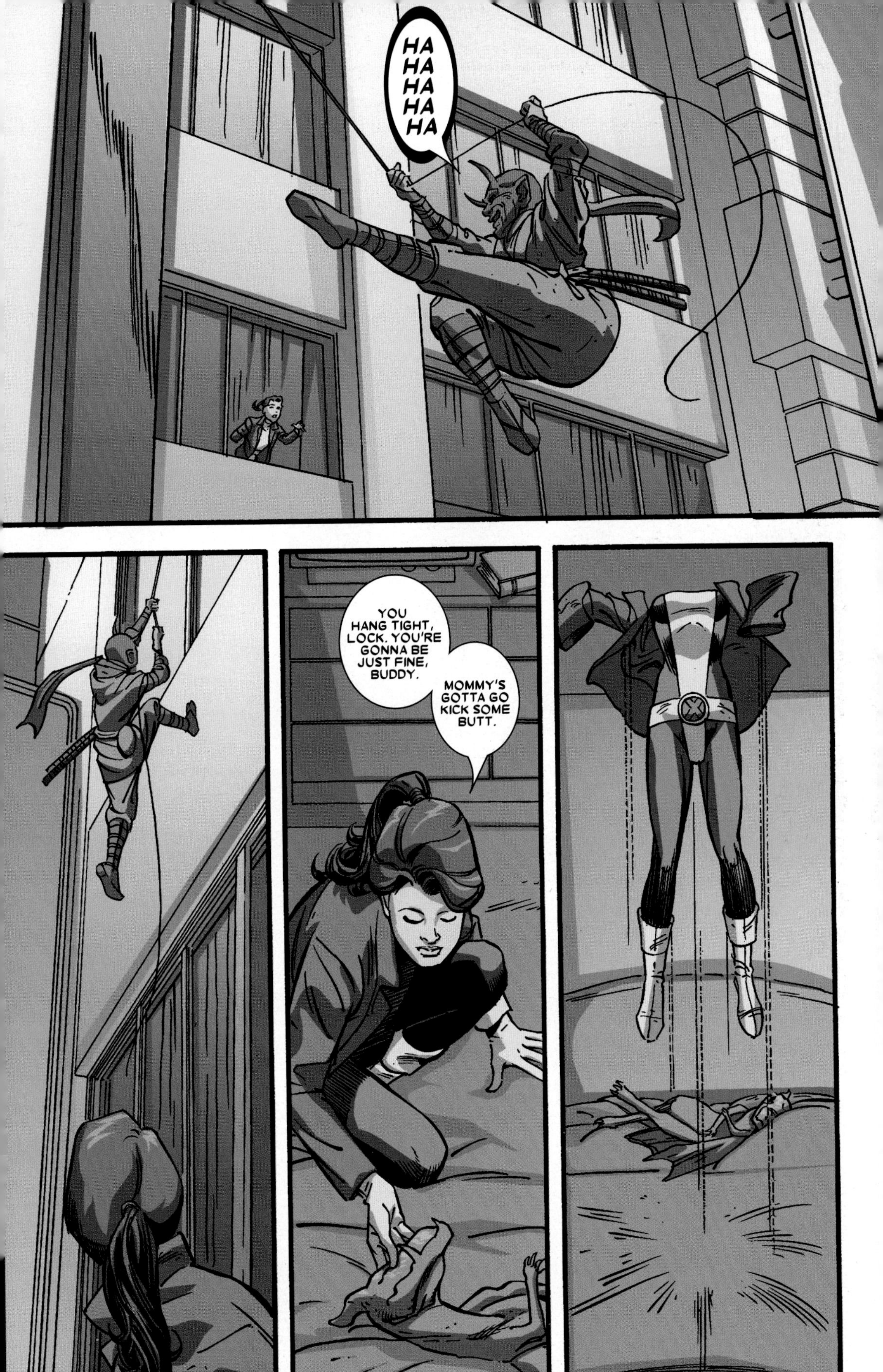
HA HA HA HA HA
YOU HANG TIGHT, LOCK. YOU'RE GONNA BE JUST FINE, BUDDY.
MOMMY'S GOTTA GO KICK SOME BUTT.

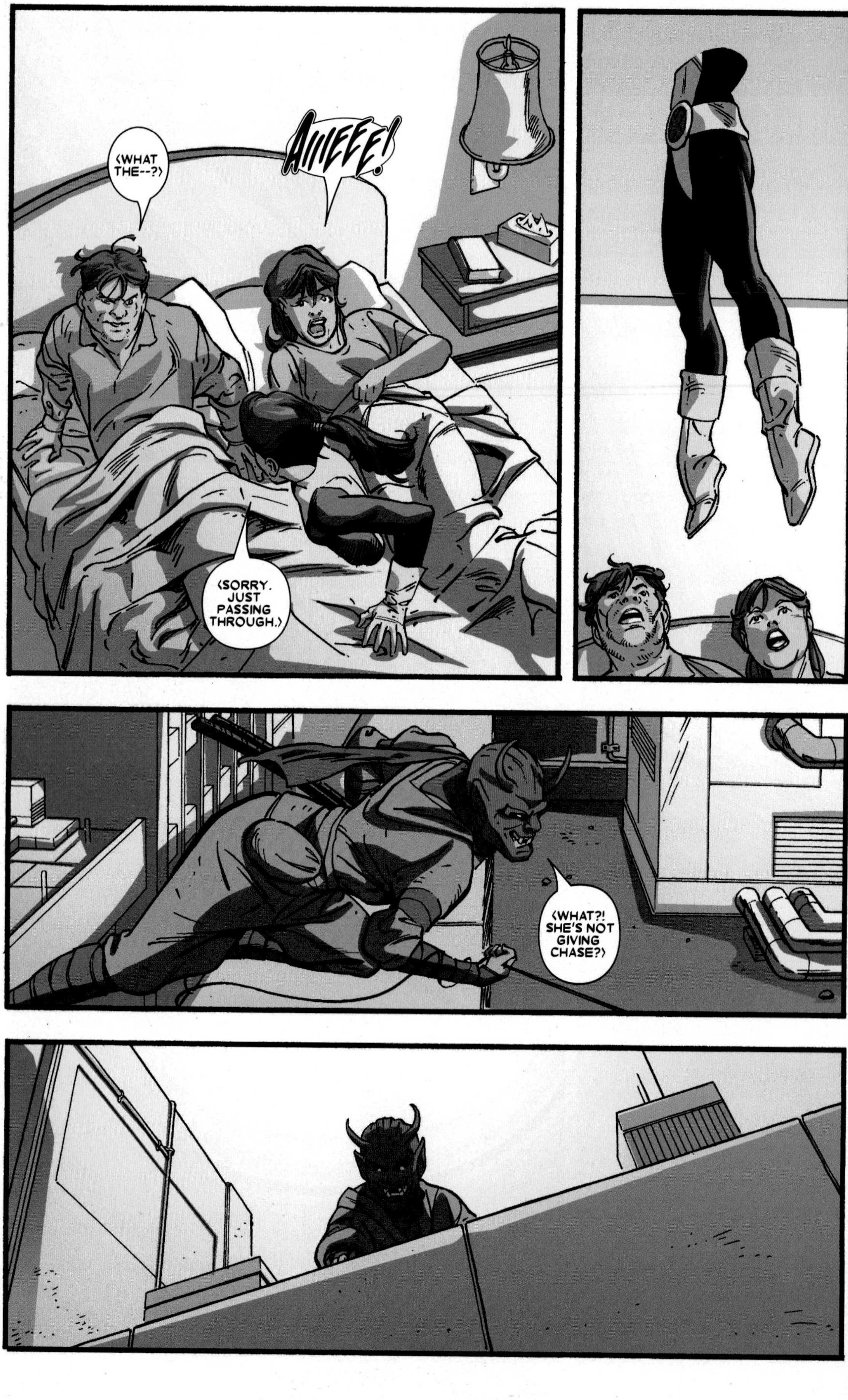
‹WHAT THE--?›
AIIIEEE!
‹SORRY. JUST PASSING THROUGH.›
‹WHAT?! SHE'S NOT GIVING CHASE?›

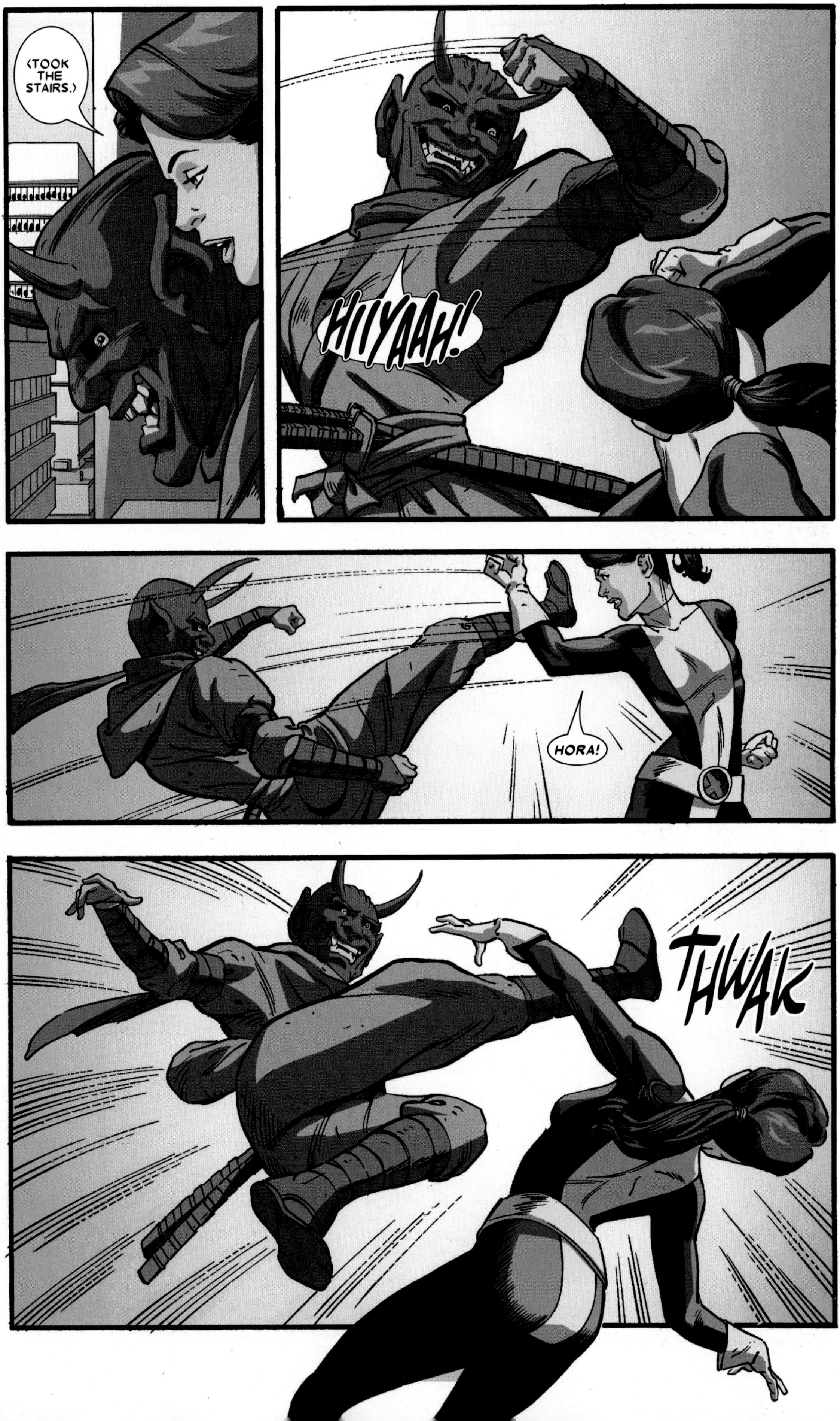

‹TOOK THE STAIRS.›
HIIYAAH!
HORA!
THWAK

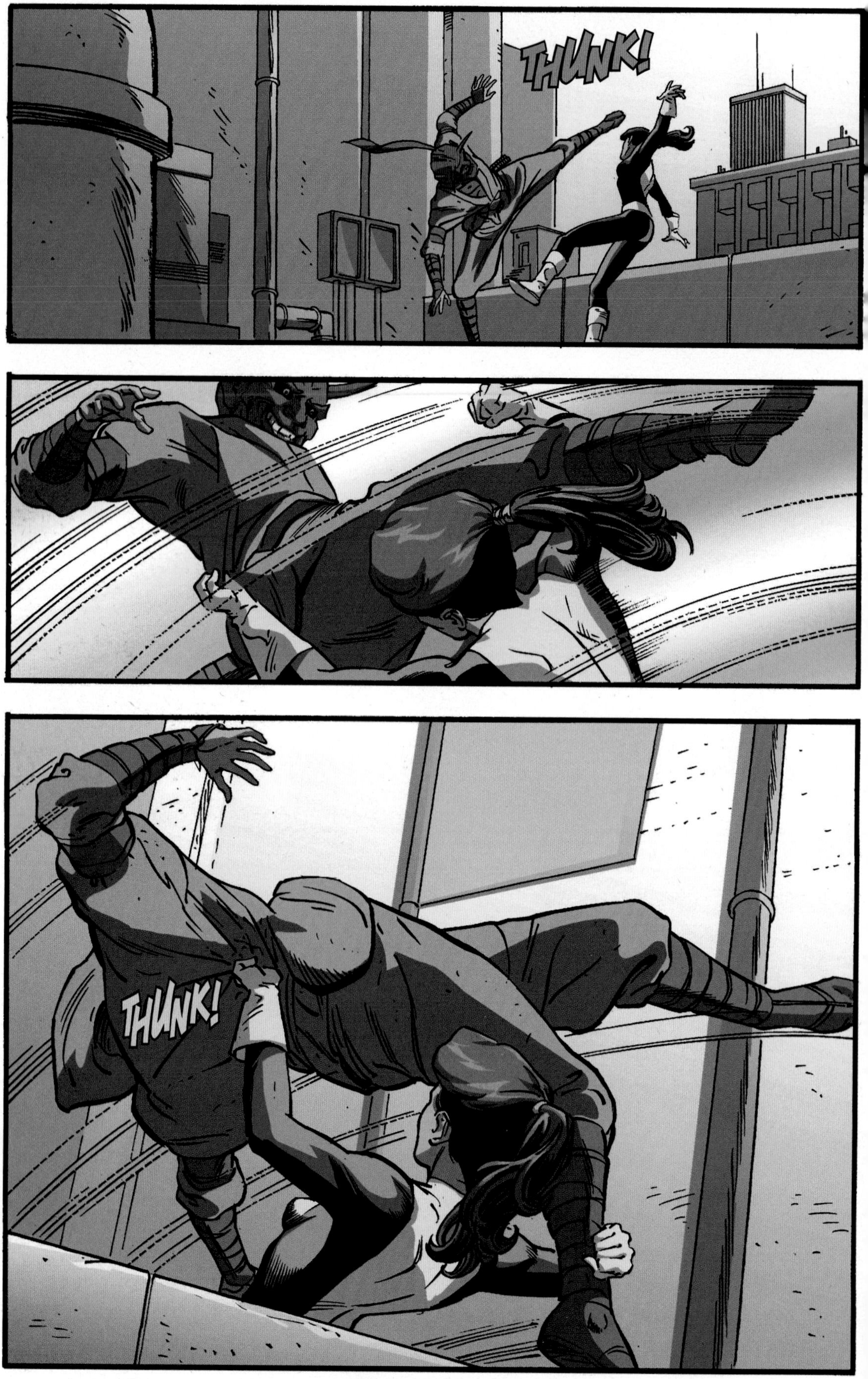
THUNK!
THUNK!

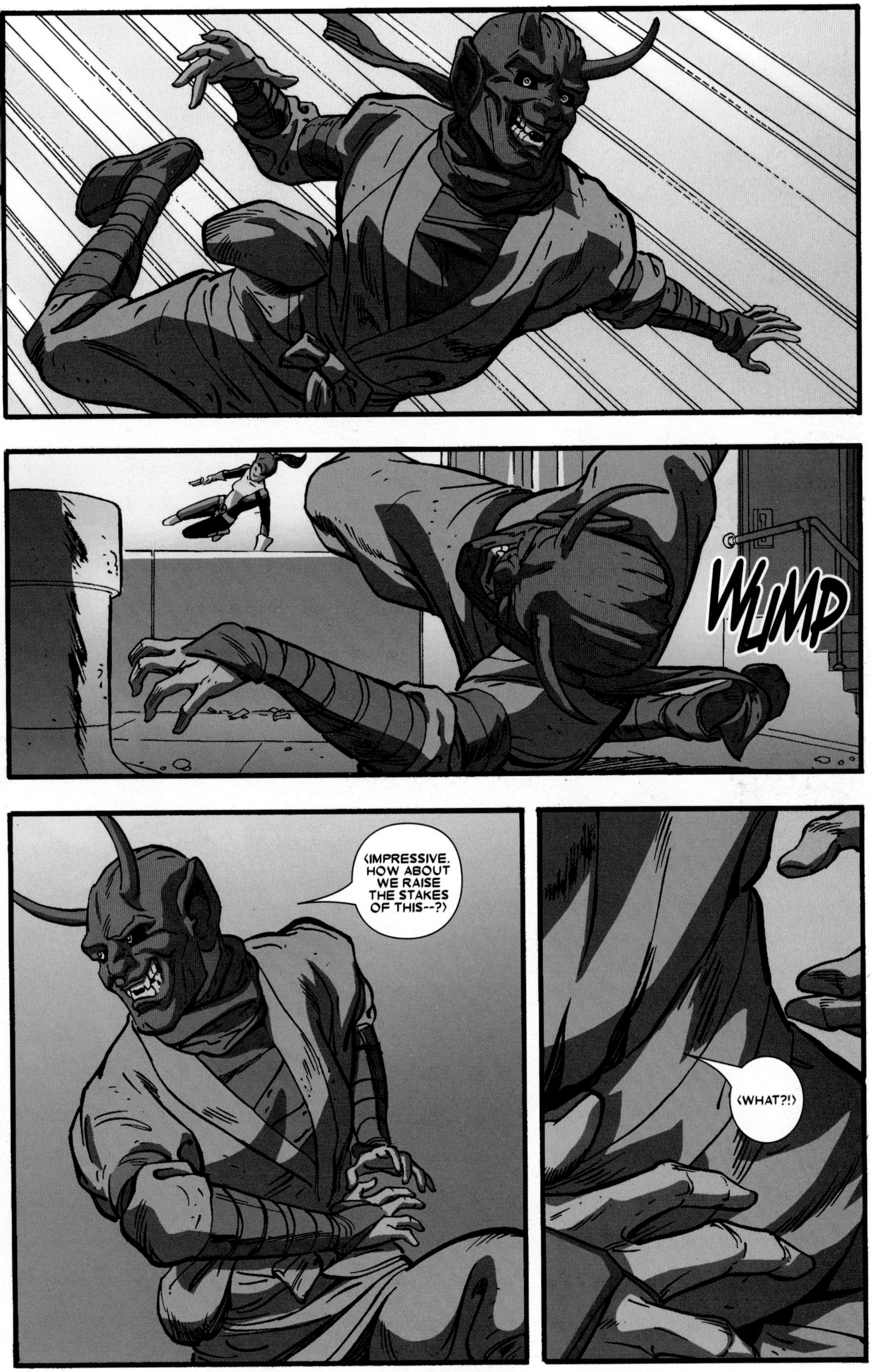
WUMP
⟨IMPRESSIVE. HOW ABOUT WE RAISE THE STAKES OF THIS--?⟩
⟨WHAT?!⟩

‹OH, YOU BROUGHT ONE FOR ME, TOO? YOU PSYCHOS CAN BE SO *THOUGHTFUL* SOMETIMES.›

CHANK

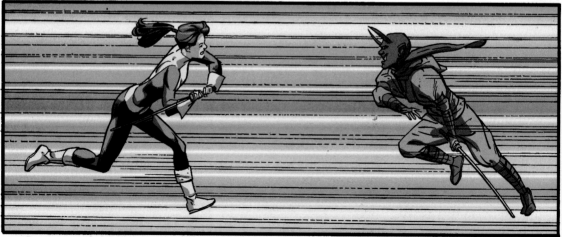

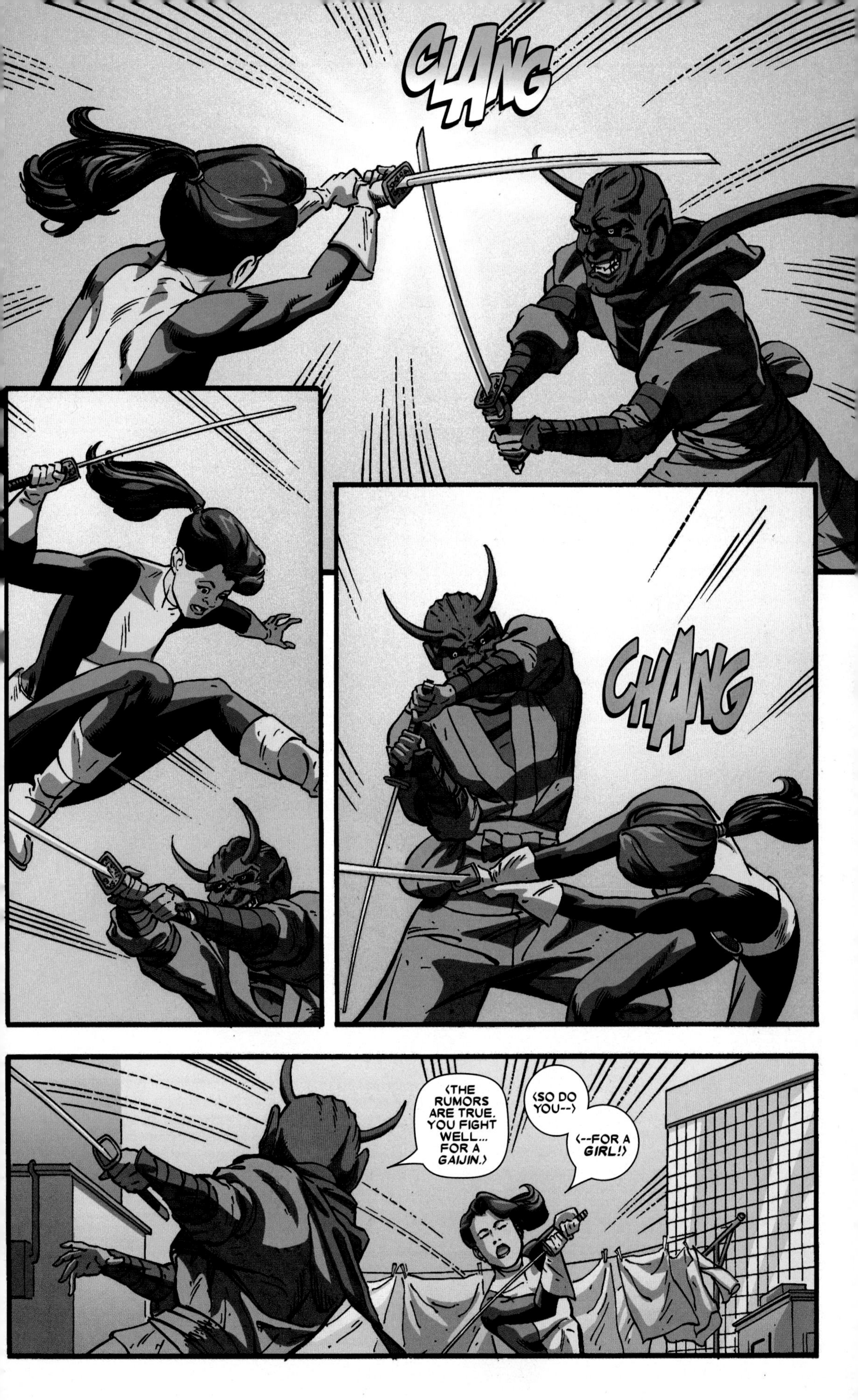
CLANG
CHANG
‹THE RUMORS ARE TRUE. YOU FIGHT WELL... FOR A GAIJIN.›
‹SO DO YOU--›
‹--FOR A GIRL!›

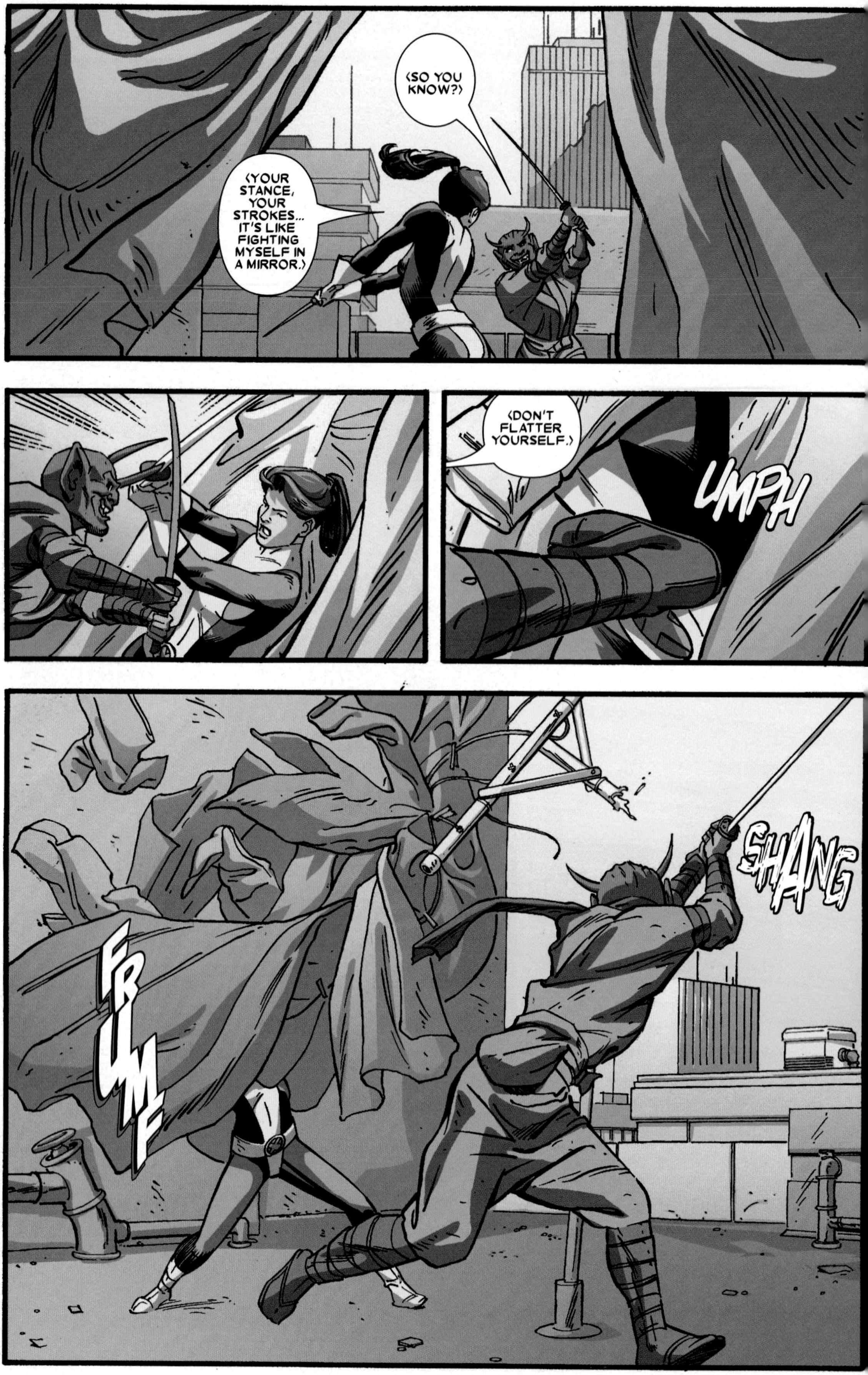

⟨SO YOU KNOW?⟩
⟨YOUR STANCE, YOUR STROKES... IT'S LIKE FIGHTING MYSELF IN A MIRROR.⟩
⟨DON'T FLATTER YOURSELF.⟩
UMPH
SHANG
FRUMF

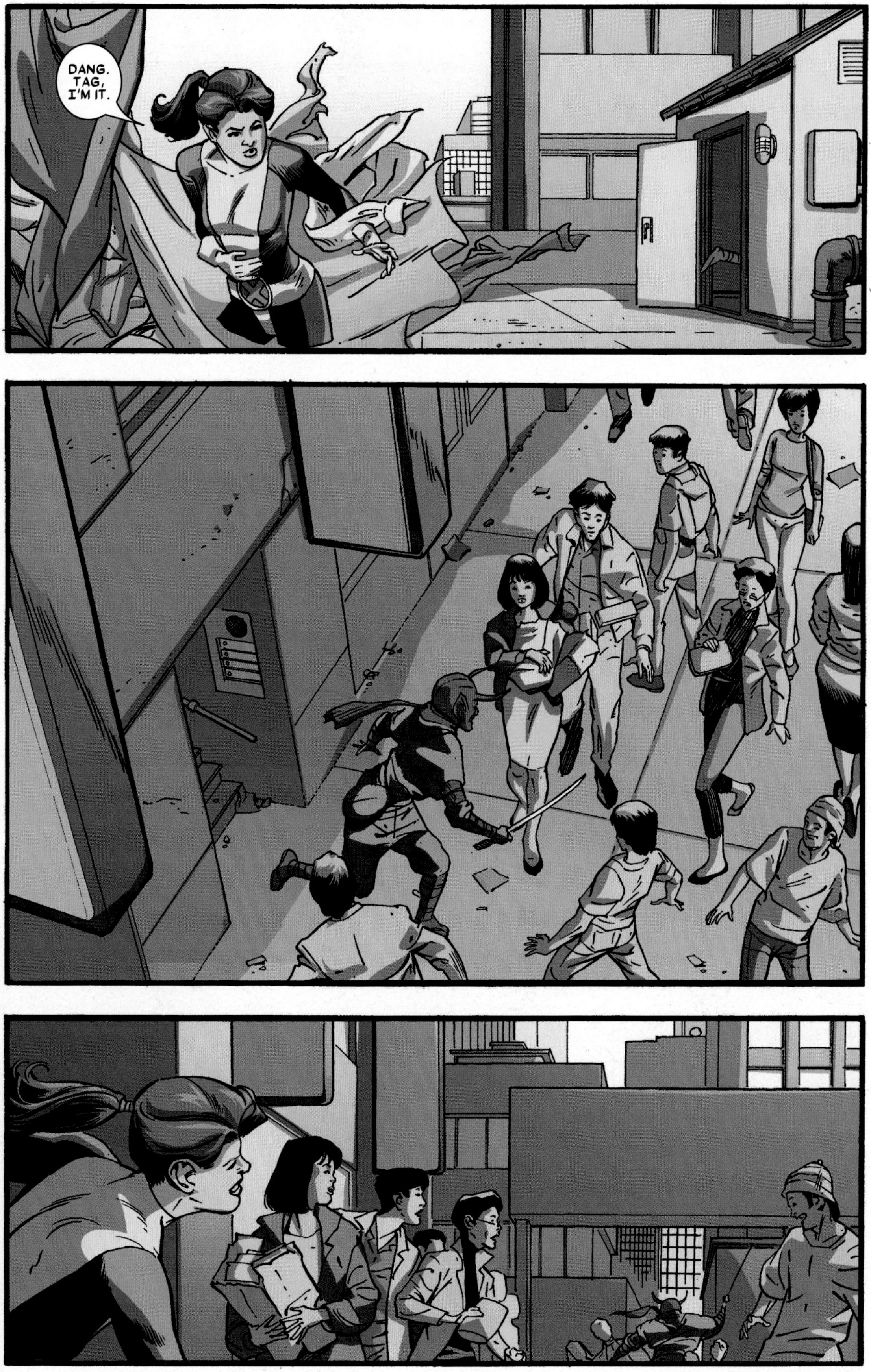
DANG. TAG, I'M IT.

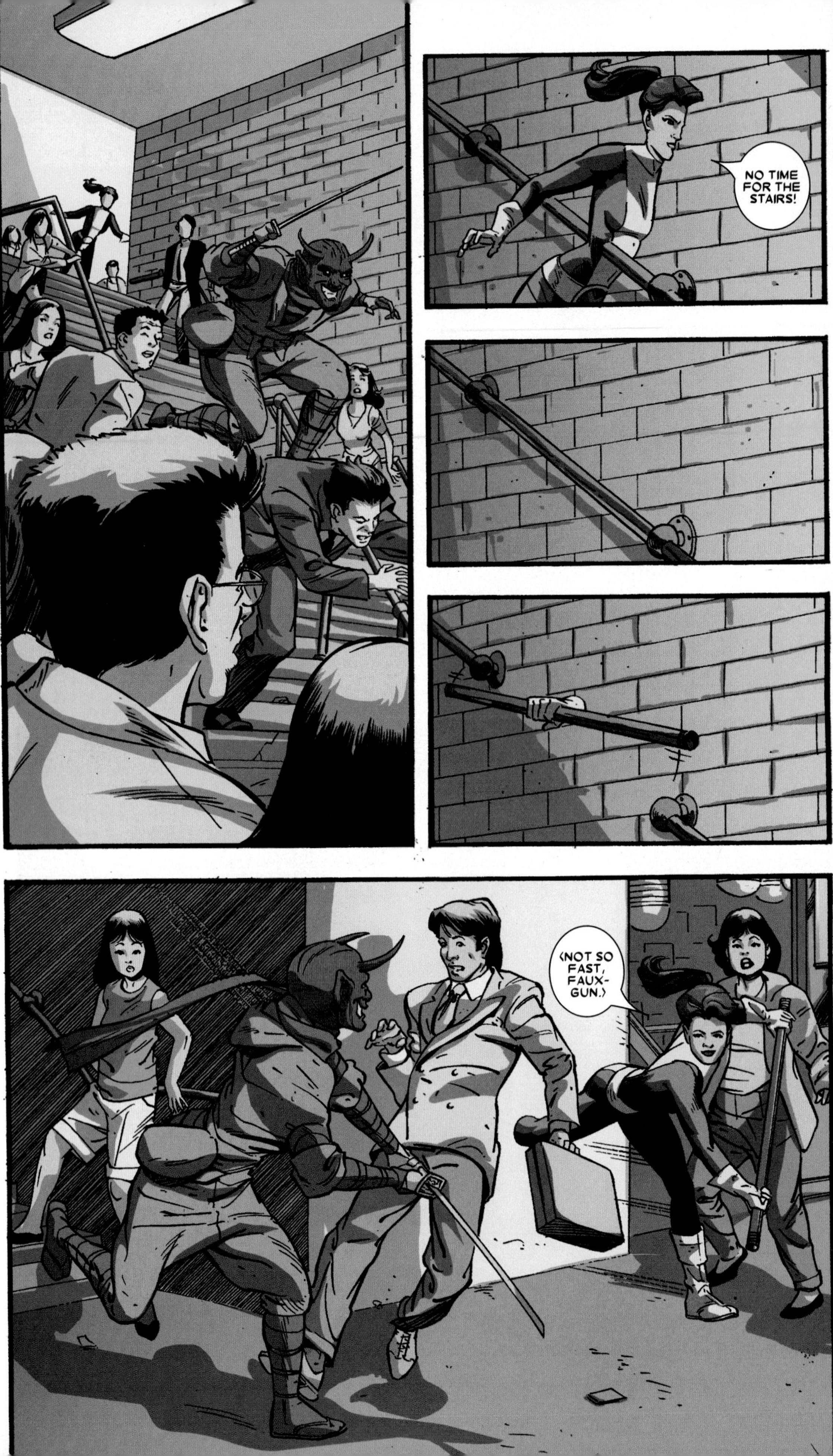
NO TIME FOR THE STAIRS!
<NOT SO FAST, FAUX-GUN.>

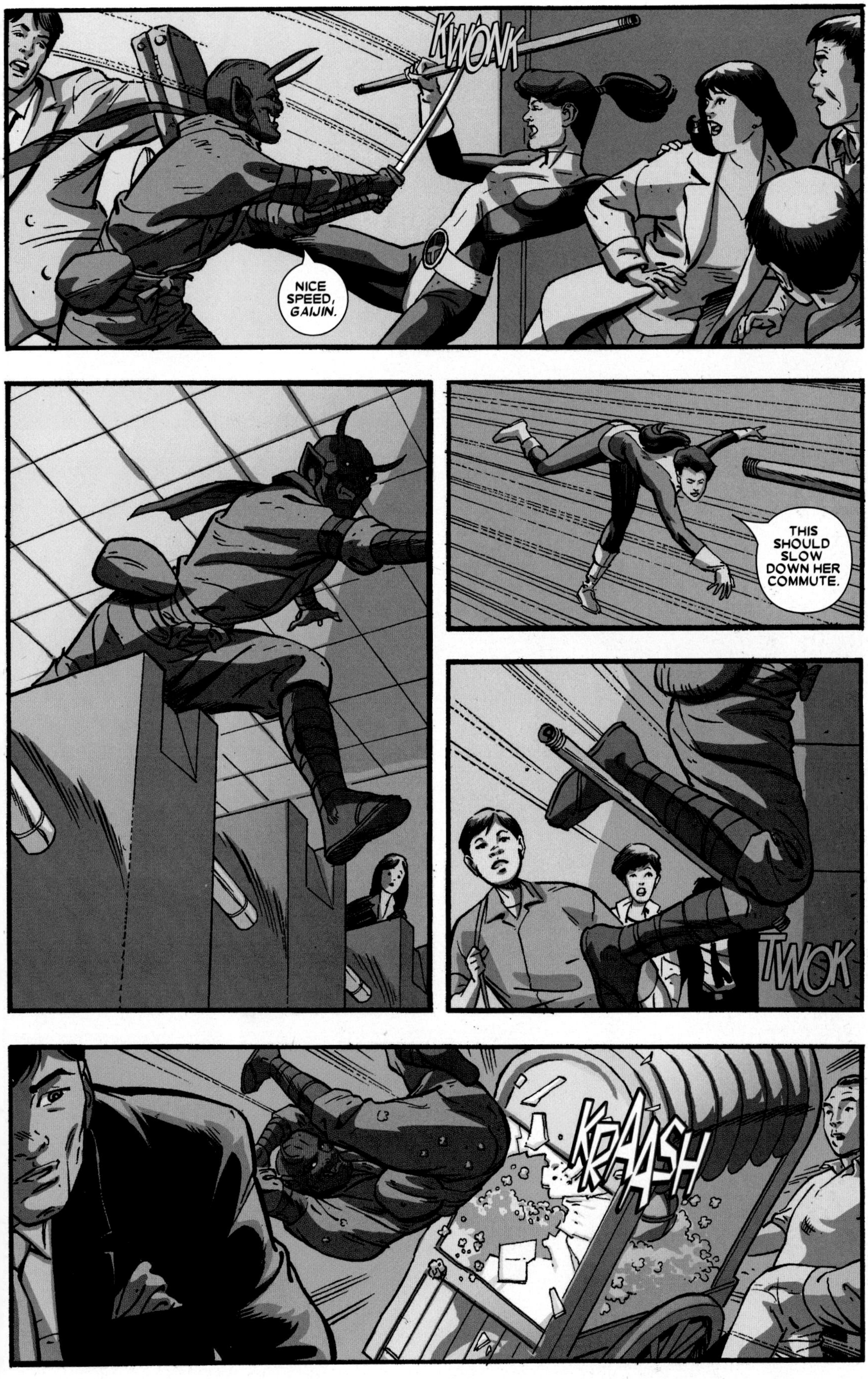
KWONK
NICE SPEED, GAIJIN.
THIS SHOULD SLOW DOWN HER COMMUTE.
TWOK
KRAASH

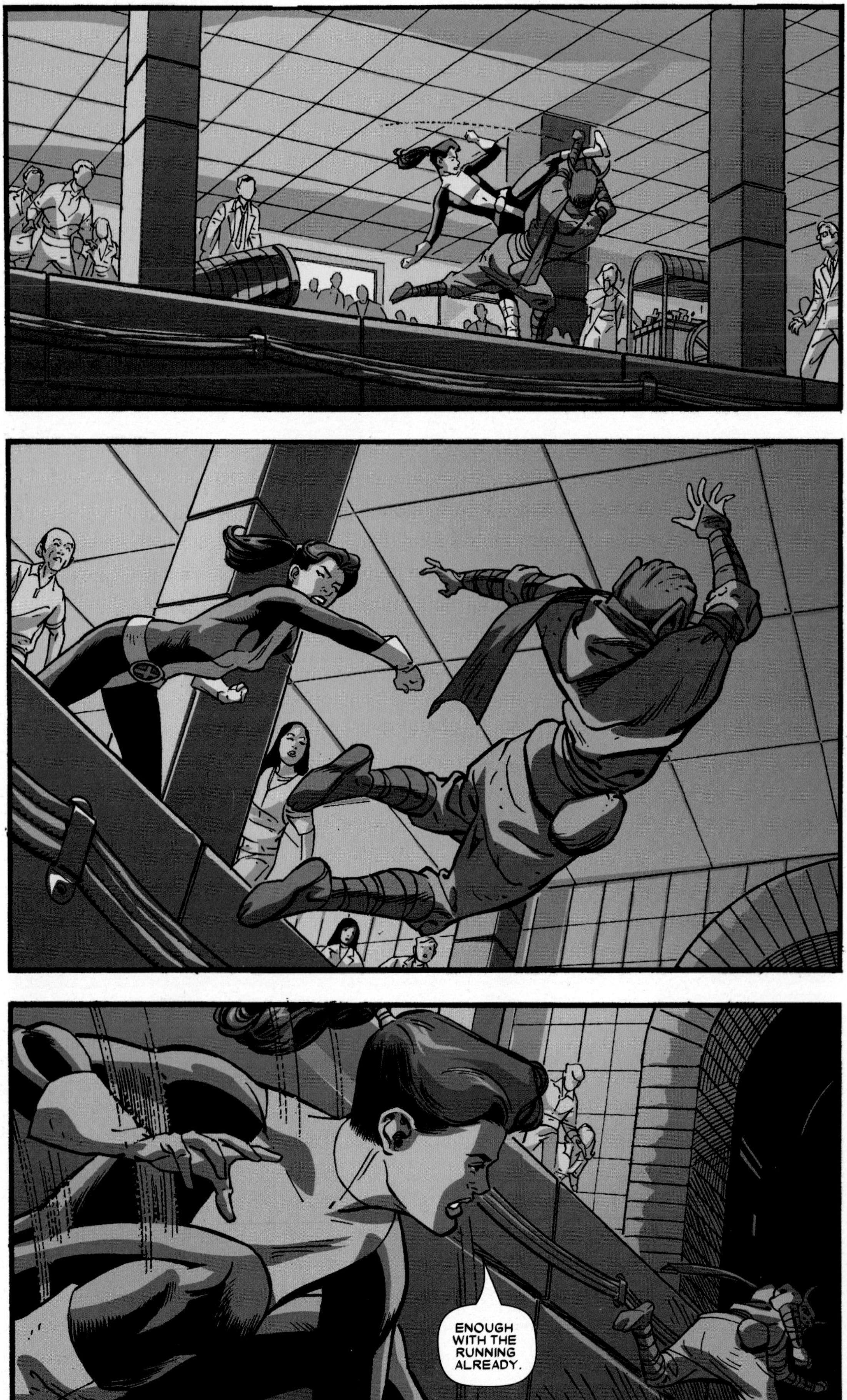
ENOUGH WITH THE RUNNING ALREADY.

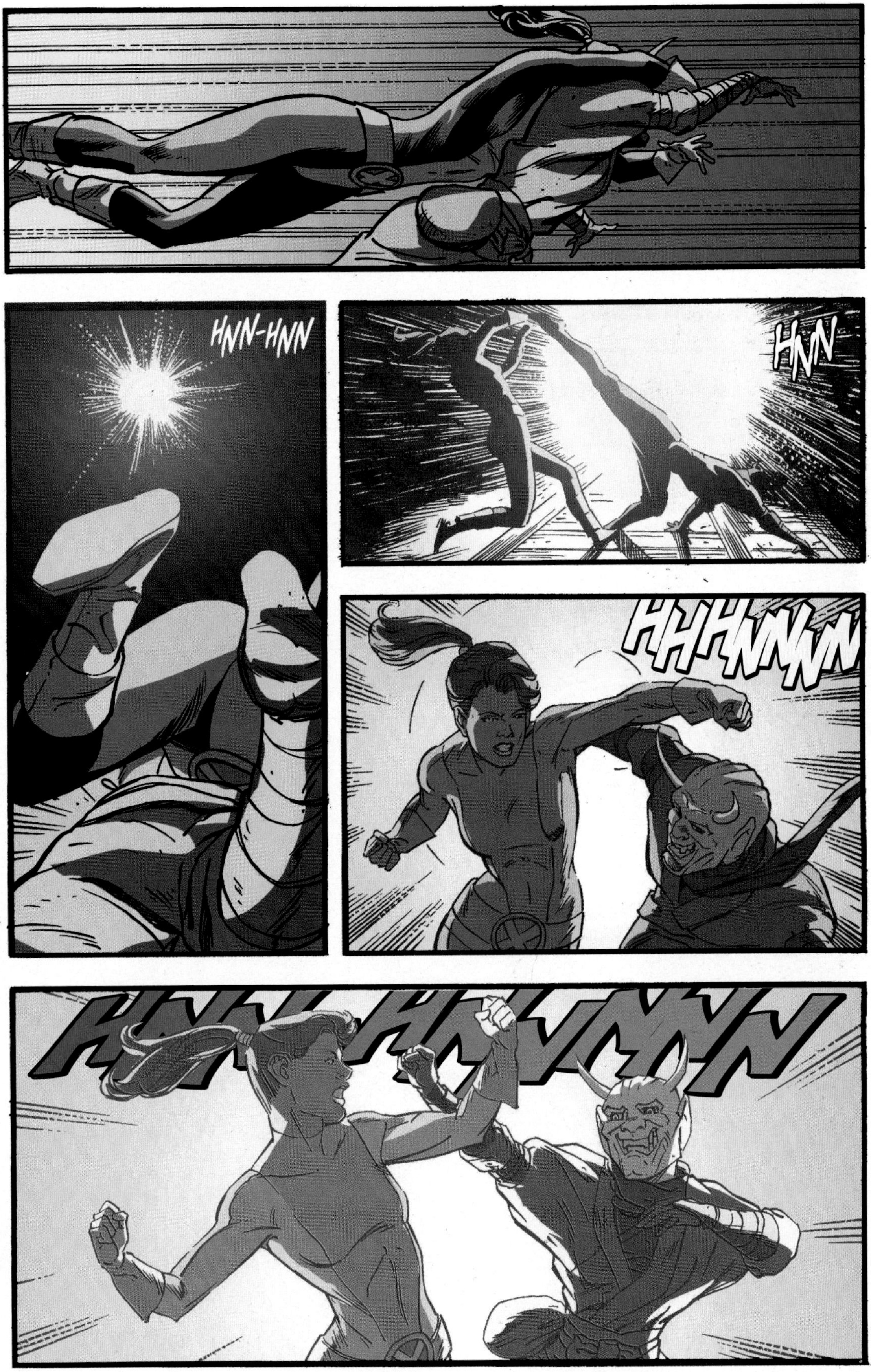
HNN-HNN
HNN
HHHNNNN

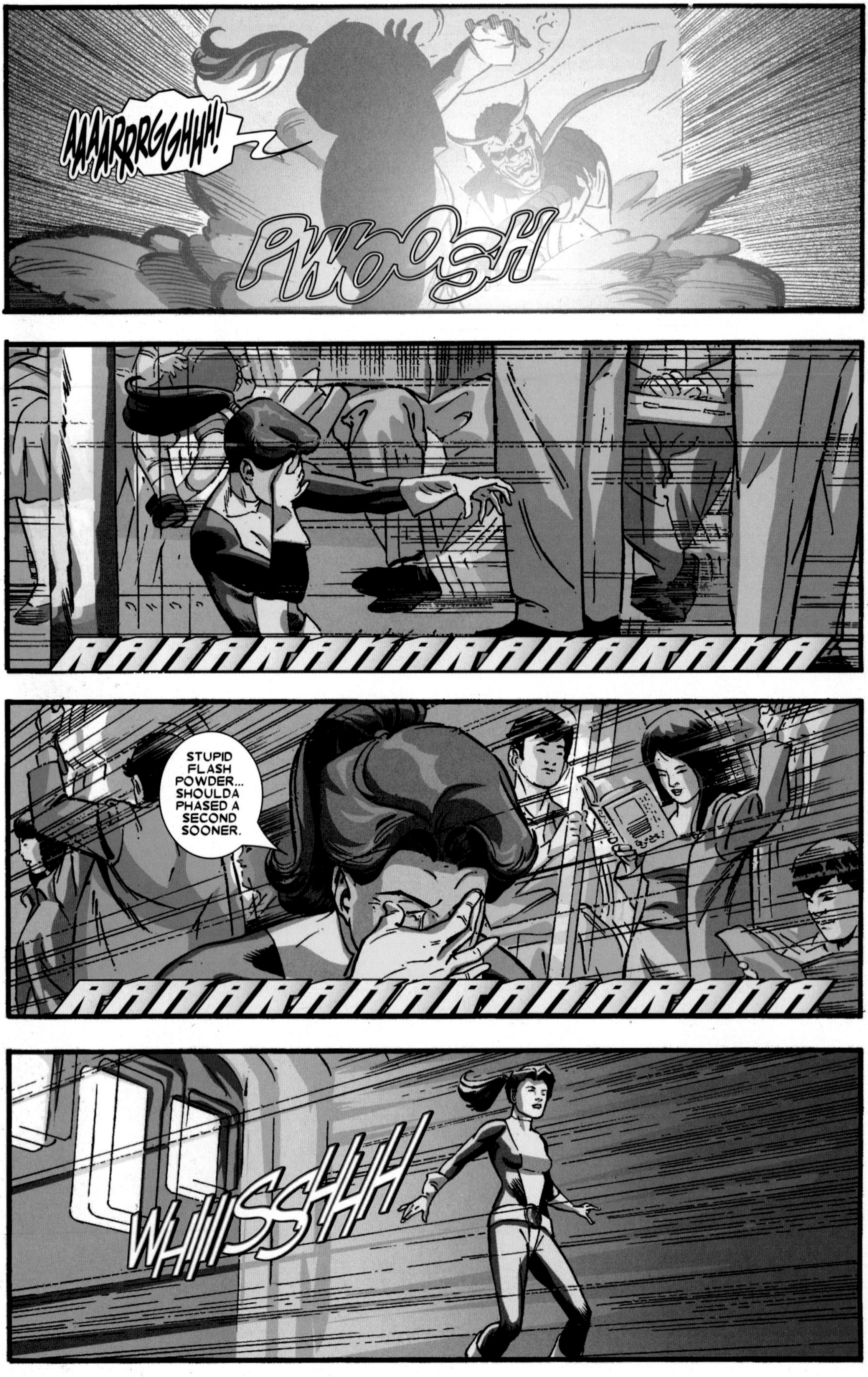
AAAARRRGHHH!
PWOOSH
RAKARAKARAKARAKARAKA
STUPID FLASH POWDER... SHOULDA PHASED A SECOND SOONER.
RAKARAKARAKARAKARAKA
WHIIISSHHH

ALRIGHT, ELMER FUDD... WHICH WAY DID SHE GO?

KRNCH

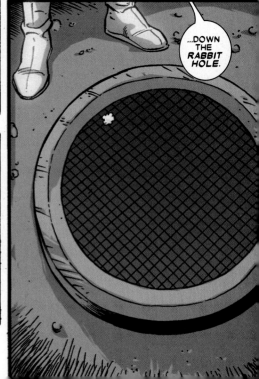

...DOWN THE RABBIT HOLE.

WELL, LOOKEE HERE...

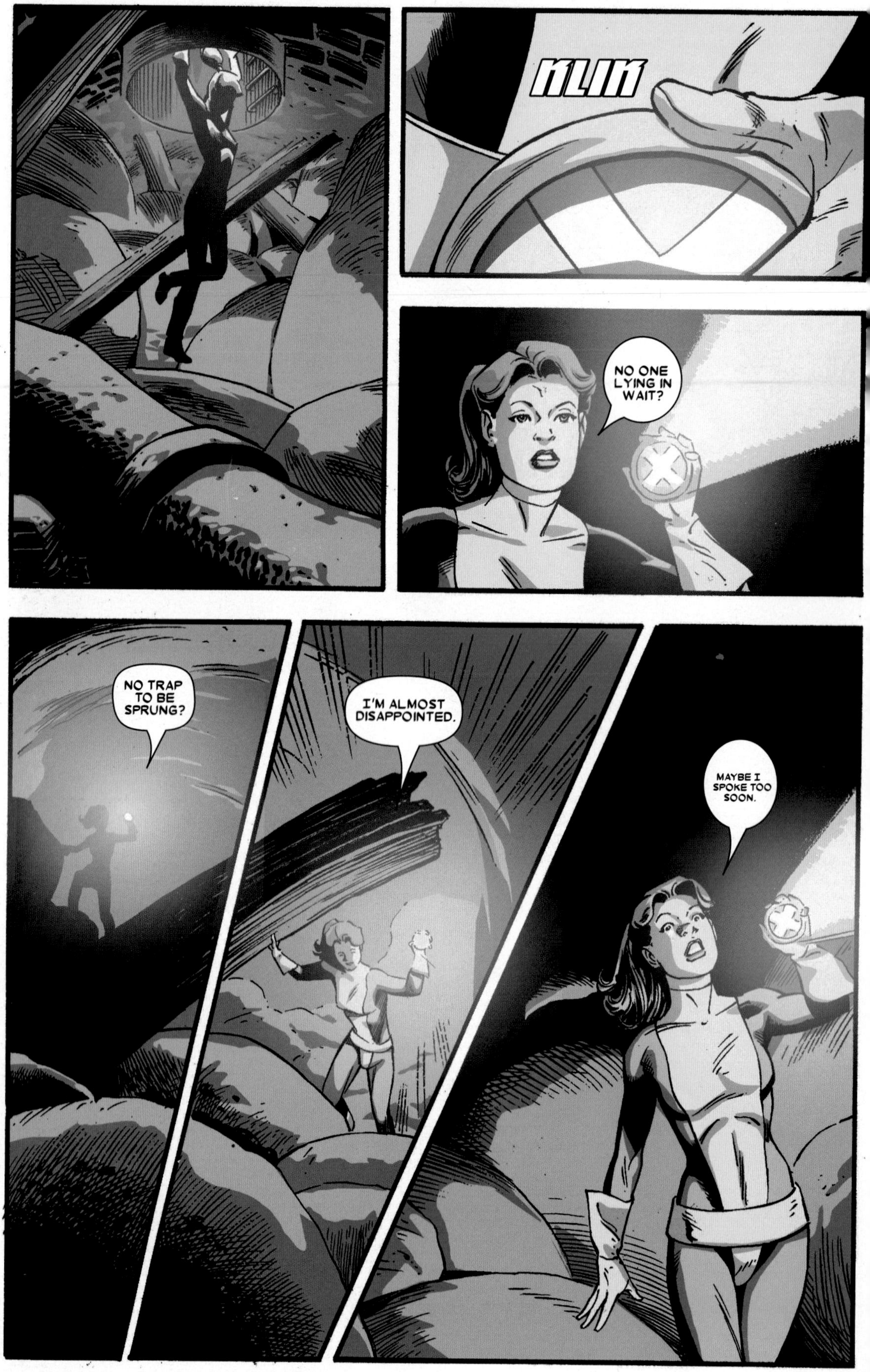
KLIK
NO ONE LYING IN WAIT?
NO TRAP TO BE SPRUNG?
I'M ALMOST DISAPPOINTED.
MAYBE I SPOKE TOO SOON.

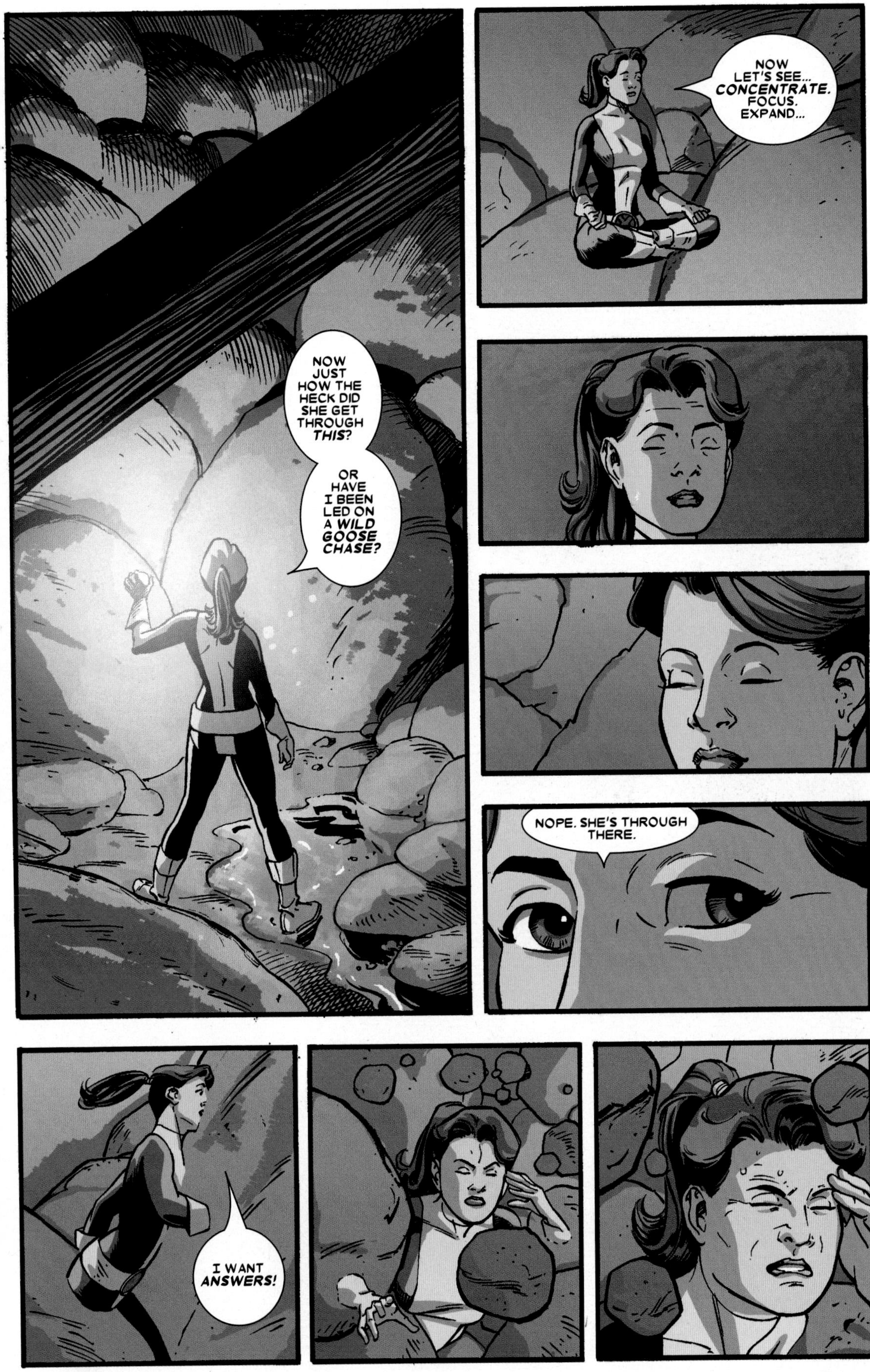
NOW JUST HOW THE HECK DID SHE GET THROUGH *THIS*?
OR HAVE I BEEN LED ON A *WILD GOOSE CHASE?*
NOW LET'S SEE... *CONCENTRATE.* FOCUS. EXPAND...
NOPE. SHE'S THROUGH THERE.
I WANT *ANSWERS!*

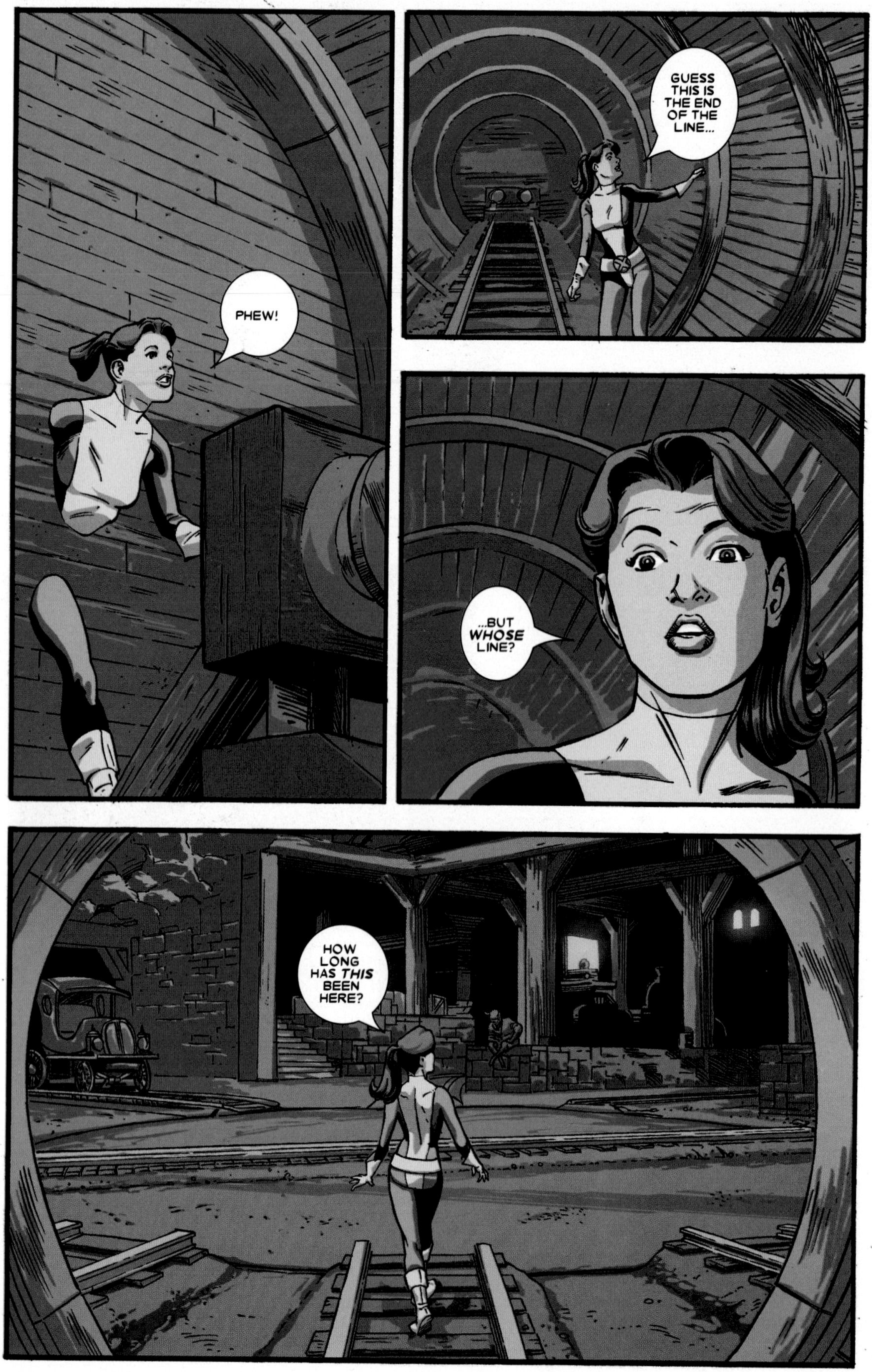
PHEW!
GUESS THIS IS THE END OF THE LINE...
...BUT *WHOSE* LINE?
HOW LONG HAS *THIS* BEEN HERE?

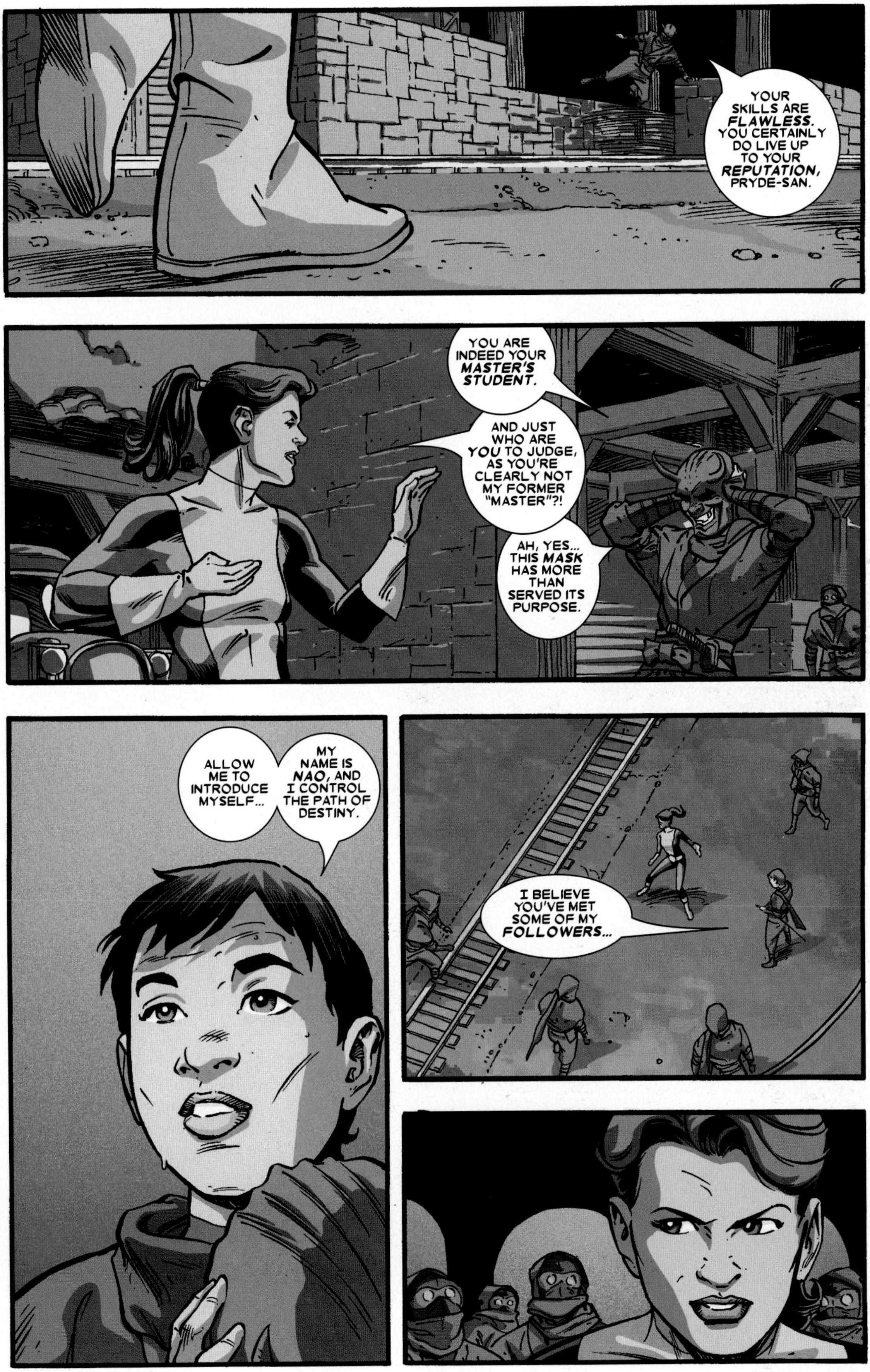

YOUR SKILLS ARE FLAWLESS. YOU CERTAINLY DO LIVE UP TO YOUR REPUTATION, PRYDE-SAN.
YOU ARE INDEED YOUR MASTER'S STUDENT.
AND JUST WHO ARE YOU TO JUDGE, AS YOU'RE CLEARLY NOT MY FORMER "MASTER"?!
AH, YES... THIS MASK HAS MORE THAN SERVED ITS PURPOSE.
ALLOW ME TO INTRODUCE MYSELF...
MY NAME IS NAO, AND I CONTROL THE PATH OF DESTINY.
I BELIEVE YOU'VE MET SOME OF MY FOLLOWERS...

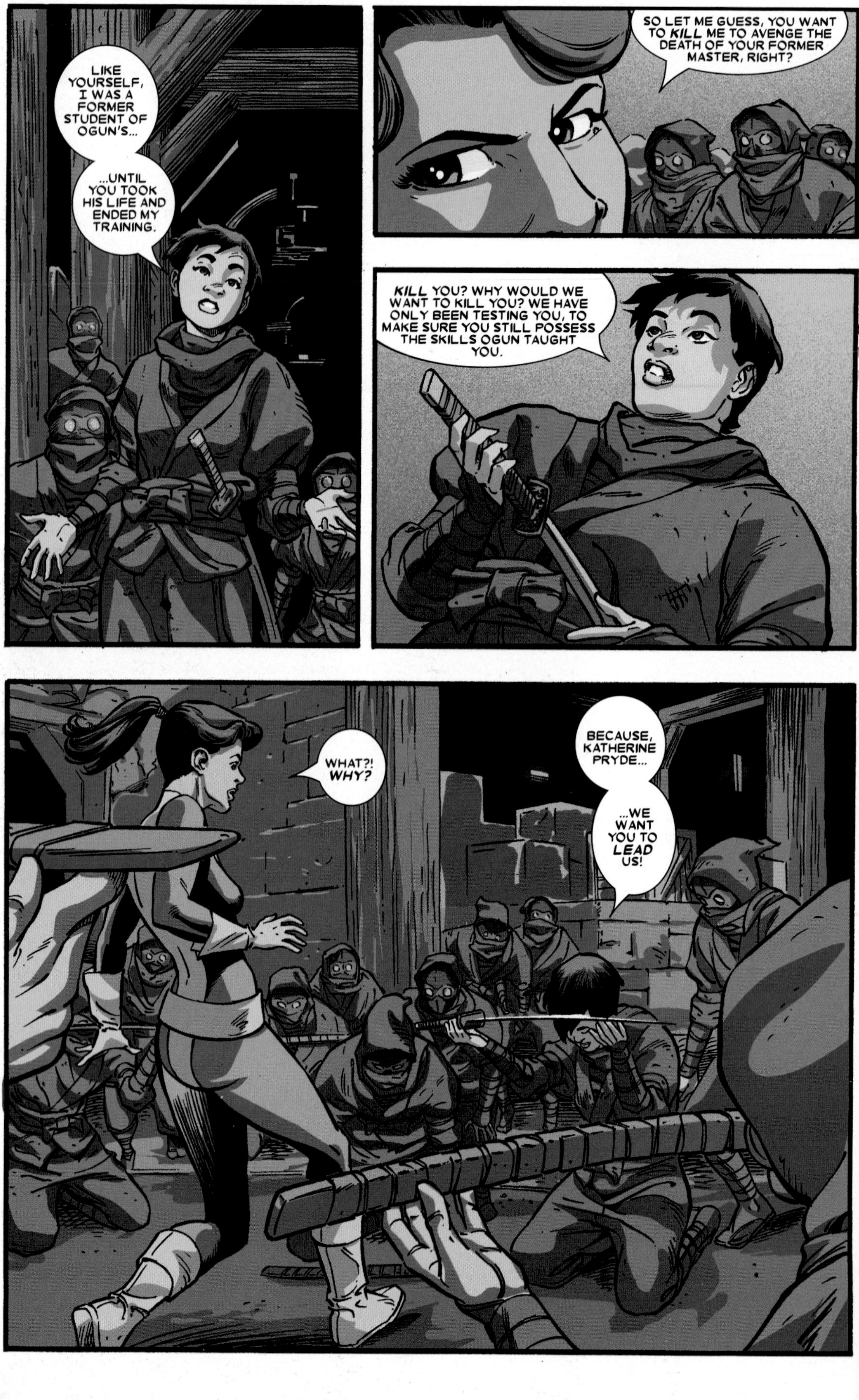
LIKE YOURSELF, I WAS A FORMER STUDENT OF OGUN'S...
...UNTIL YOU TOOK HIS LIFE AND ENDED MY TRAINING.
SO LET ME GUESS, YOU WANT TO **KILL** ME TO AVENGE THE DEATH OF YOUR FORMER MASTER, RIGHT?
KILL YOU? WHY WOULD WE WANT TO KILL YOU? WE HAVE ONLY BEEN TESTING YOU, TO MAKE SURE YOU STILL POSSESS THE SKILLS OGUN TAUGHT YOU.
WHAT?! **WHY?**
BECAUSE, KATHERINE PRYDE...
...WE WANT YOU TO **LEAD** US!

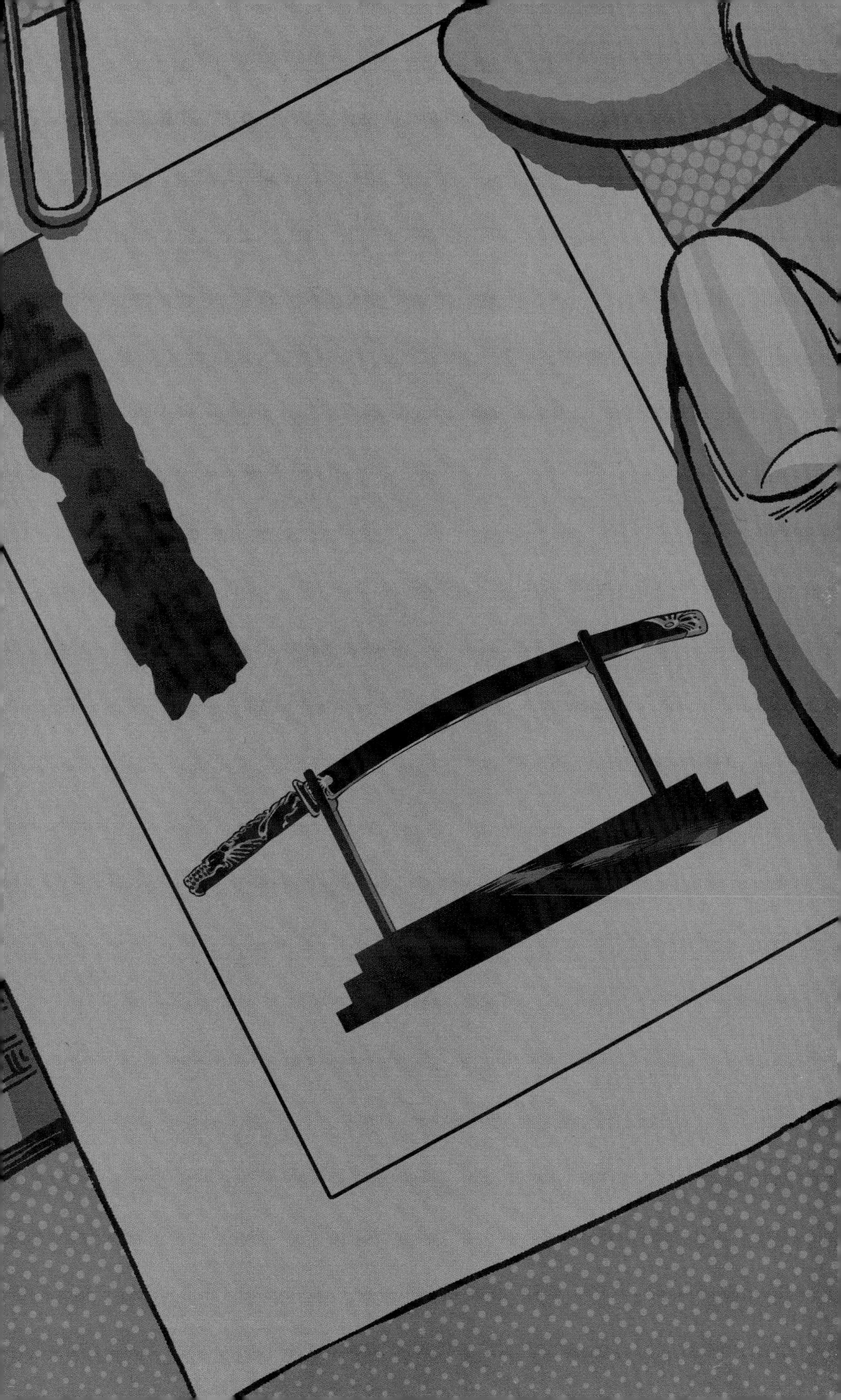

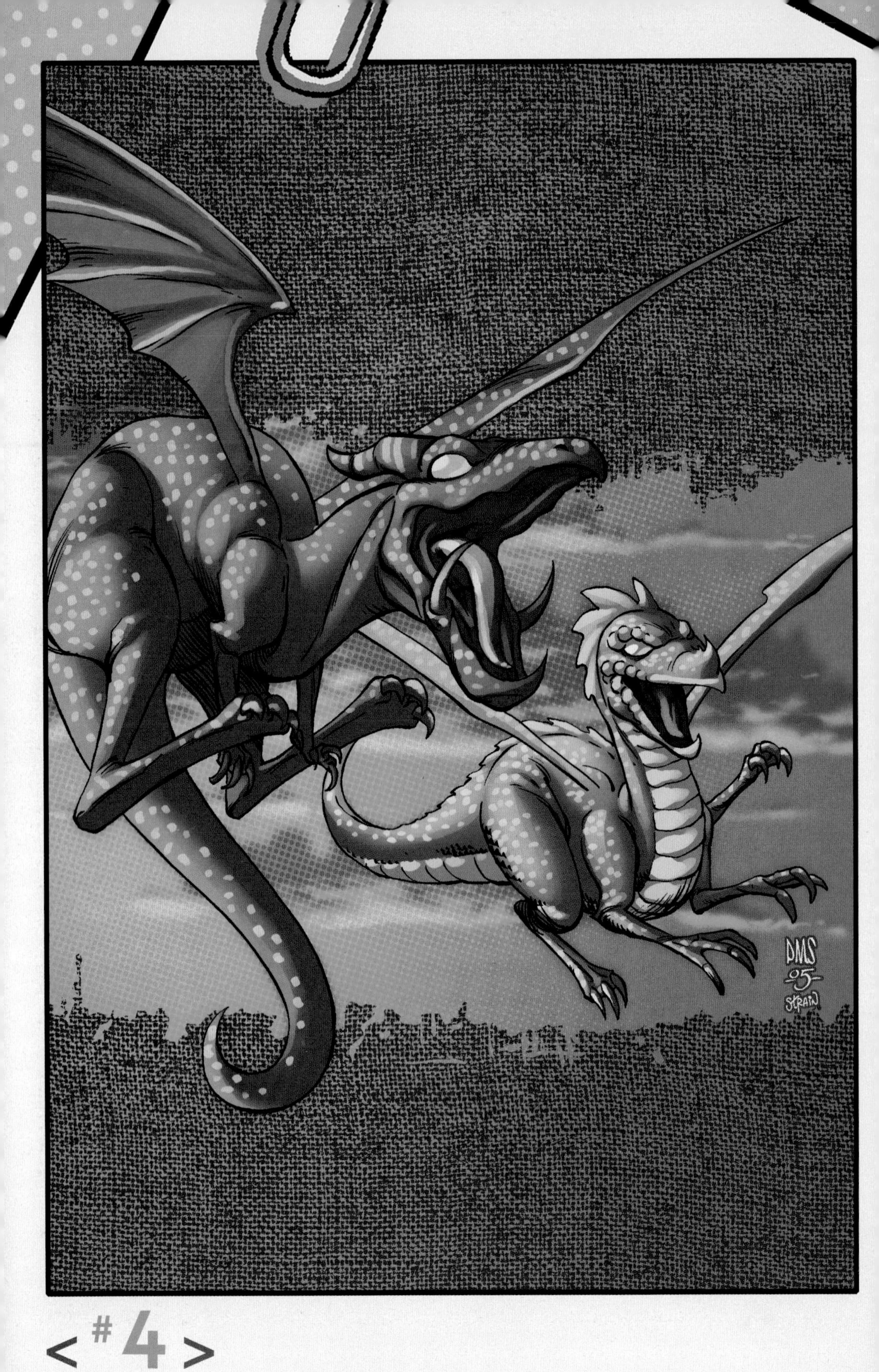
DMS
05
STRAIN

< #4 >

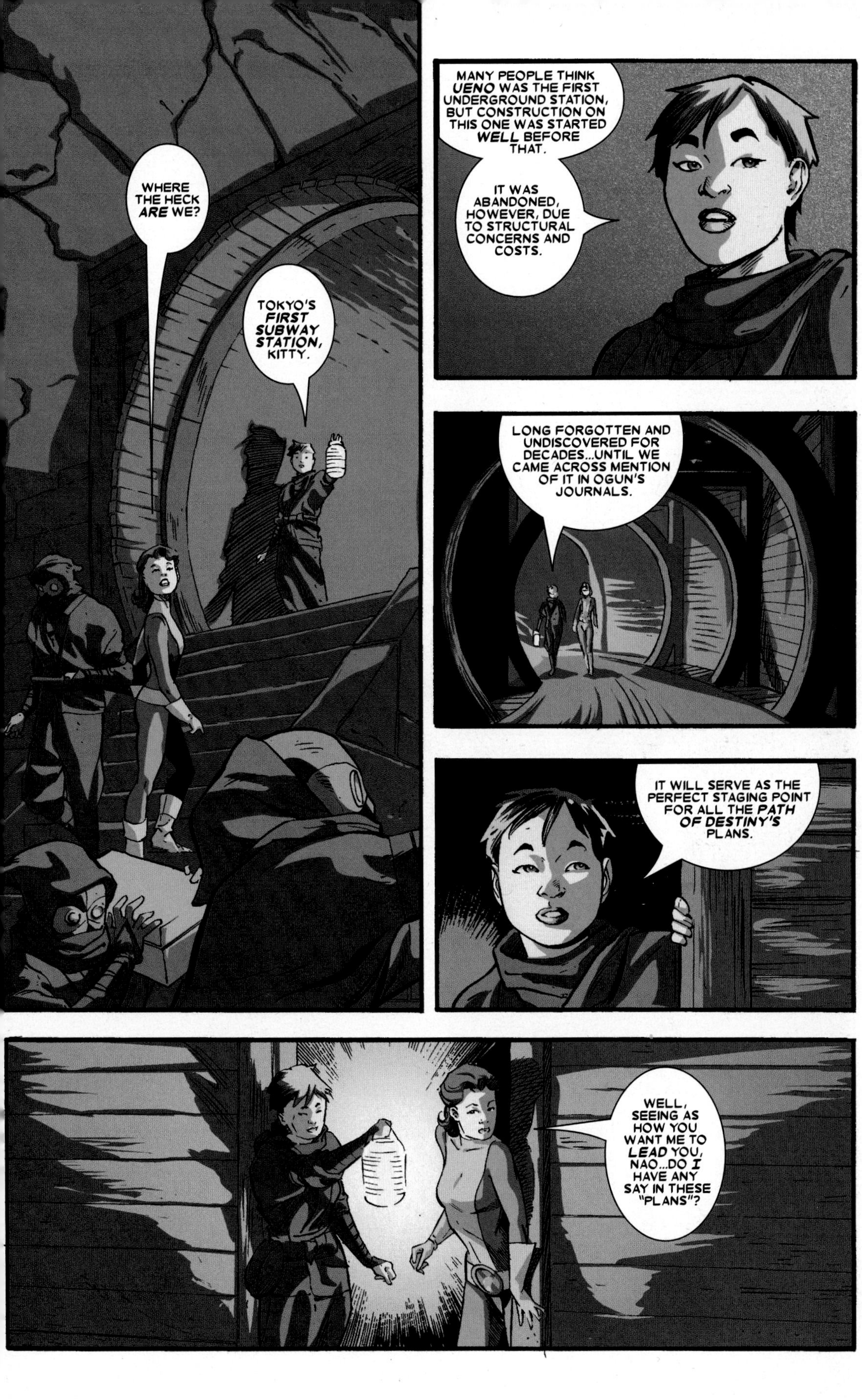
WHERE THE HECK ARE WE?
TOKYO'S FIRST SUBWAY STATION, KITTY.
MANY PEOPLE THINK UENO WAS THE FIRST UNDERGROUND STATION, BUT CONSTRUCTION ON THIS ONE WAS STARTED WELL BEFORE THAT.
IT WAS ABANDONED, HOWEVER, DUE TO STRUCTURAL CONCERNS AND COSTS.
LONG FORGOTTEN AND UNDISCOVERED FOR DECADES...UNTIL WE CAME ACROSS MENTION OF IT IN OGUN'S JOURNALS.
IT WILL SERVE AS THE PERFECT STAGING POINT FOR ALL THE PATH OF DESTINY'S PLANS.
WELL, SEEING AS HOW YOU WANT ME TO LEAD YOU, NAO...DO I HAVE ANY SAY IN THESE "PLANS"?

THAT WILL DEPEND...

ON *WHAT?*

UNLIKE *THE HAND,* WHICH CONSIDERED THEMSELVES JAPANESE PURISTS AND SOUGHT TO DRIVE THE FOREIGNERS FROM OUR LAND--

--THE PATH OF DESTINY CHOSE TO MAINTAIN TRADITIONAL JAPANESE VALUES WHILE INCORPORATING THEM WITH WESTERN PHILOSOPHIES.

WE EMBRACED THE BEST OF *BOTH WORLDS* FOR OUR OWN ADVANCEMENT IN THE JAPANESE UNDERWORLD.

YOUR *COMMITMENT* TO OUR CAUSE.

THE PATH IS AN ORGANIZATION WITH A *RICH HISTORY,* DATING BACK TO THE TIMES OF THE MEIJI RESTORATION, WHEN JAPAN WAS JUST STARTING TO OPEN ITS SHORES TO FOREIGN INFLUENCE.

ALSO UNLIKE OTHER CLANS AT THAT TIME, WHICH ACTED AS MERCENARIES AND SOLD THEIR SKILLS TO THE HIGHEST BIDDERS, THE PATH CHOSE TO REMAIN *HIDDEN* AND FOLLOW THEIR *OWN AGENDAS,* ACTING ONLY WHEN NECESSARY, UNDER THE DIRECT LEADERSHIP OF *OGUN.*

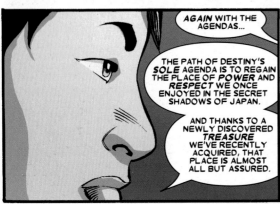

AGAIN WITH THE AGENDAS...

THE PATH OF DESTINY'S *SOLE* AGENDA IS TO REGAIN THE PLACE OF *POWER* AND *RESPECT* WE ONCE ENJOYED IN THE SECRET SHADOWS OF JAPAN.

AND THANKS TO A NEWLY DISCOVERED *TREASURE* WE'VE RECENTLY ACQUIRED, THAT PLACE IS ALMOST ALL BUT ASSURED.

YOU MEAN A TREASURE OTHER THAN *ME?* I'M A LITTLE DISAPPOINTED.

CUTE. SEE FOR YOURSELF.

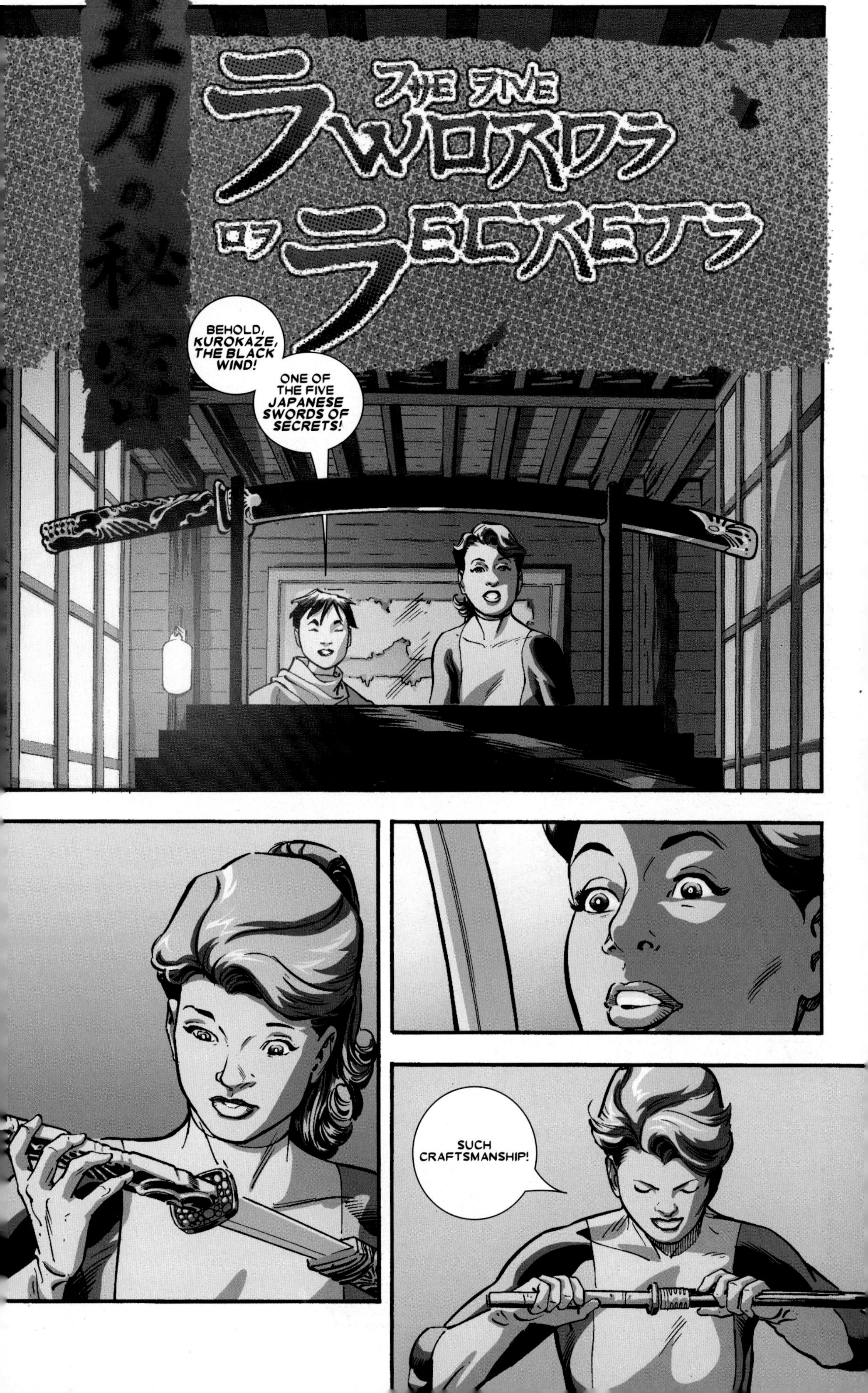

五刀の秘
THE FIVE SWORDS OF SECRETS
BEHOLD, KUROKAZE, THE BLACK WIND!
ONE OF THE FIVE JAPANESE SWORDS OF SECRETS!
SUCH CRAFTSMANSHIP!

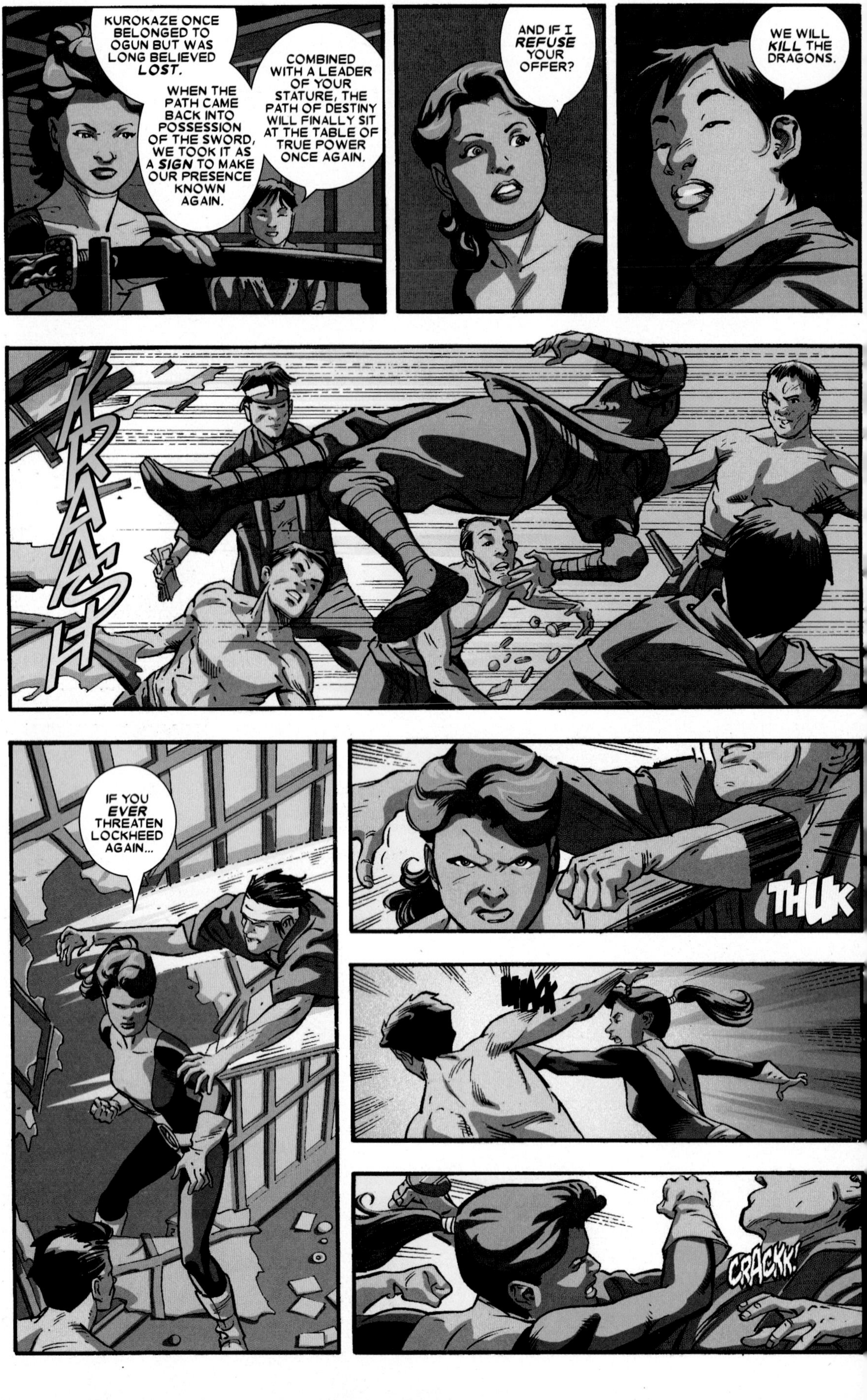
KUROKAZE ONCE BELONGED TO OGUN BUT WAS LONG BELIEVED LOST.
WHEN THE PATH CAME BACK INTO POSSESSION OF THE SWORD, WE TOOK IT AS A SIGN TO MAKE OUR PRESENCE KNOWN AGAIN.
COMBINED WITH A LEADER OF YOUR STATURE, THE PATH OF DESTINY WILL FINALLY SIT AT THE TABLE OF TRUE POWER ONCE AGAIN.
AND IF I REFUSE YOUR OFFER?
WE WILL KILL THE DRAGONS.
KRAASH
IF YOU EVER THREATEN LOCKHEED AGAIN...
THUK
CRACKK!

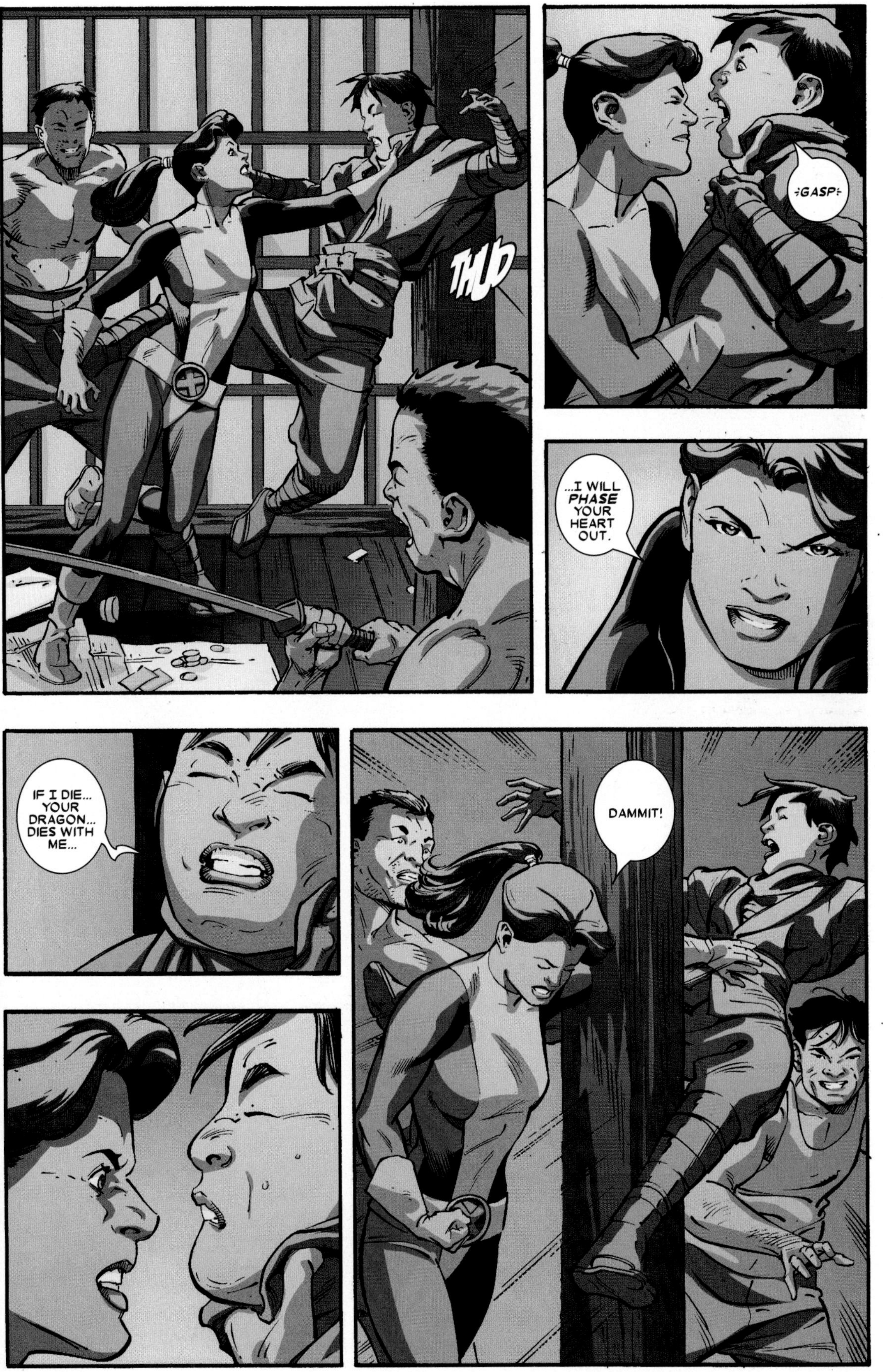

THUD
GASP
...I WILL PHASE YOUR HEART OUT.
IF I DIE... YOUR DRAGON... DIES WITH ME...
DAMMIT!

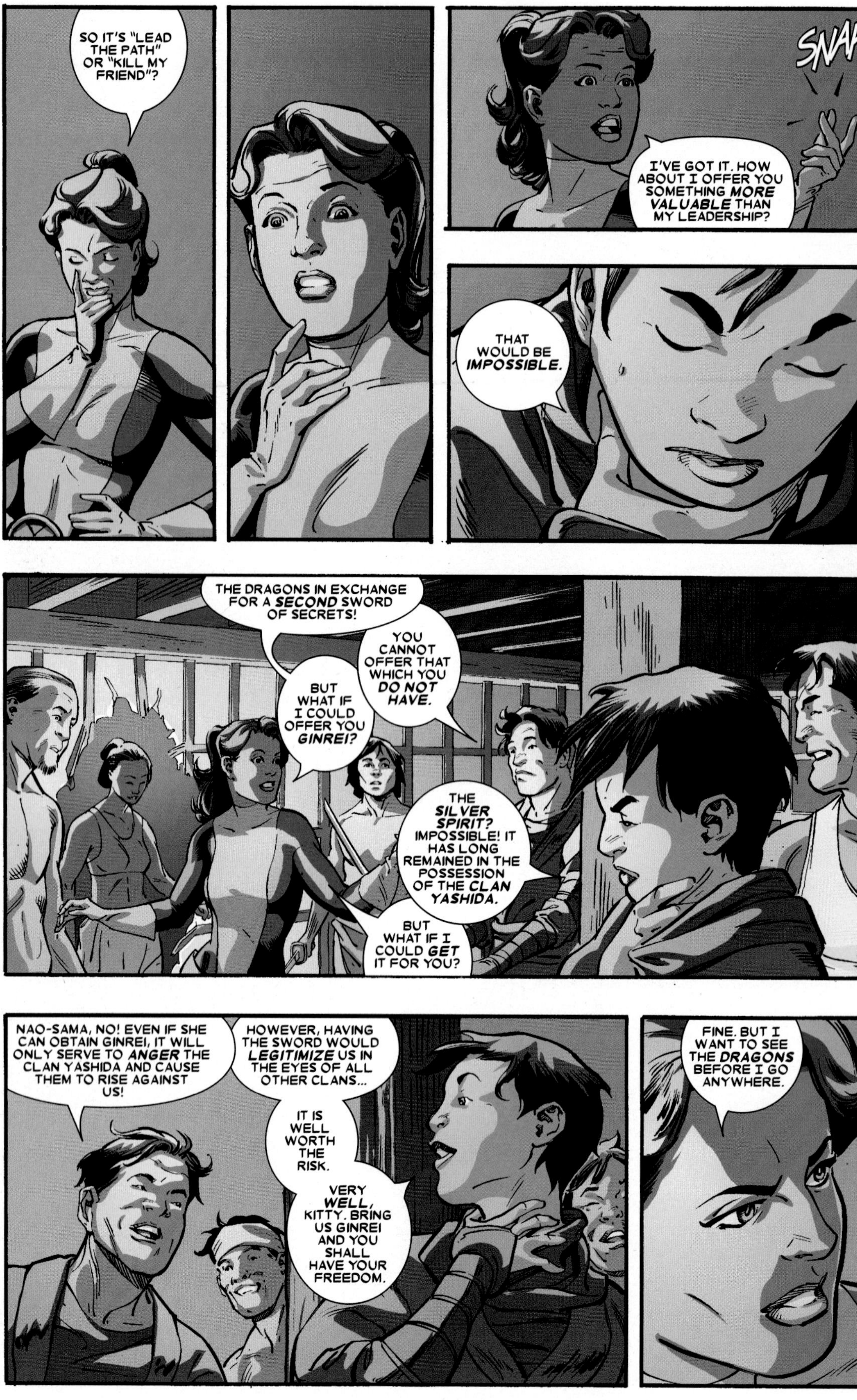

SO IT'S "LEAD THE PATH" OR "KILL MY FRIEND"?
SNAP
I'VE GOT IT. HOW ABOUT I OFFER YOU SOMETHING MORE VALUABLE THAN MY LEADERSHIP?
THAT WOULD BE IMPOSSIBLE.
THE DRAGONS IN EXCHANGE FOR A SECOND SWORD OF SECRETS!
YOU CANNOT OFFER THAT WHICH YOU DO NOT HAVE.
BUT WHAT IF I COULD OFFER YOU GINREI?
THE SILVER SPIRIT? IMPOSSIBLE! IT HAS LONG REMAINED IN THE POSSESSION OF THE CLAN YASHIDA.
BUT WHAT IF I COULD GET IT FOR YOU?
NAO-SAMA, NO! EVEN IF SHE CAN OBTAIN GINREI, IT WILL ONLY SERVE TO ANGER THE CLAN YASHIDA AND CAUSE THEM TO RISE AGAINST US!
HOWEVER, HAVING THE SWORD WOULD LEGITIMIZE US IN THE EYES OF ALL OTHER CLANS...
IT IS WELL WORTH THE RISK.
VERY WELL, KITTY. BRING US GINREI AND YOU SHALL HAVE YOUR FREEDOM.
FINE. BUT I WANT TO SEE THE DRAGONS BEFORE I GO ANYWHERE.

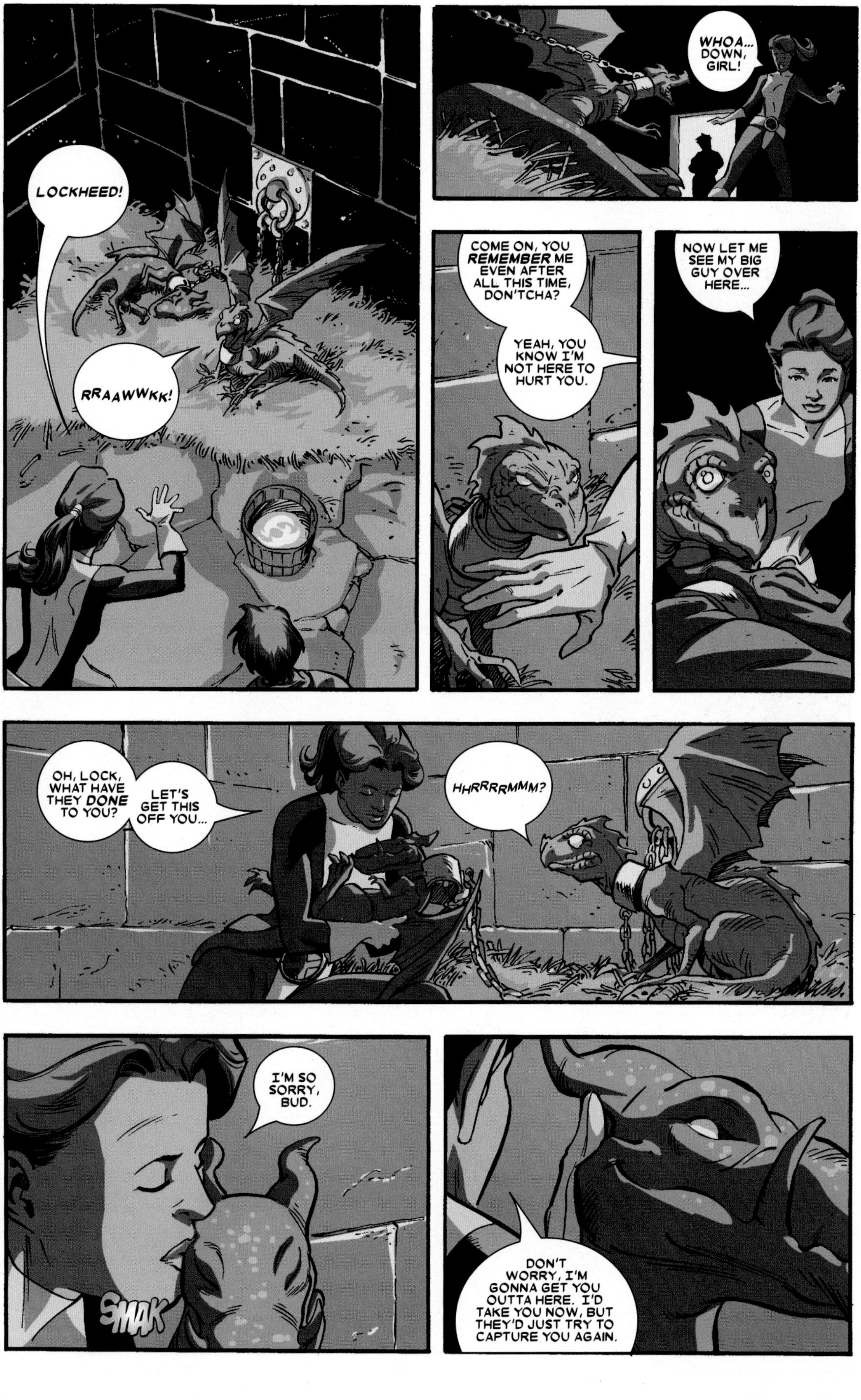

LOCKHEED!
RRAAWWKK!
WHOA... DOWN, GIRL!
COME ON, YOU *REMEMBER* ME EVEN AFTER ALL THIS TIME, DON'TCHA?
YEAH, YOU KNOW I'M NOT HERE TO HURT YOU.
NOW LET ME SEE MY BIG GUY OVER HERE...
OH, LOCK, WHAT HAVE THEY *DONE* TO YOU?
LET'S GET THIS OFF YOU...
HHRRRRMMM?
I'M SO SORRY, BUD.
SMAK
DON'T WORRY, I'M GONNA GET YOU OUTTA HERE. I'D TAKE YOU NOW, BUT THEY'D JUST TRY TO CAPTURE YOU AGAIN.

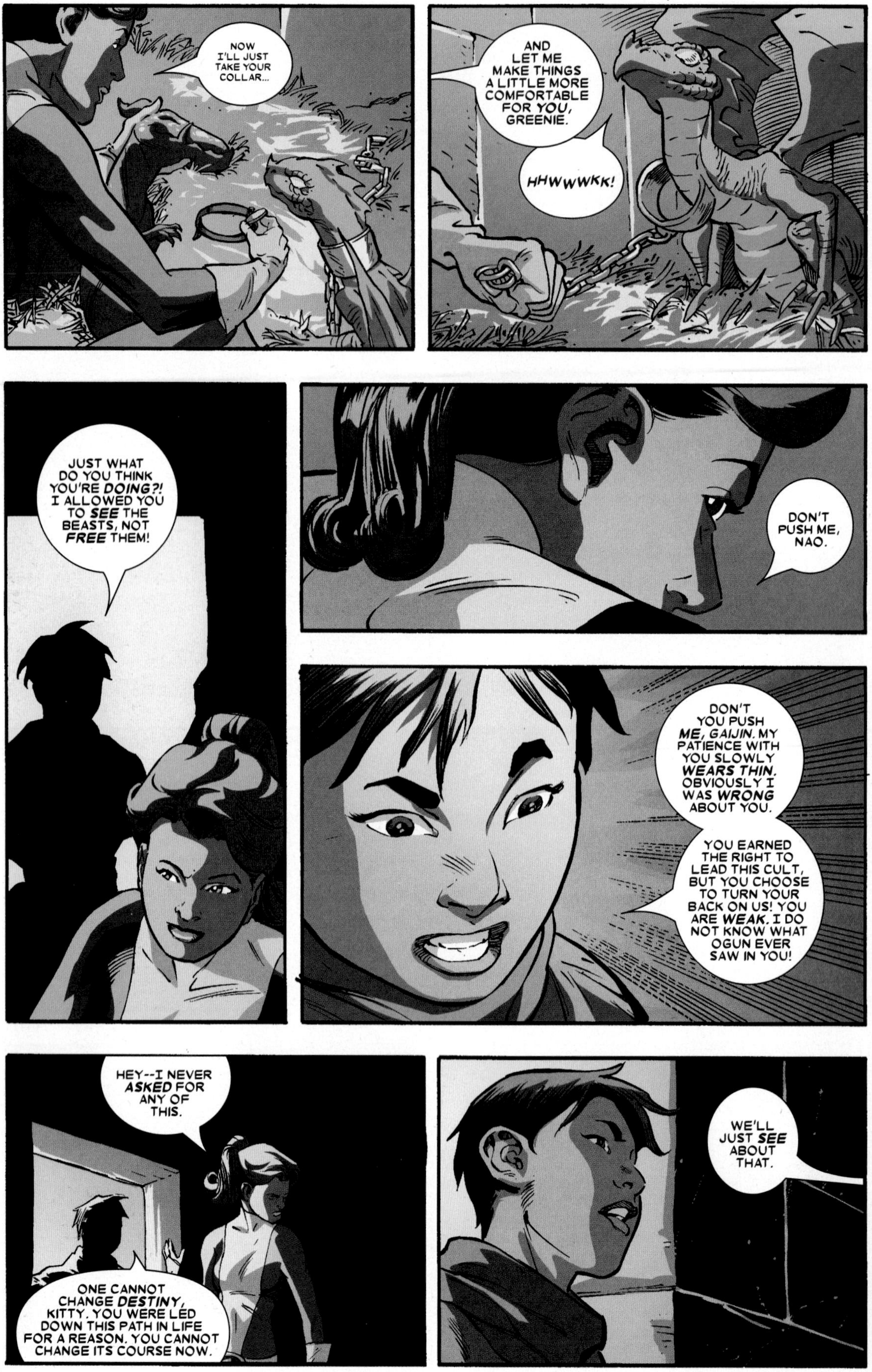
NOW I'LL JUST TAKE YOUR COLLAR...
AND LET ME MAKE THINGS A LITTLE MORE COMFORTABLE FOR YOU, GREENIE.
HHWWWKK!
JUST WHAT DO YOU THINK YOU'RE DOING?! I ALLOWED YOU TO SEE THE BEASTS, NOT FREE THEM!
DON'T PUSH ME, NAO.
DON'T YOU PUSH ME, GAIJIN. MY PATIENCE WITH YOU SLOWLY WEARS THIN. OBVIOUSLY I WAS WRONG ABOUT YOU.
YOU EARNED THE RIGHT TO LEAD THIS CULT, BUT YOU CHOOSE TO TURN YOUR BACK ON US! YOU ARE WEAK. I DO NOT KNOW WHAT OGUN EVER SAW IN YOU!
HEY--I NEVER ASKED FOR ANY OF THIS.
ONE CANNOT CHANGE DESTINY, KITTY. YOU WERE LED DOWN THIS PATH IN LIFE FOR A REASON. YOU CANNOT CHANGE ITS COURSE NOW.
WE'LL JUST SEE ABOUT THAT.

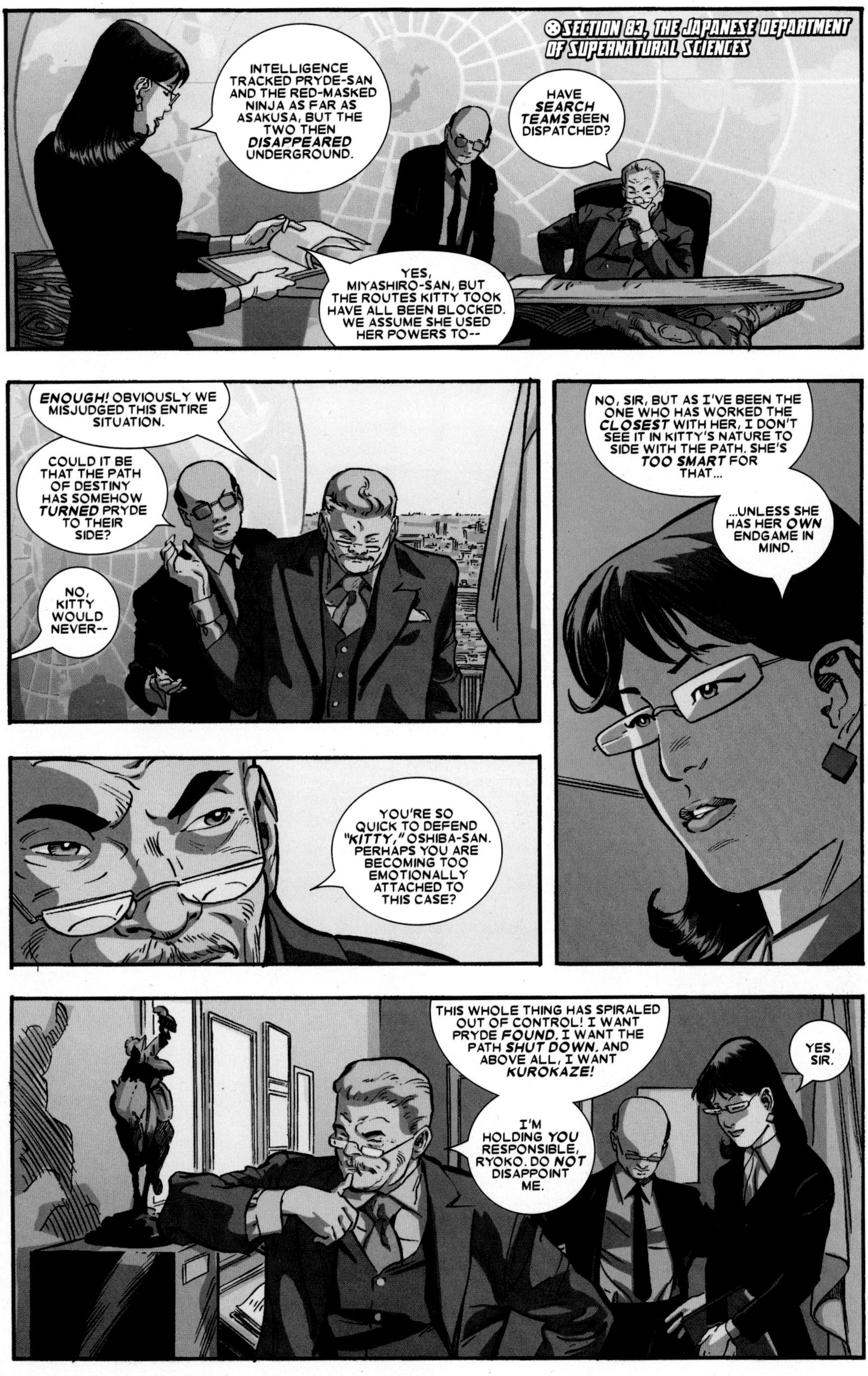
SECTION 83, THE JAPANESE DEPARTMENT OF SUPERNATURAL SCIENCES
INTELLIGENCE TRACKED PRYDE-SAN AND THE RED-MASKED NINJA AS FAR AS ASAKUSA, BUT THE TWO THEN DISAPPEARED UNDERGROUND.
HAVE SEARCH TEAMS BEEN DISPATCHED?
YES, MIYASHIRO-SAN, BUT THE ROUTES KITTY TOOK HAVE ALL BEEN BLOCKED. WE ASSUME SHE USED HER POWERS TO--
ENOUGH! OBVIOUSLY WE MISJUDGED THIS ENTIRE SITUATION.
COULD IT BE THAT THE PATH OF DESTINY HAS SOMEHOW TURNED PRYDE TO THEIR SIDE?
NO, KITTY WOULD NEVER--
YOU'RE SO QUICK TO DEFEND "KITTY," OSHIBA-SAN. PERHAPS YOU ARE BECOMING TOO EMOTIONALLY ATTACHED TO THIS CASE?
NO, SIR, BUT AS I'VE BEEN THE ONE WHO HAS WORKED THE CLOSEST WITH HER, I DON'T SEE IT IN KITTY'S NATURE TO SIDE WITH THE PATH. SHE'S TOO SMART FOR THAT...
...UNLESS SHE HAS HER OWN ENDGAME IN MIND.
THIS WHOLE THING HAS SPIRALED OUT OF CONTROL! I WANT PRYDE FOUND. I WANT THE PATH SHUT DOWN. AND ABOVE ALL, I WANT KUROKAZE!
I'M HOLDING YOU RESPONSIBLE, RYOKO. DO NOT DISAPPOINT ME.
YES, SIR.

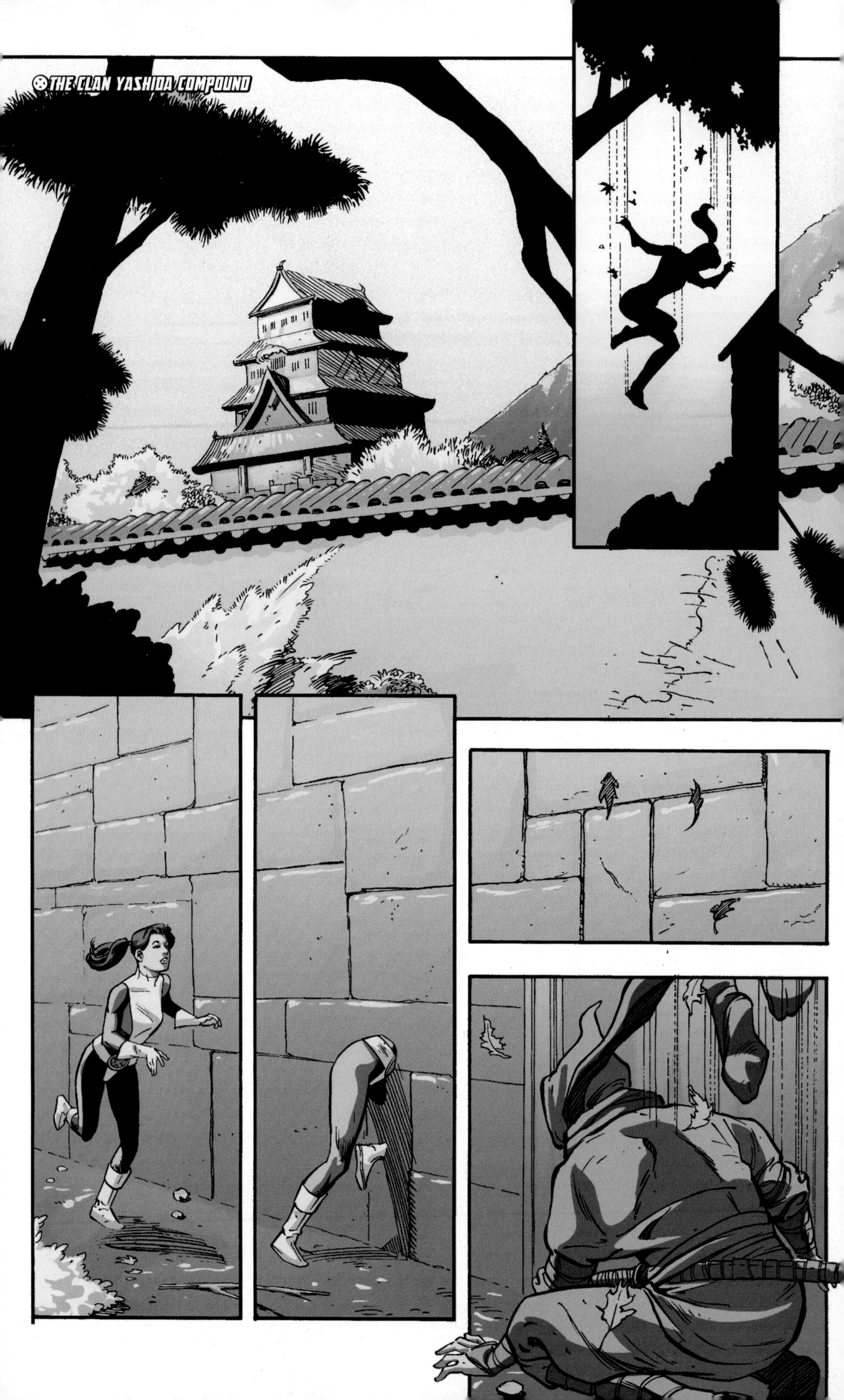
THE CLAN YASHIDA COMPOUND

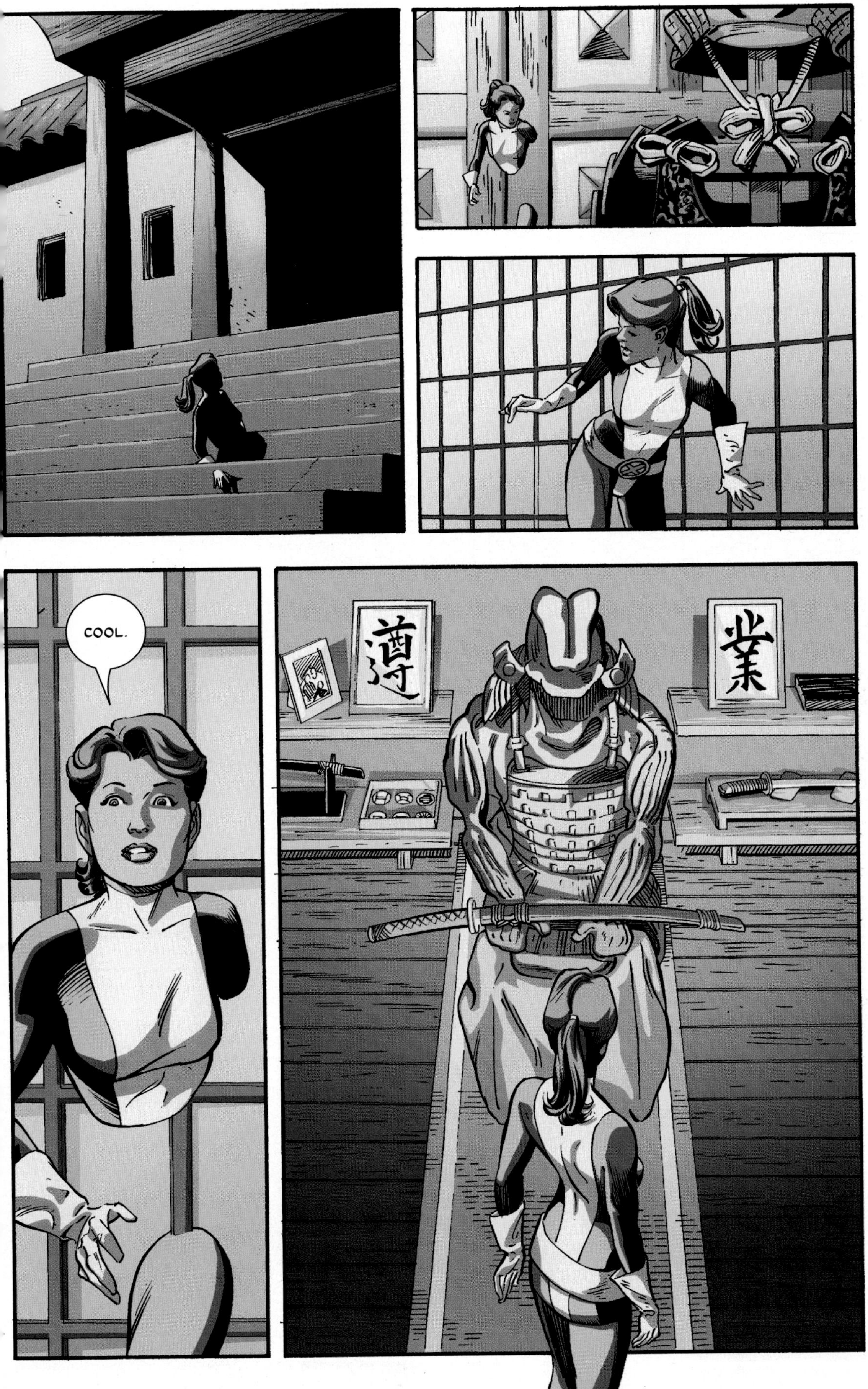

COOL.

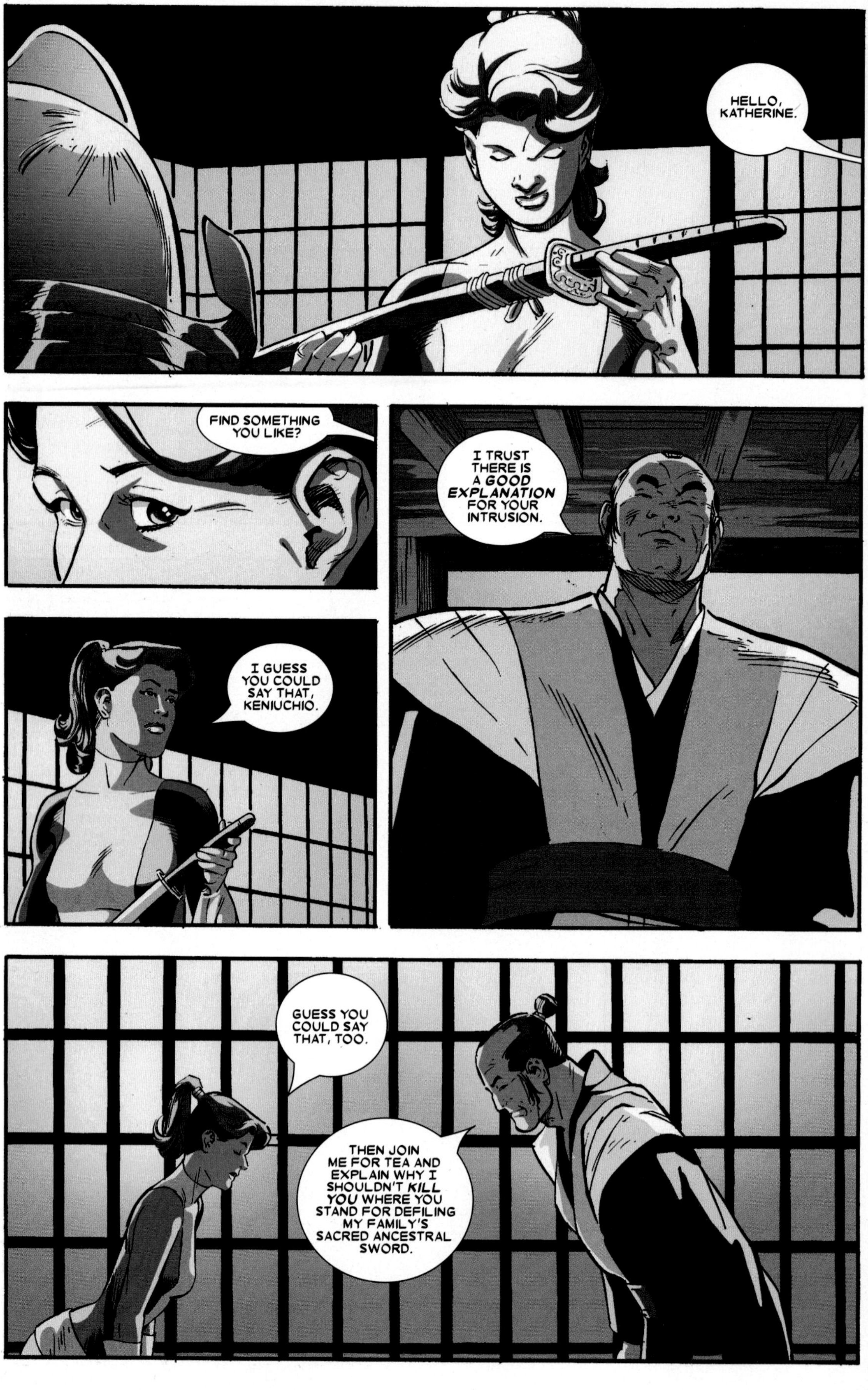
HELLO, KATHERINE.
FIND SOMETHING YOU LIKE?
I TRUST THERE IS A GOOD EXPLANATION FOR YOUR INTRUSION.
I GUESS YOU COULD SAY THAT, KENIUCHIO.
GUESS YOU COULD SAY THAT, TOO.
THEN JOIN ME FOR TEA AND EXPLAIN WHY I SHOULDN'T KILL YOU WHERE YOU STAND FOR DEFILING MY FAMILY'S SACRED ANCESTRAL SWORD.

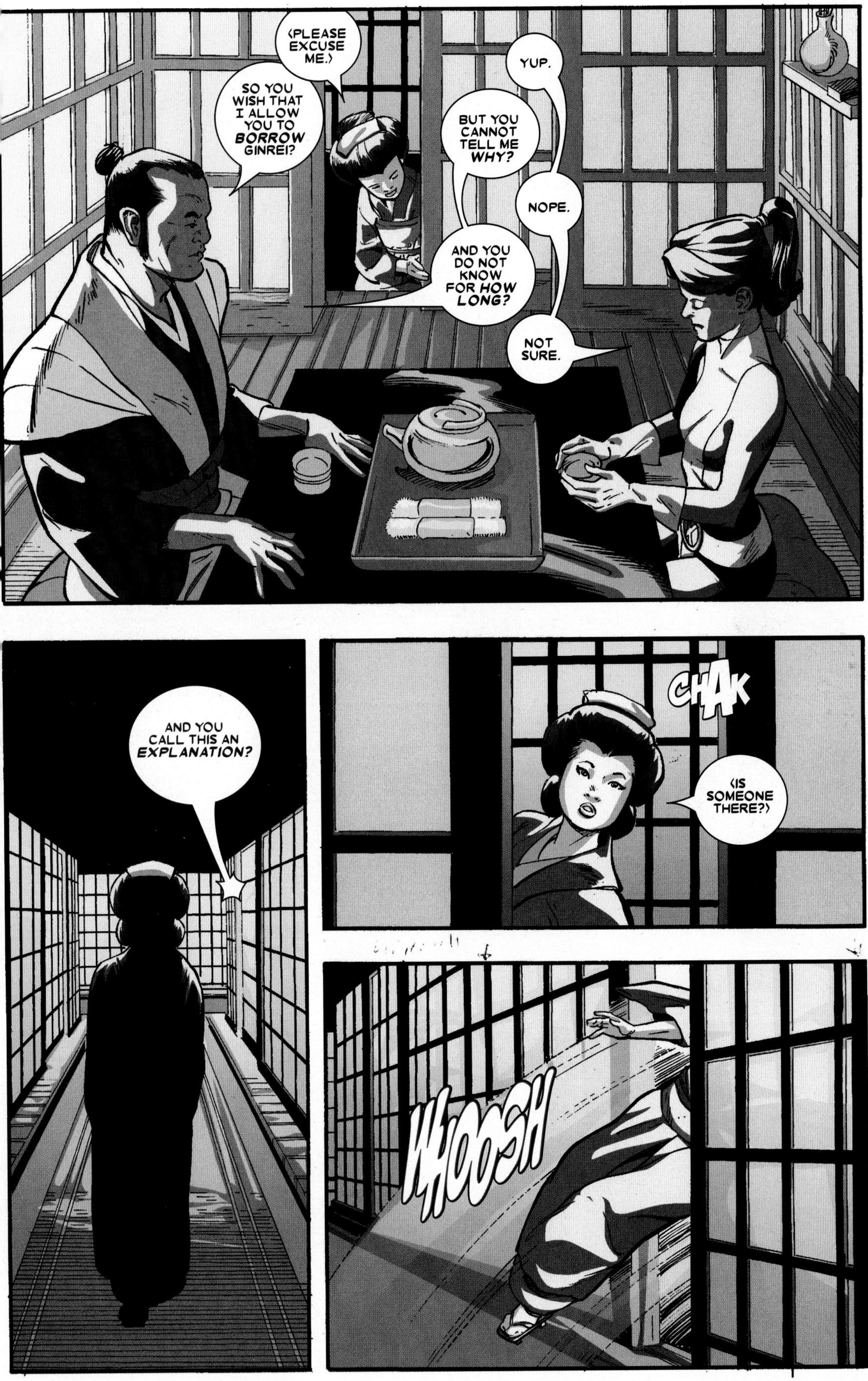
SO YOU WISH THAT I ALLOW YOU TO BORROW GINREI?
‹PLEASE EXCUSE ME.›
YUP.
BUT YOU CANNOT TELL ME WHY?
NOPE.
AND YOU DO NOT KNOW FOR HOW LONG?
NOT SURE.
AND YOU CALL THIS AN EXPLANATION?
CHAK
‹IS SOMEONE THERE?›
WHOOSH

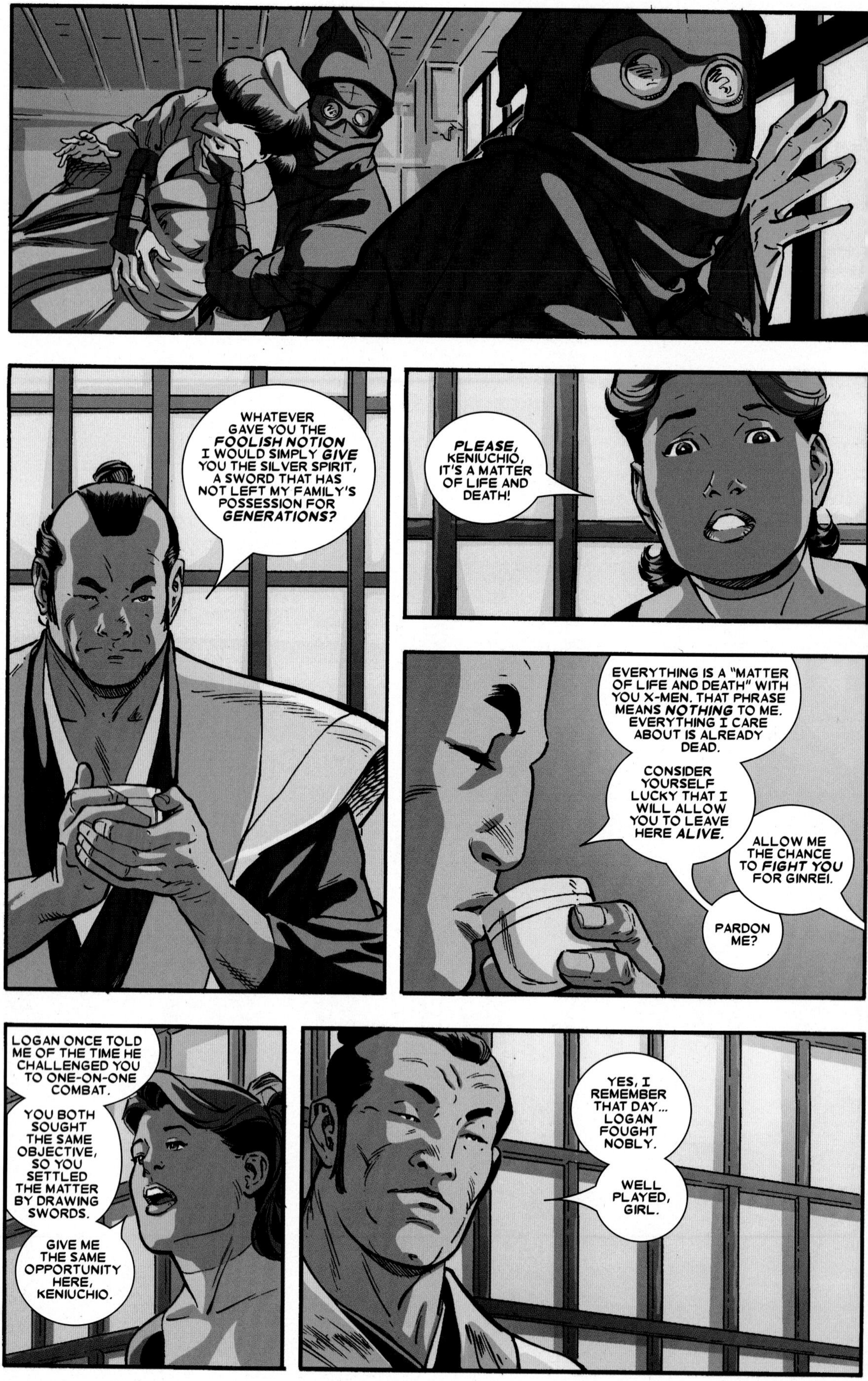

WHATEVER GAVE YOU THE FOOLISH NOTION I WOULD SIMPLY GIVE YOU THE SILVER SPIRIT, A SWORD THAT HAS NOT LEFT MY FAMILY'S POSSESSION FOR GENERATIONS?
PLEASE, KENIUCHIO, IT'S A MATTER OF LIFE AND DEATH!
EVERYTHING IS A "MATTER OF LIFE AND DEATH" WITH YOU X-MEN. THAT PHRASE MEANS NOTHING TO ME. EVERYTHING I CARE ABOUT IS ALREADY DEAD.
CONSIDER YOURSELF LUCKY THAT I WILL ALLOW YOU TO LEAVE HERE ALIVE.
ALLOW ME THE CHANCE TO FIGHT YOU FOR GINREI.
PARDON ME?
LOGAN ONCE TOLD ME OF THE TIME HE CHALLENGED YOU TO ONE-ON-ONE COMBAT.
YOU BOTH SOUGHT THE SAME OBJECTIVE, SO YOU SETTLED THE MATTER BY DRAWING SWORDS.
GIVE ME THE SAME OPPORTUNITY HERE, KENIUCHIO.
YES, I REMEMBER THAT DAY... LOGAN FOUGHT NOBLY.
WELL PLAYED, GIRL.

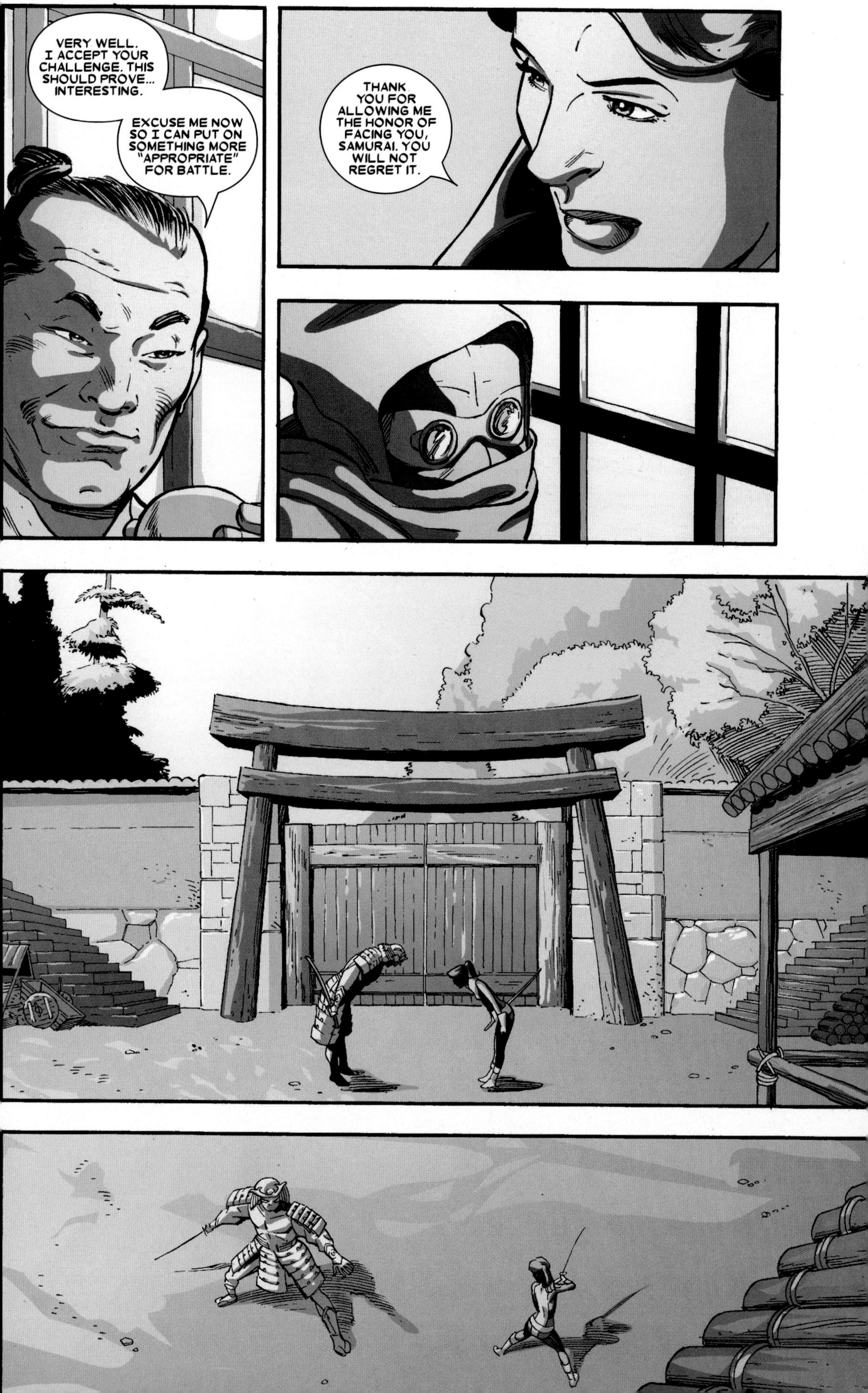
VERY WELL. I ACCEPT YOUR CHALLENGE. THIS SHOULD PROVE... INTERESTING.
EXCUSE ME NOW SO I CAN PUT ON SOMETHING MORE "APPROPRIATE" FOR BATTLE.
THANK YOU FOR ALLOWING ME THE HONOR OF FACING YOU, SAMURAI. YOU WILL NOT REGRET IT.

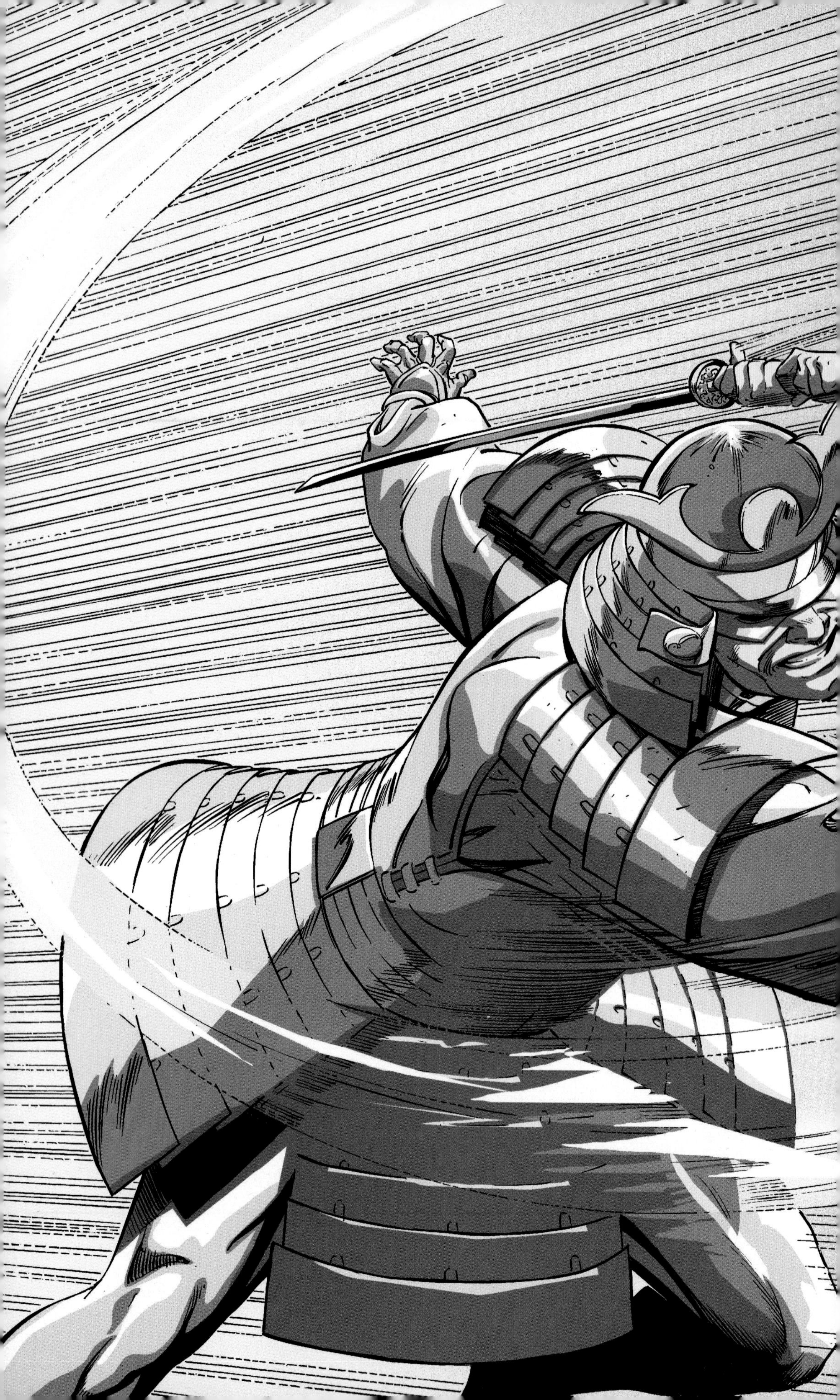

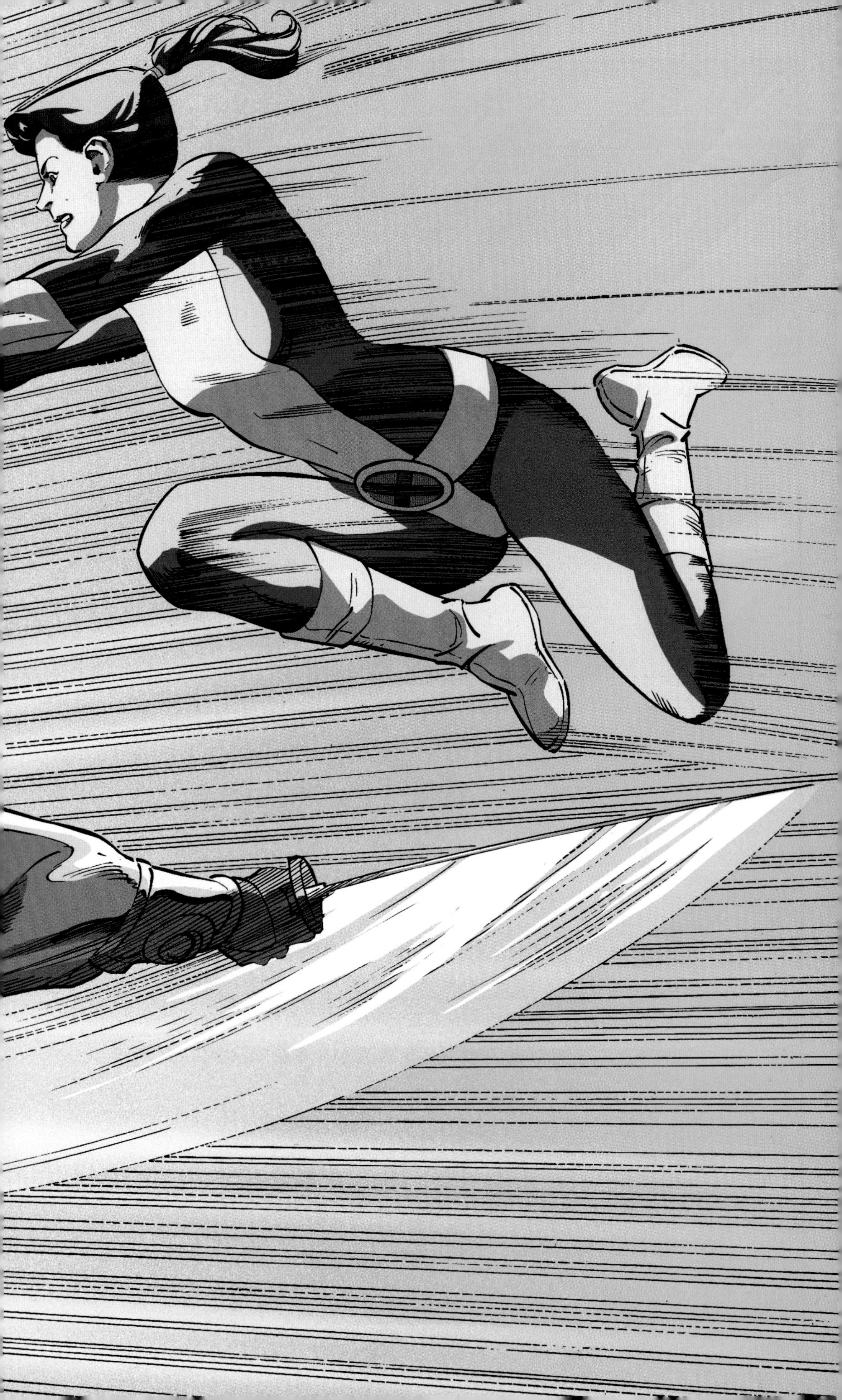

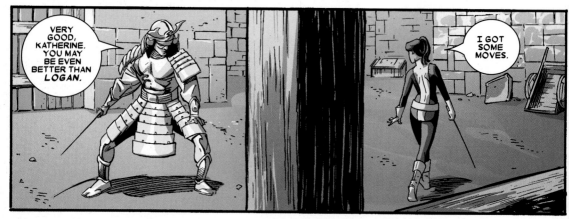

VERY GOOD, KATHERINE. YOU MAY BE EVEN BETTER THAN *LOGAN*.

I GOT SOME MOVES.

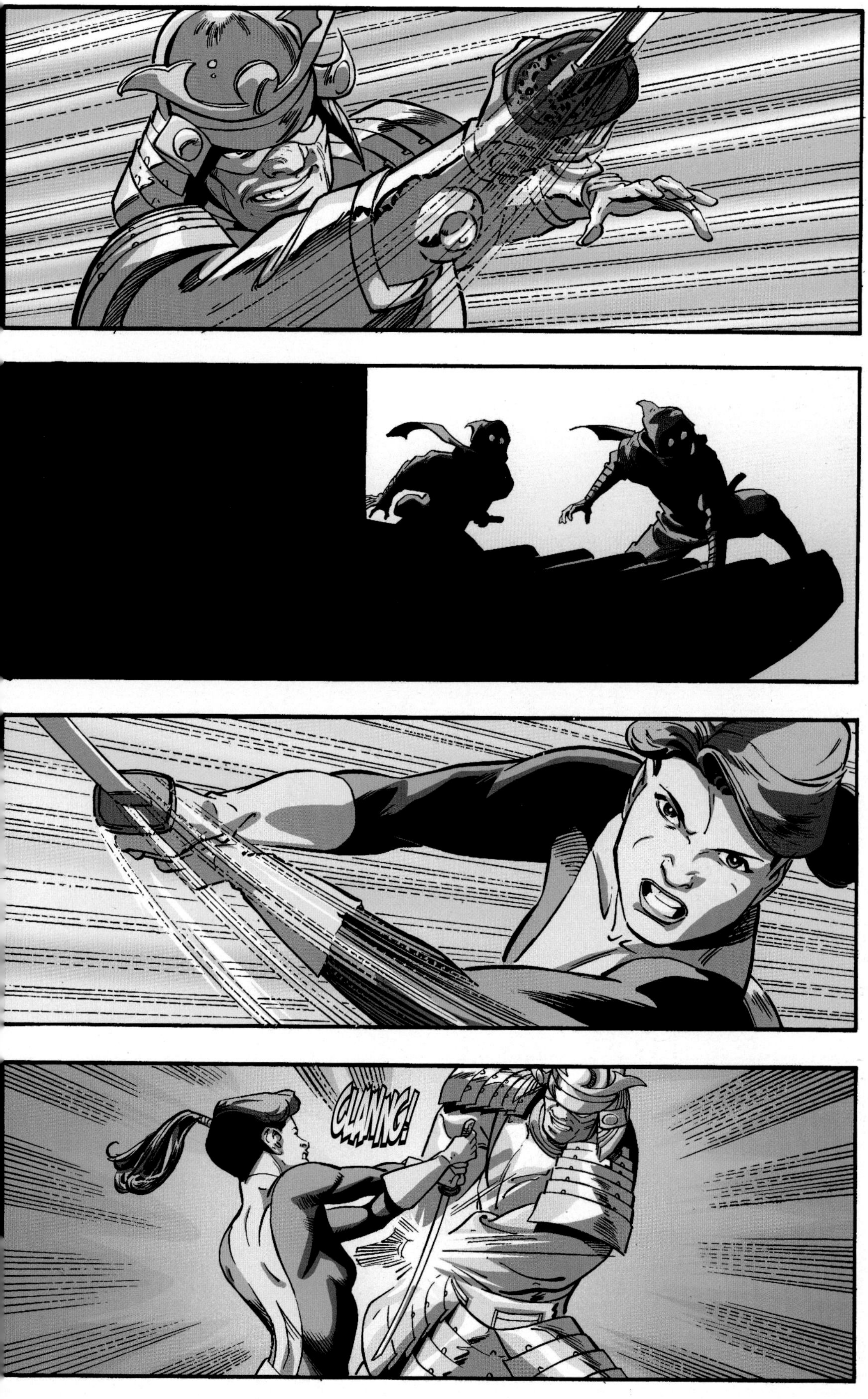
CLANNG!

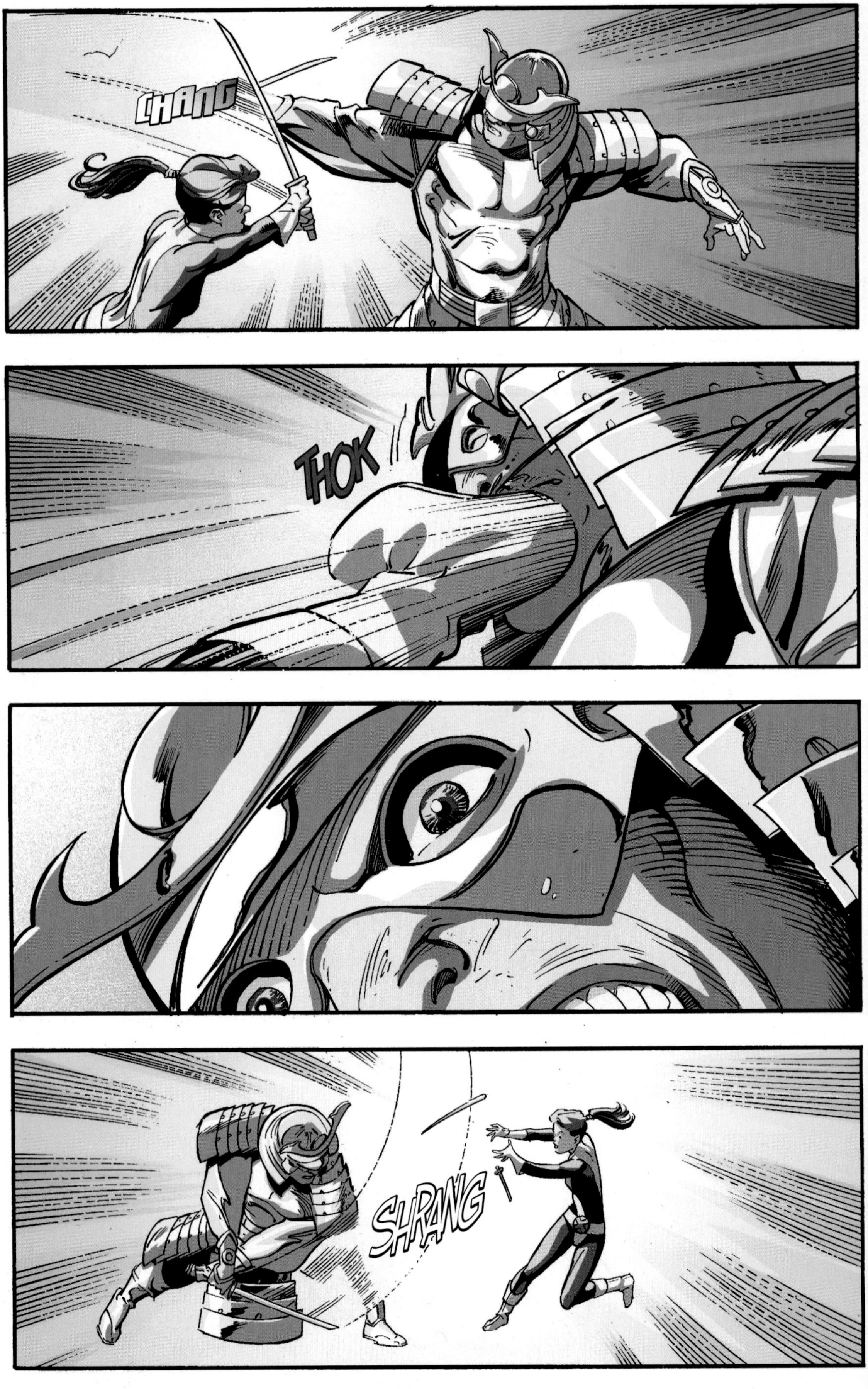
CHANG
THOK
SHRANG

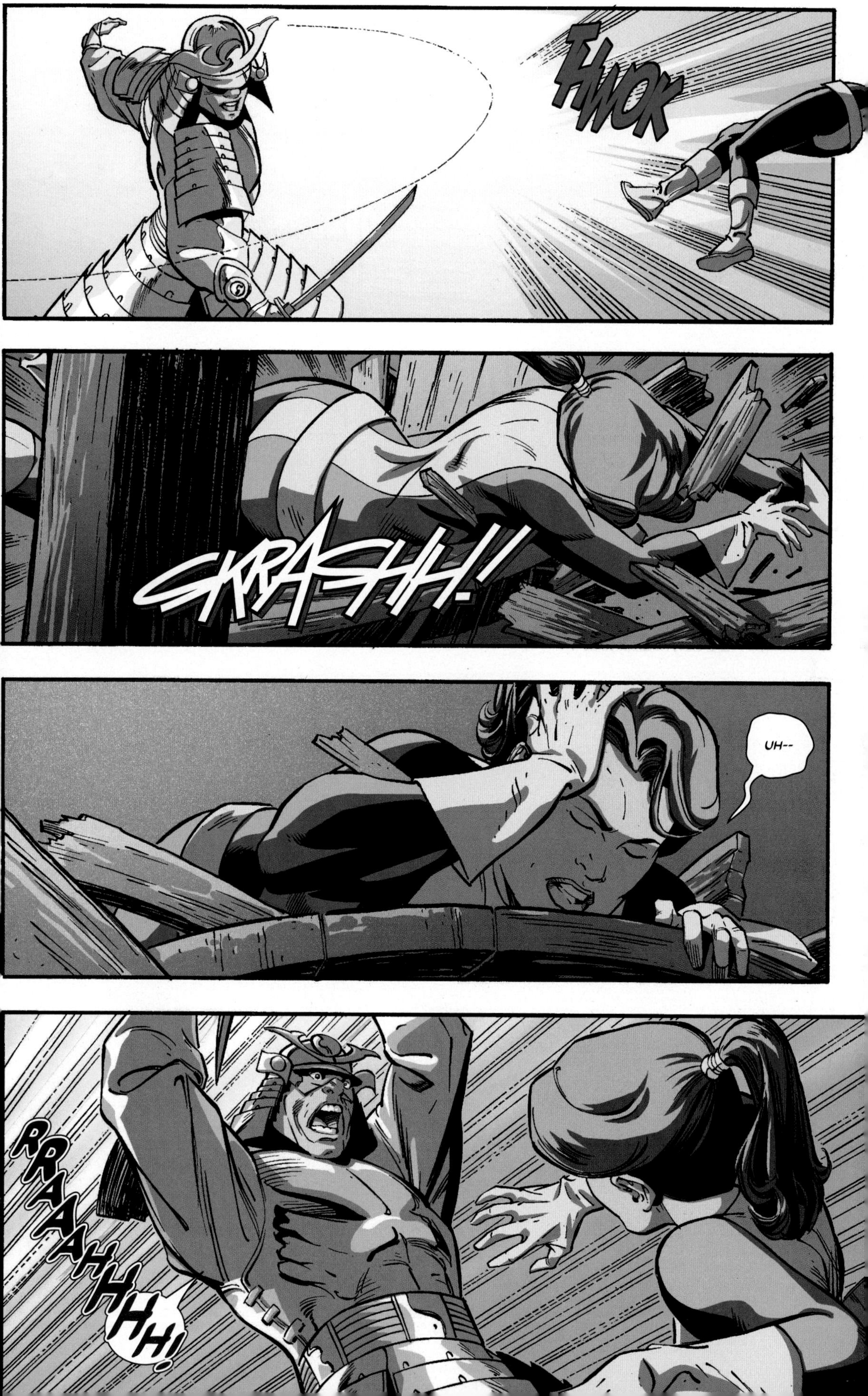

THWOK
SKRASHH!
UH--
RRAAAHHHH!

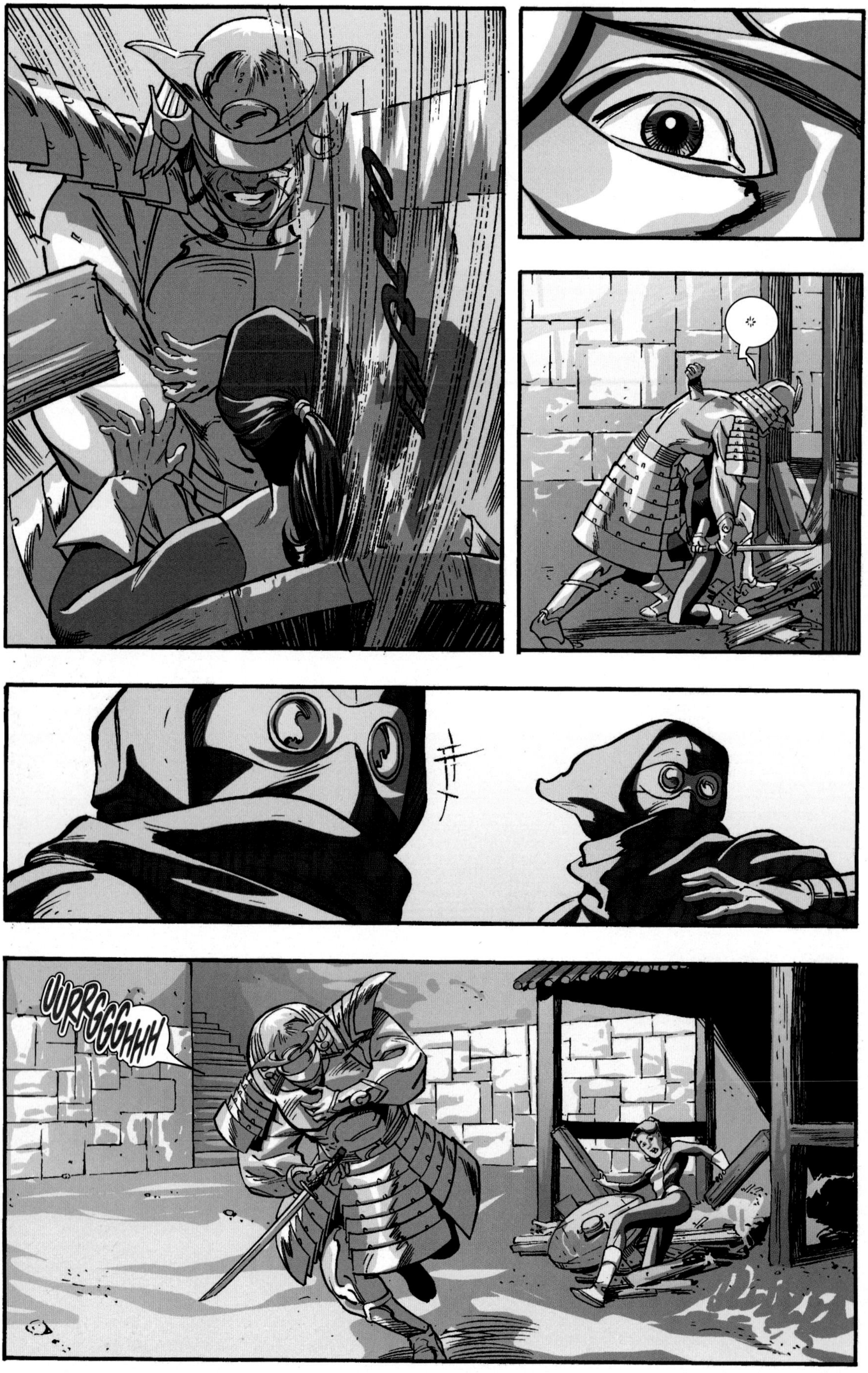
UURRGGGHHH

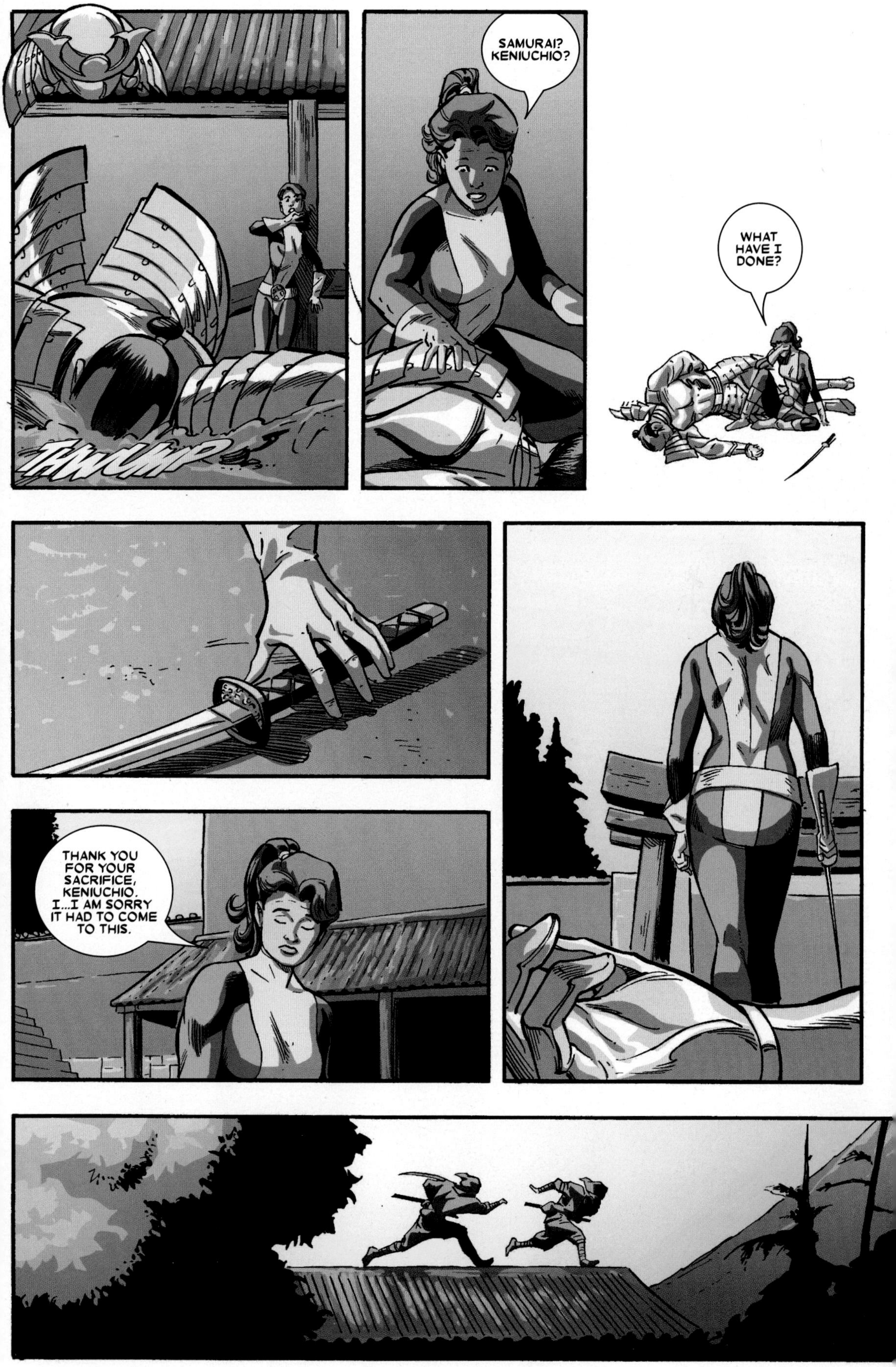
THWUMP
SAMURAI? KENIUCHIO?
WHAT HAVE I DONE?
THANK YOU FOR YOUR SACRIFICE, KENIUCHIO. I...I AM SORRY IT HAD TO COME TO THIS.

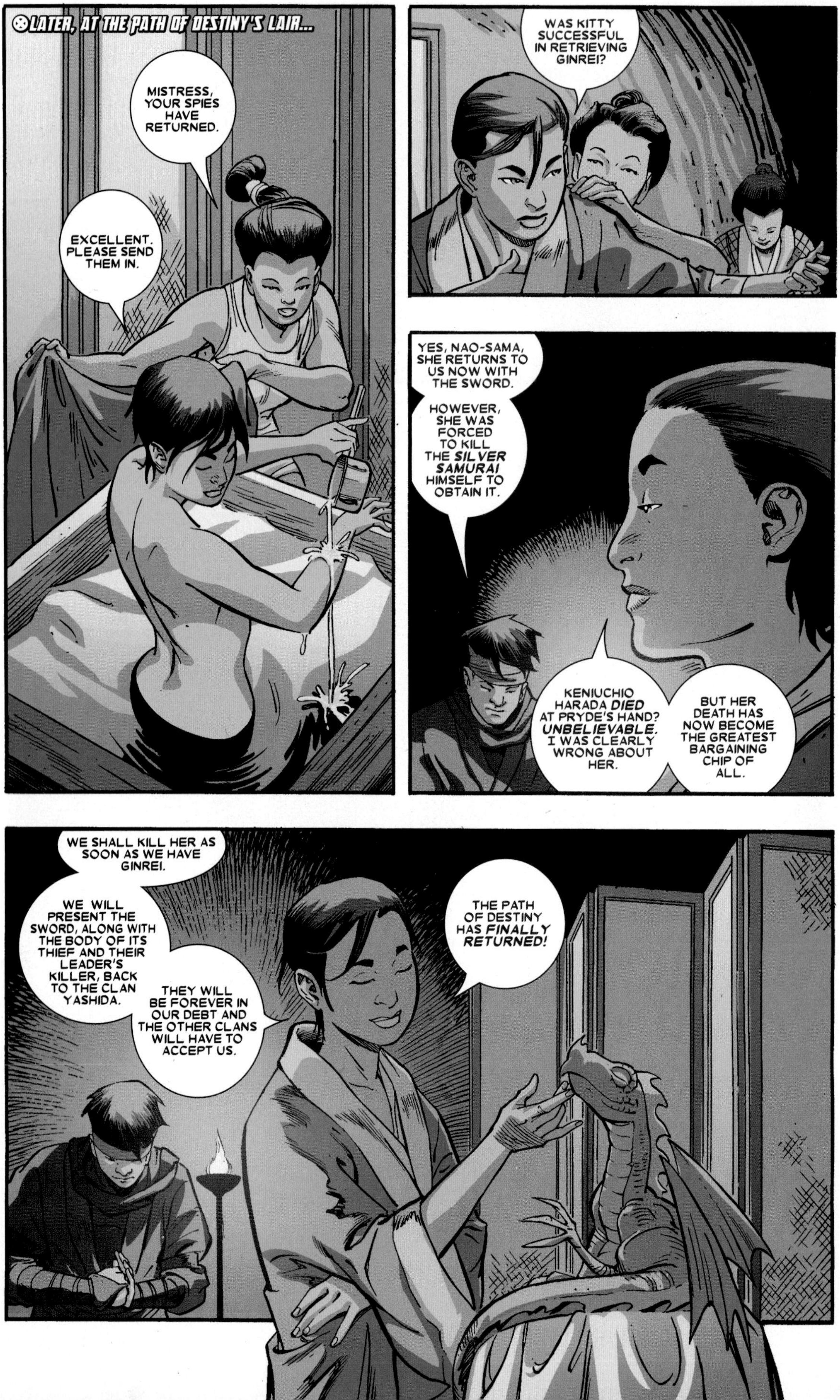
LATER, AT THE PATH OF DESTINY'S LAIR...
MISTRESS, YOUR SPIES HAVE RETURNED.
EXCELLENT. PLEASE SEND THEM IN.
WAS KITTY SUCCESSFUL IN RETRIEVING GINREI?
YES, NAO-SAMA, SHE RETURNS TO US NOW WITH THE SWORD.
HOWEVER, SHE WAS FORCED TO KILL THE SILVER SAMURAI HIMSELF TO OBTAIN IT.
KENIUCHIO HARADA DIED AT PRYDE'S HAND? UNBELIEVABLE. I WAS CLEARLY WRONG ABOUT HER.
BUT HER DEATH HAS NOW BECOME THE GREATEST BARGAINING CHIP OF ALL.
WE SHALL KILL HER AS SOON AS WE HAVE GINREI.
WE WILL PRESENT THE SWORD, ALONG WITH THE BODY OF ITS THIEF AND THEIR LEADER'S KILLER, BACK TO THE CLAN YASHIDA.
THEY WILL BE FOREVER IN OUR DEBT AND THE OTHER CLANS WILL HAVE TO ACCEPT US.
THE PATH OF DESTINY HAS FINALLY RETURNED!

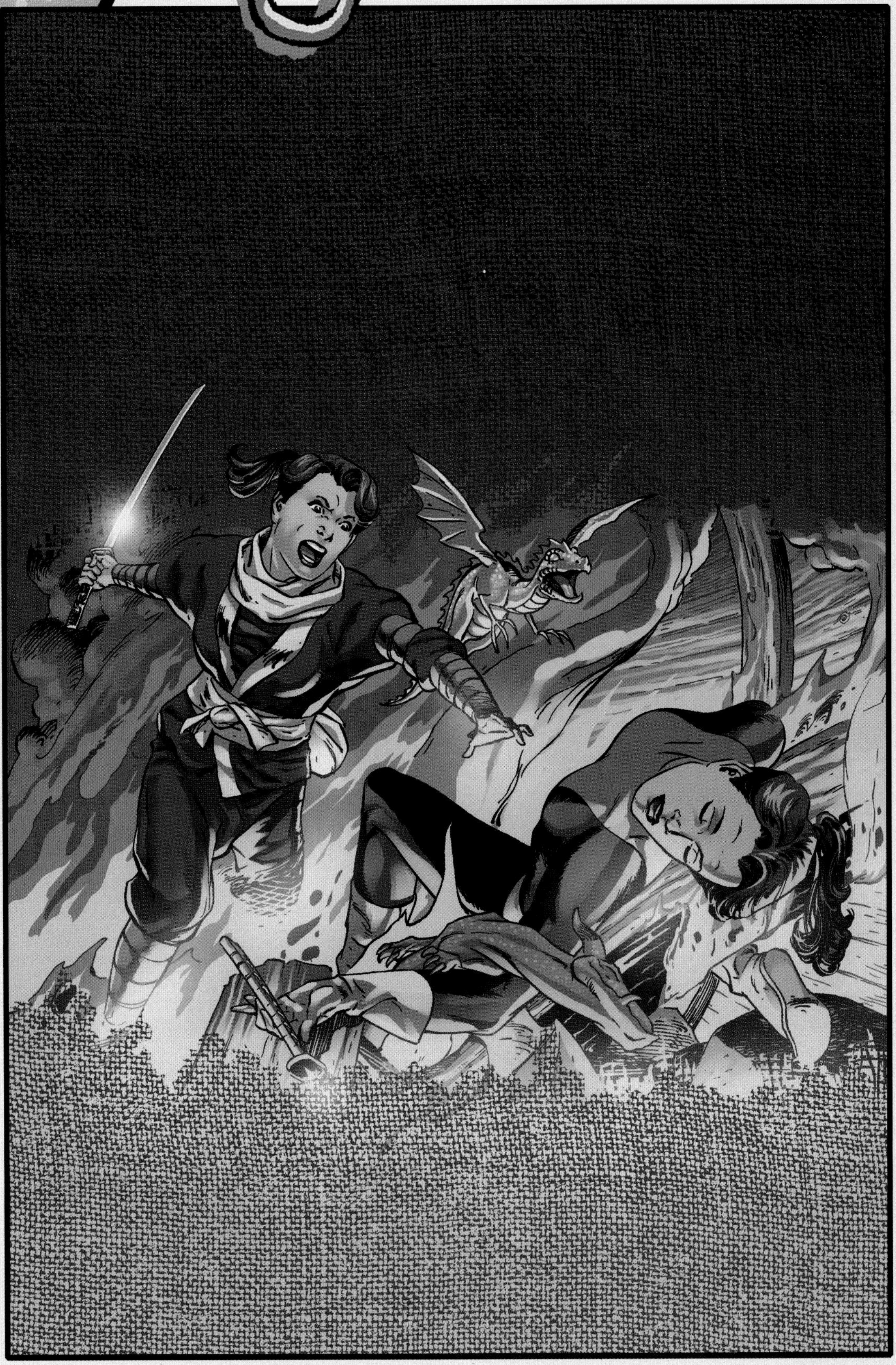

<#5>

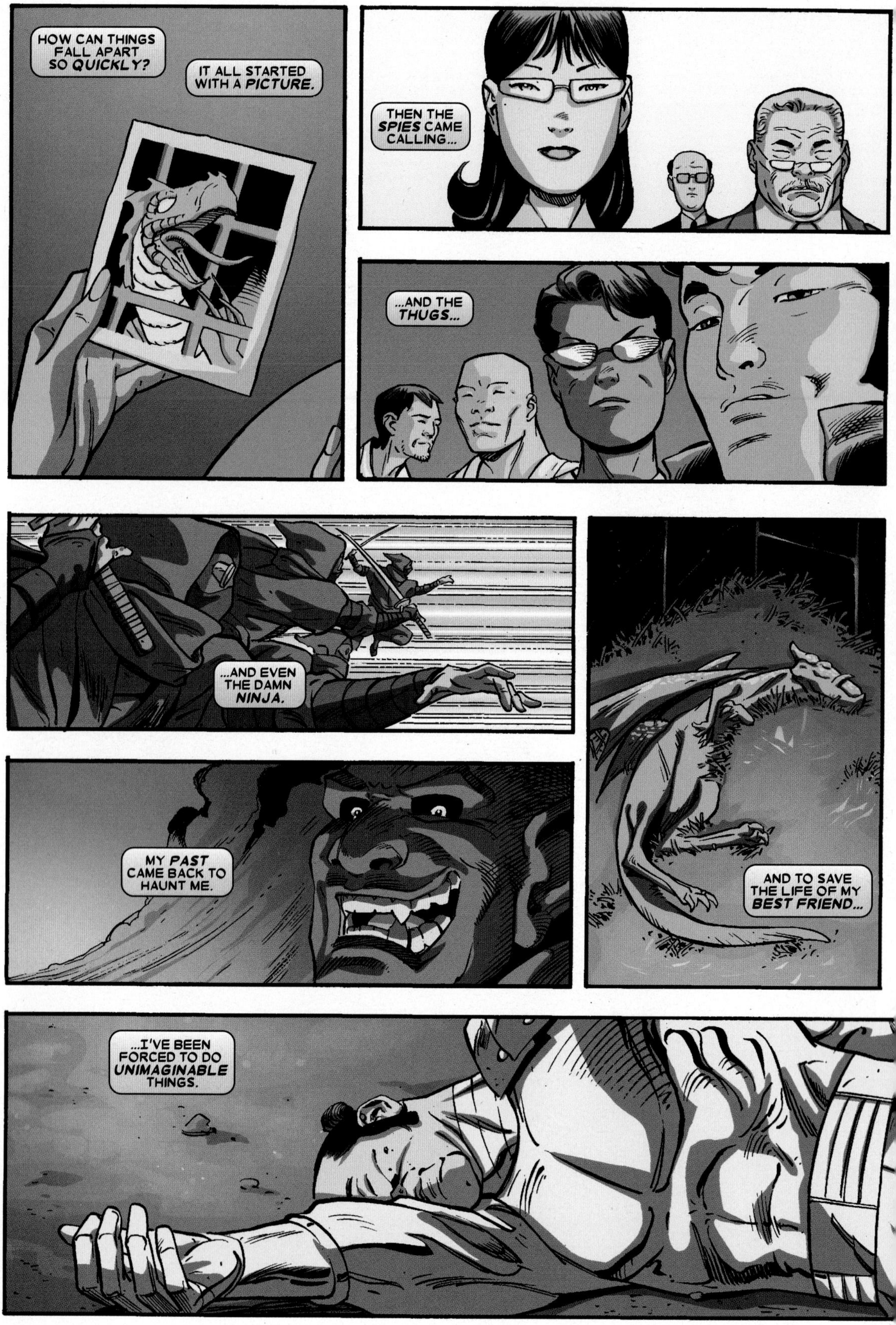
HOW CAN THINGS FALL APART SO QUICKLY?
IT ALL STARTED WITH A PICTURE.
THEN THE SPIES CAME CALLING...
...AND THE THUGS...
...AND EVEN THE DAMN NINJA.
MY PAST CAME BACK TO HAUNT ME.
AND TO SAVE THE LIFE OF MY BEST FRIEND...
...I'VE BEEN FORCED TO DO UNIMAGINABLE THINGS.

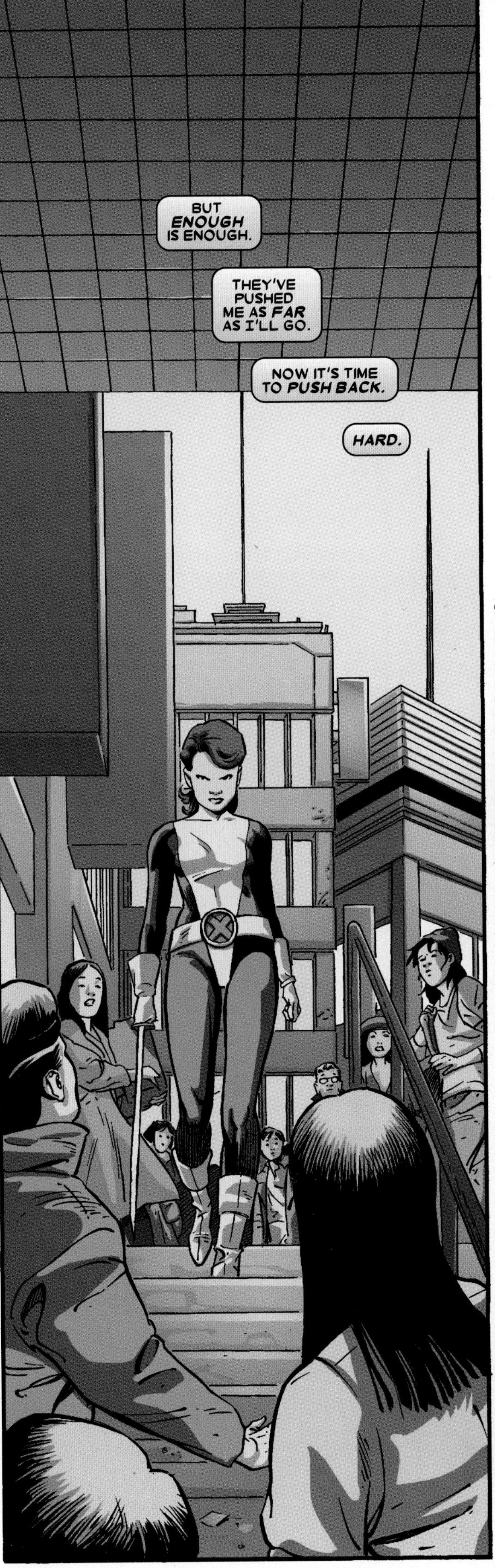
BUT ENOUGH IS ENOUGH.
THEY'VE PUSHED ME AS FAR AS I'LL GO.
NOW IT'S TIME TO PUSH BACK.
HARD.

SHADOW AND FLAME CONCLUSION

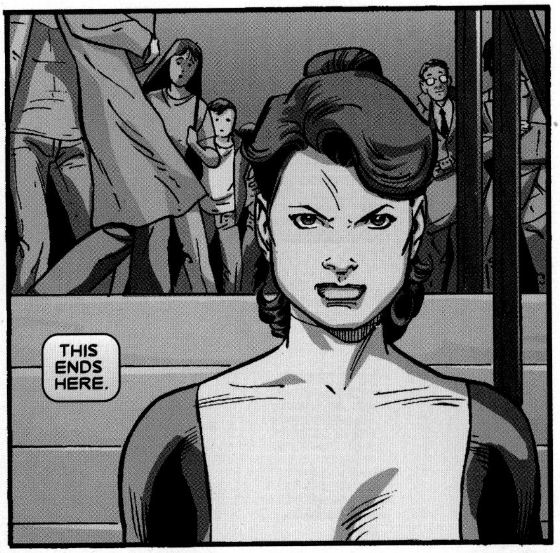
THIS ENDS HERE.

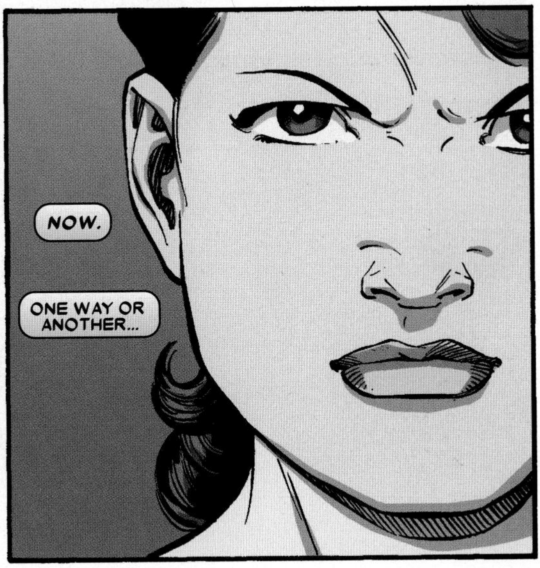
NOW.
ONE WAY OR ANOTHER...

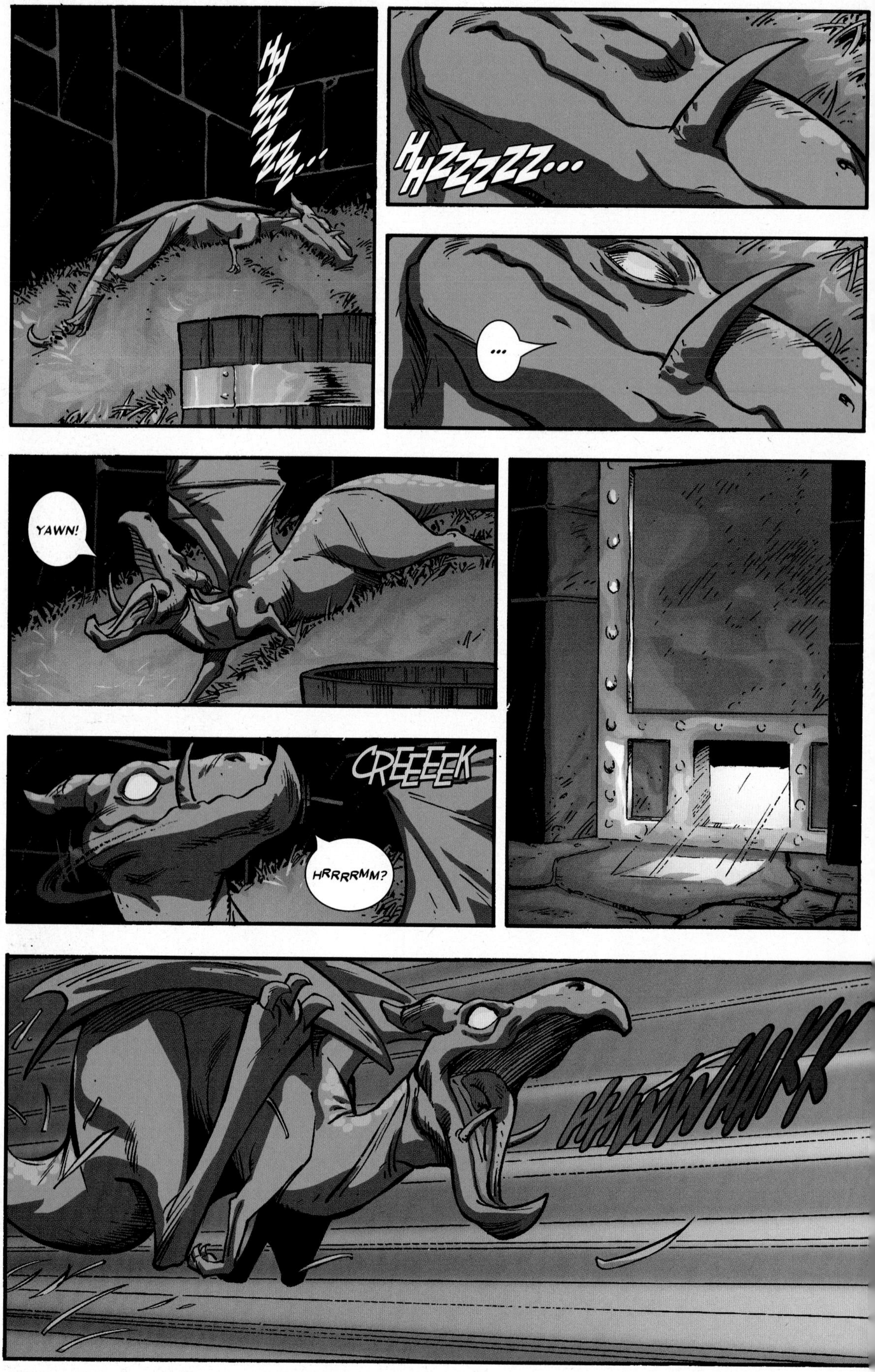
HHZZZZZZ...
HHZZZZZZ...
...
YAWN!
CREEEEEK
HRRRRMM?
HHWWAAKK

WHIIISH

HHHZZZ!!
HHHZZ?

EEP!

CLONK

⟨PATHETIC PURPLE CREATURE...⟩

HHRRROOOOO?

⟨YOU'LL BE PUT OUT OF YOUR MISERY SOON ENOUGH.⟩

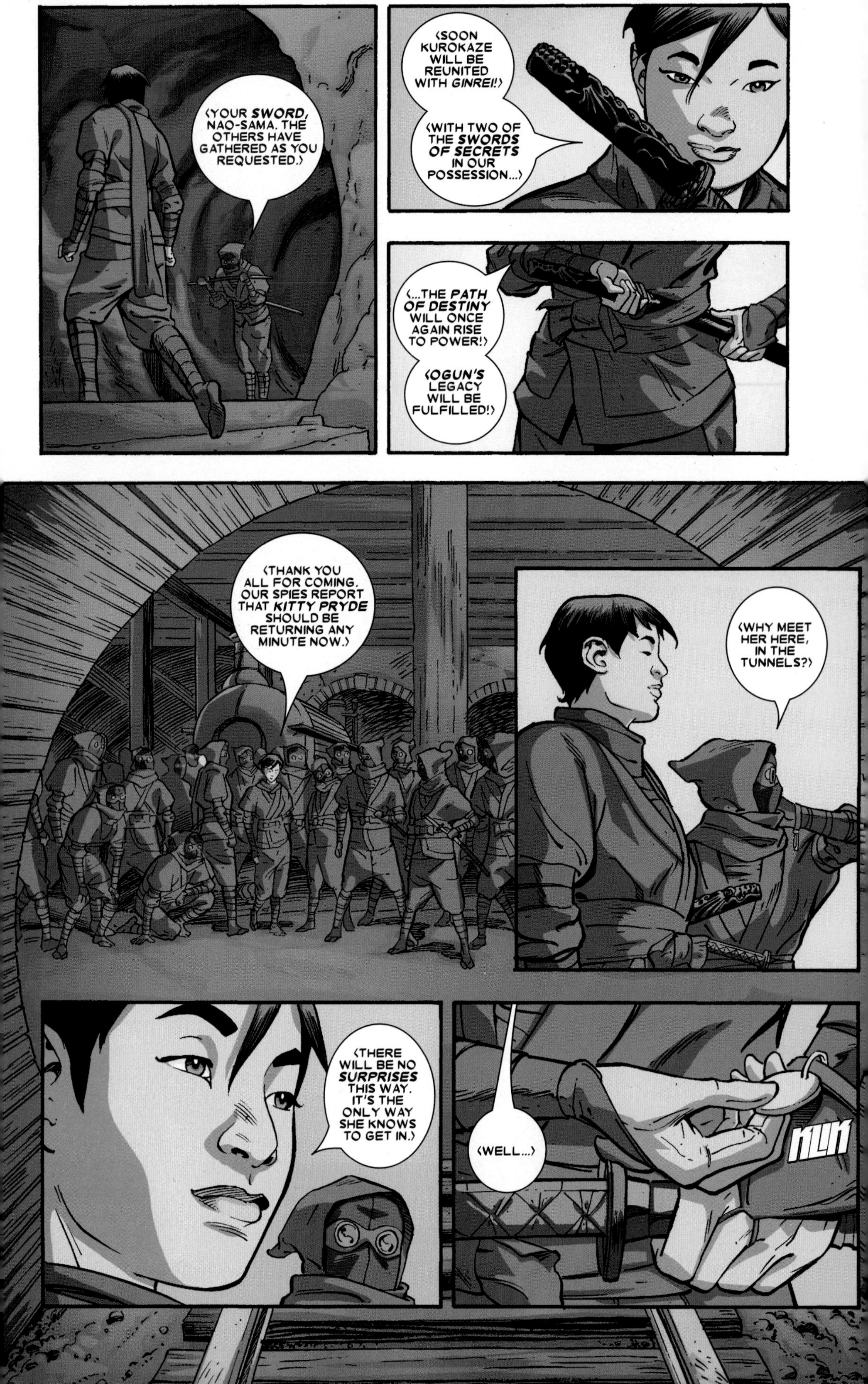

‹YOUR SWORD, NAO-SAMA. THE OTHERS HAVE GATHERED AS YOU REQUESTED.›
‹SOON KUROKAZE WILL BE REUNITED WITH GINREI!›
‹WITH TWO OF THE SWORDS OF SECRETS IN OUR POSSESSION...›
‹...THE PATH OF DESTINY WILL ONCE AGAIN RISE TO POWER!›
‹OGUN'S LEGACY WILL BE FULFILLED!›
‹THANK YOU ALL FOR COMING. OUR SPIES REPORT THAT KITTY PRYDE SHOULD BE RETURNING ANY MINUTE NOW.›
‹WHY MEET HER HERE, IN THE TUNNELS?›
‹THERE WILL BE NO SURPRISES THIS WAY. IT'S THE ONLY WAY SHE KNOWS TO GET IN.›
‹WELL...›
KLIK

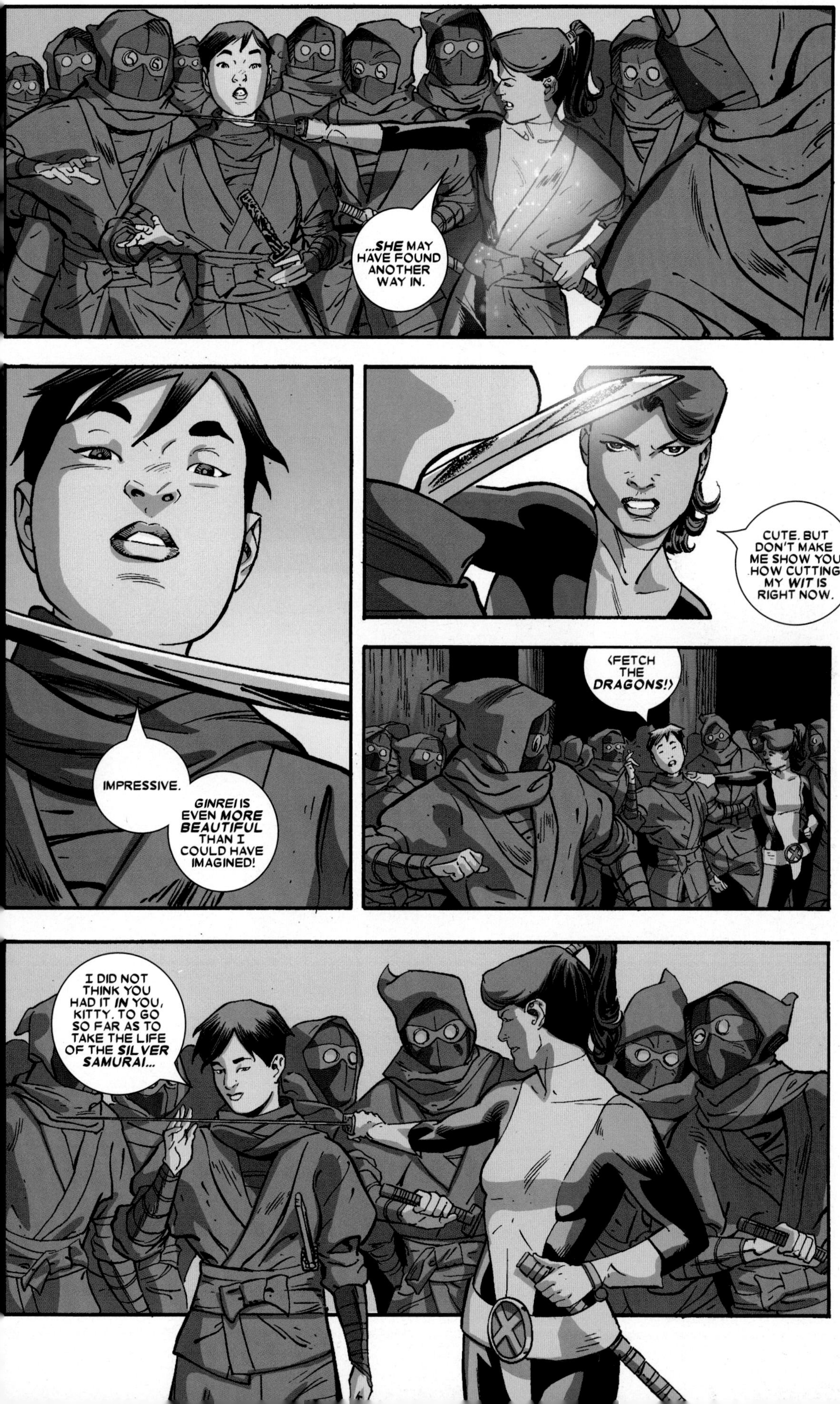
...SHE MAY HAVE FOUND ANOTHER WAY IN.
IMPRESSIVE.
GINREI IS EVEN MORE BEAUTIFUL THAN I COULD HAVE IMAGINED!
CUTE. BUT DON'T MAKE ME SHOW YOU HOW CUTTING MY WIT IS RIGHT NOW.
<FETCH THE DRAGONS!>
I DID NOT THINK YOU HAD IT IN YOU, KITTY. TO GO SO FAR AS TO TAKE THE LIFE OF THE SILVER SAMURAI...

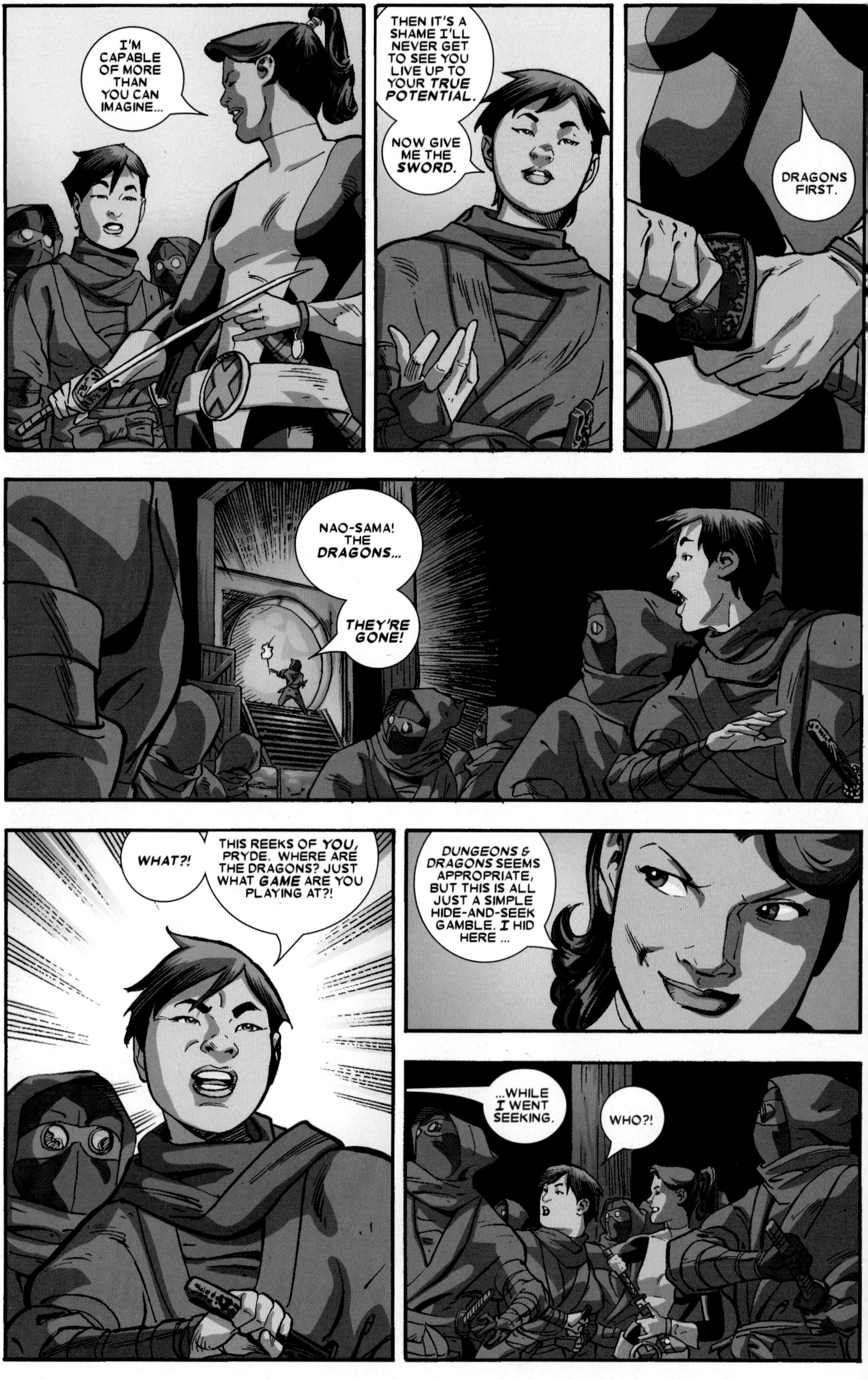
I'M CAPABLE OF MORE THAN YOU CAN IMAGINE...
THEN IT'S A SHAME I'LL NEVER GET TO SEE YOU LIVE UP TO YOUR *TRUE POTENTIAL*.
NOW GIVE ME THE *SWORD*.
DRAGONS FIRST.
NAO-SAMA! THE *DRAGONS*...
THEY'RE GONE!
WHAT?!
THIS REEKS OF *YOU*, PRYDE. WHERE ARE THE DRAGONS? JUST WHAT *GAME* ARE YOU PLAYING AT?!
DUNGEONS & DRAGONS SEEMS APPROPRIATE, BUT THIS IS ALL JUST A SIMPLE HIDE-AND-SEEK GAMBLE. *I* HID HERE ...
...WHILE *I* WENT SEEKING.
WHO?!

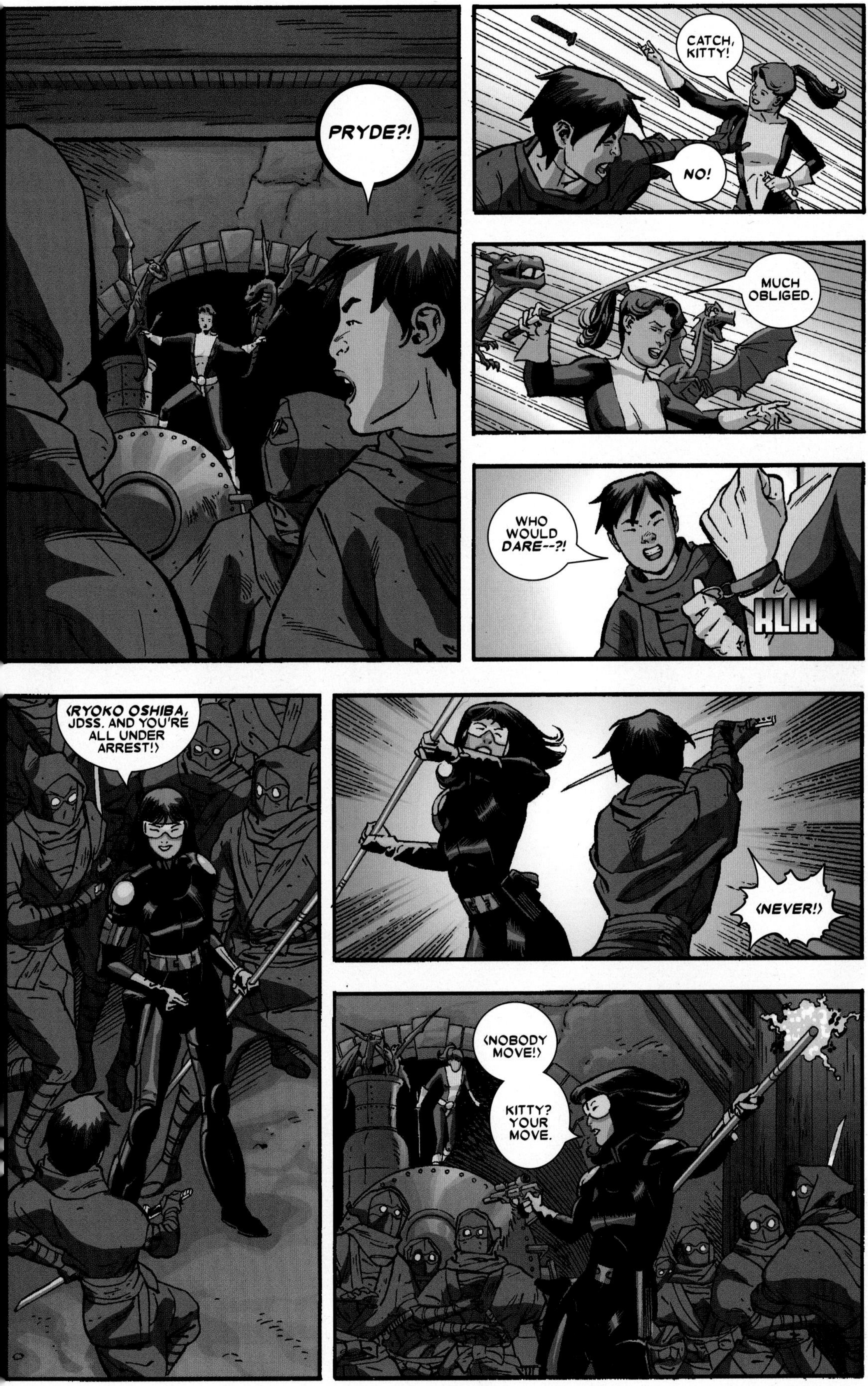
PRYDE?!
CATCH, KITTY!
NO!
MUCH OBLIGED.
WHO WOULD DARE--?!
KLIK
‹RYOKO OSHIBA, JDSS. AND YOU'RE ALL UNDER ARREST!›
‹NEVER!›
‹NOBODY MOVE!›
KITTY? YOUR MOVE.

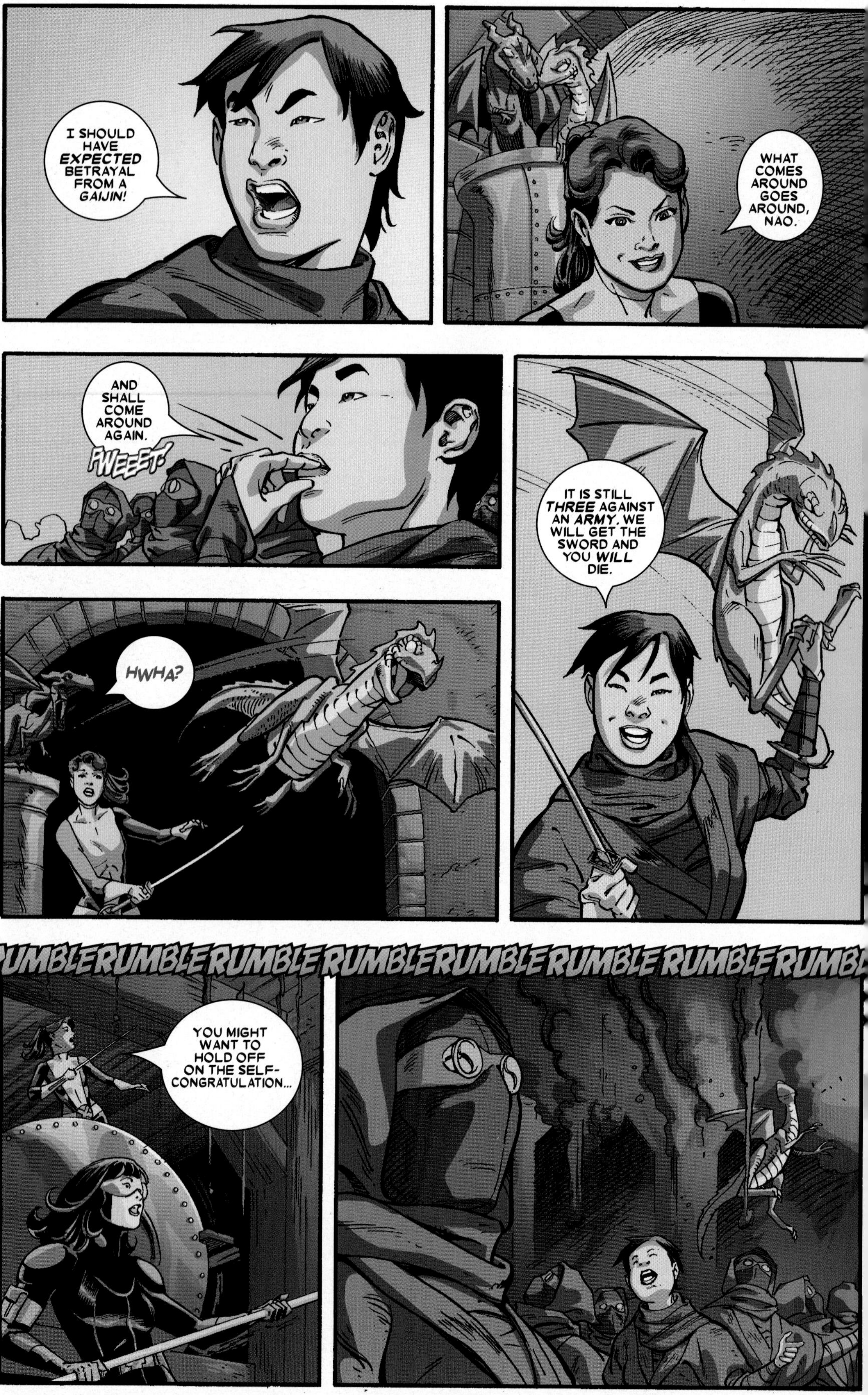

I SHOULD HAVE *EXPECTED* BETRAYAL FROM A *GAIJIN!*
WHAT COMES AROUND GOES AROUND, NAO.
AND SHALL COME AROUND AGAIN.
PWEEEET!
IT IS STILL *THREE* AGAINST AN *ARMY*. WE WILL GET THE SWORD AND YOU *WILL* DIE.
HWHA?
RUMBLE RUMBLE RUMBLE RUMBLE RUMBLE RUMBLE RUMBLE
YOU MIGHT WANT TO HOLD OFF ON THE SELF-CONGRATULATION...

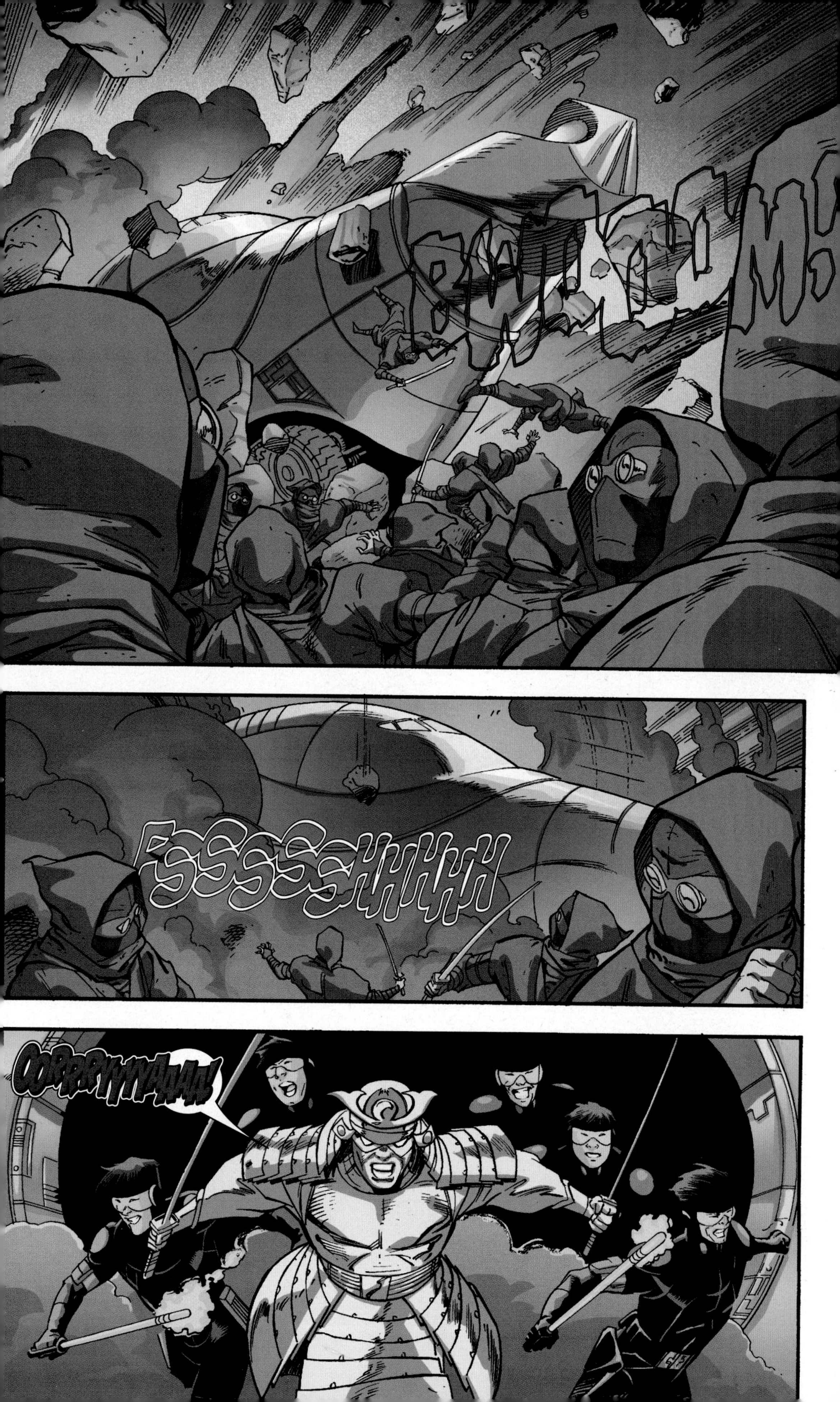
BWOOOOM!
FSSSSSHHHHH
OORRRYYYAAAA!

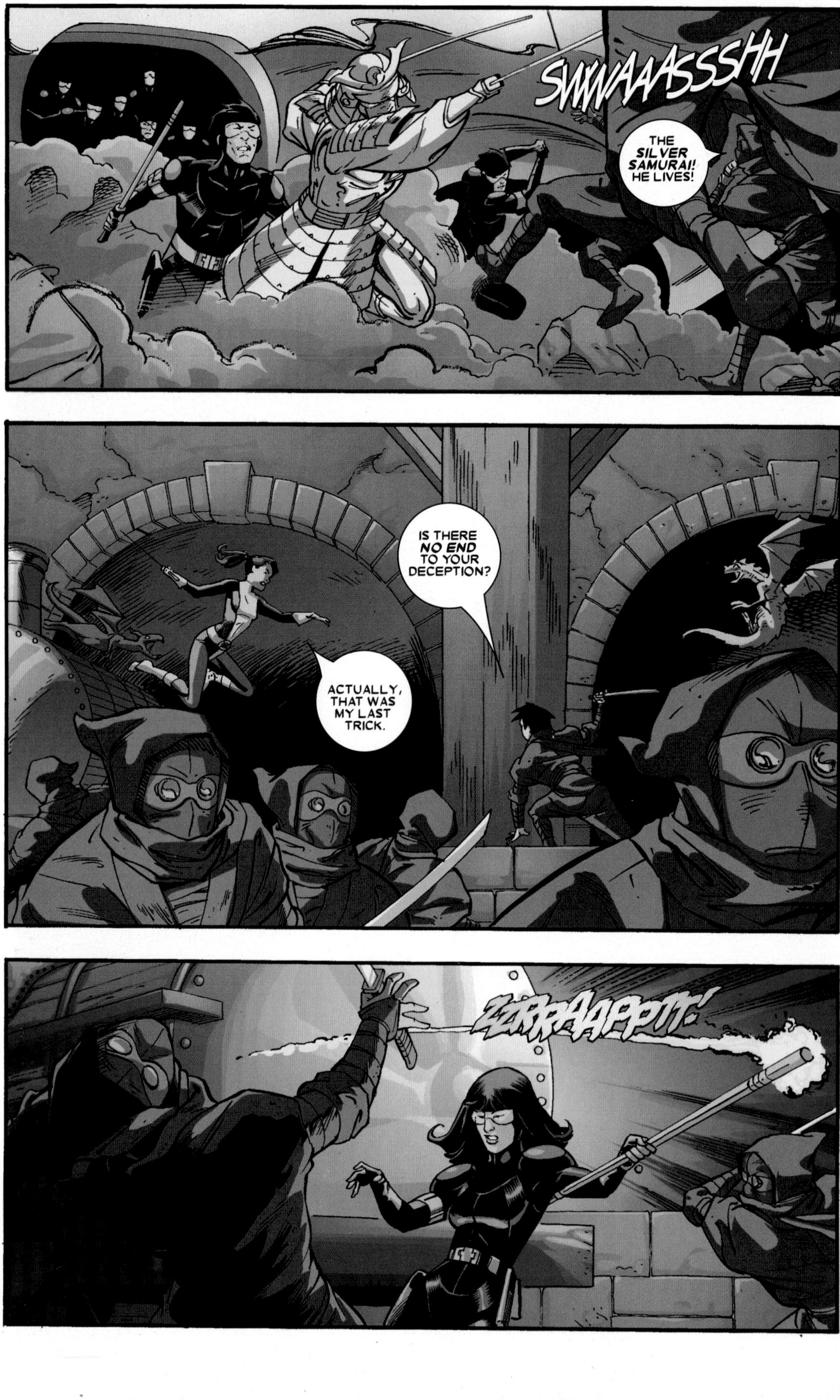
SWWAAASSSHH
THE SILVER SAMURAI! HE LIVES!
IS THERE NO END TO YOUR DECEPTION?
ACTUALLY, THAT WAS MY LAST TRICK.
ZZRRAAPPTT!

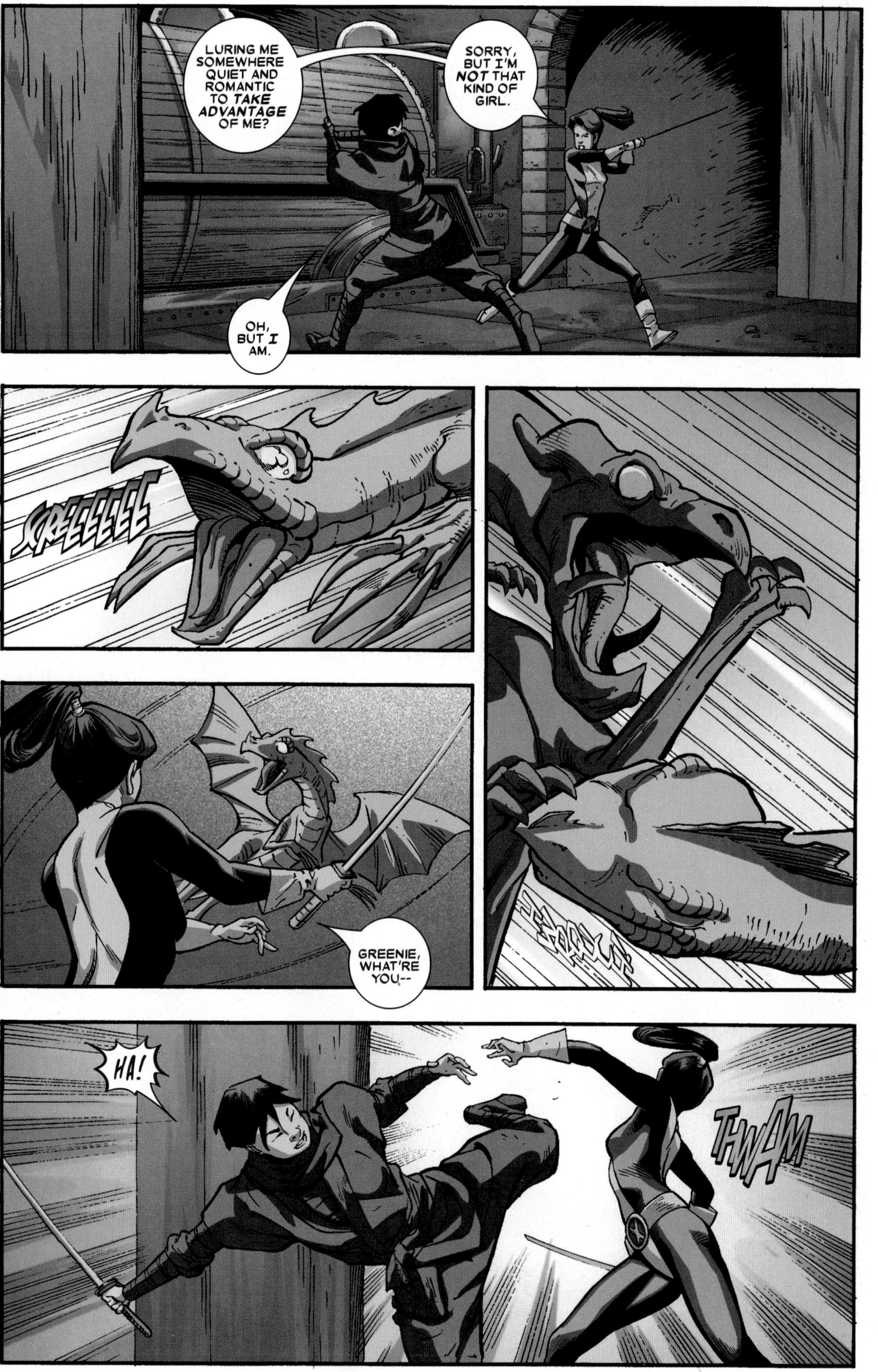
LURING ME SOMEWHERE QUIET AND ROMANTIC TO TAKE ADVANTAGE OF ME?
SORRY, BUT I'M NOT THAT KIND OF GIRL.
OH, BUT I AM.
SCREEEEEE
GREENIE, WHAT'RE YOU--
HA!
THWAM

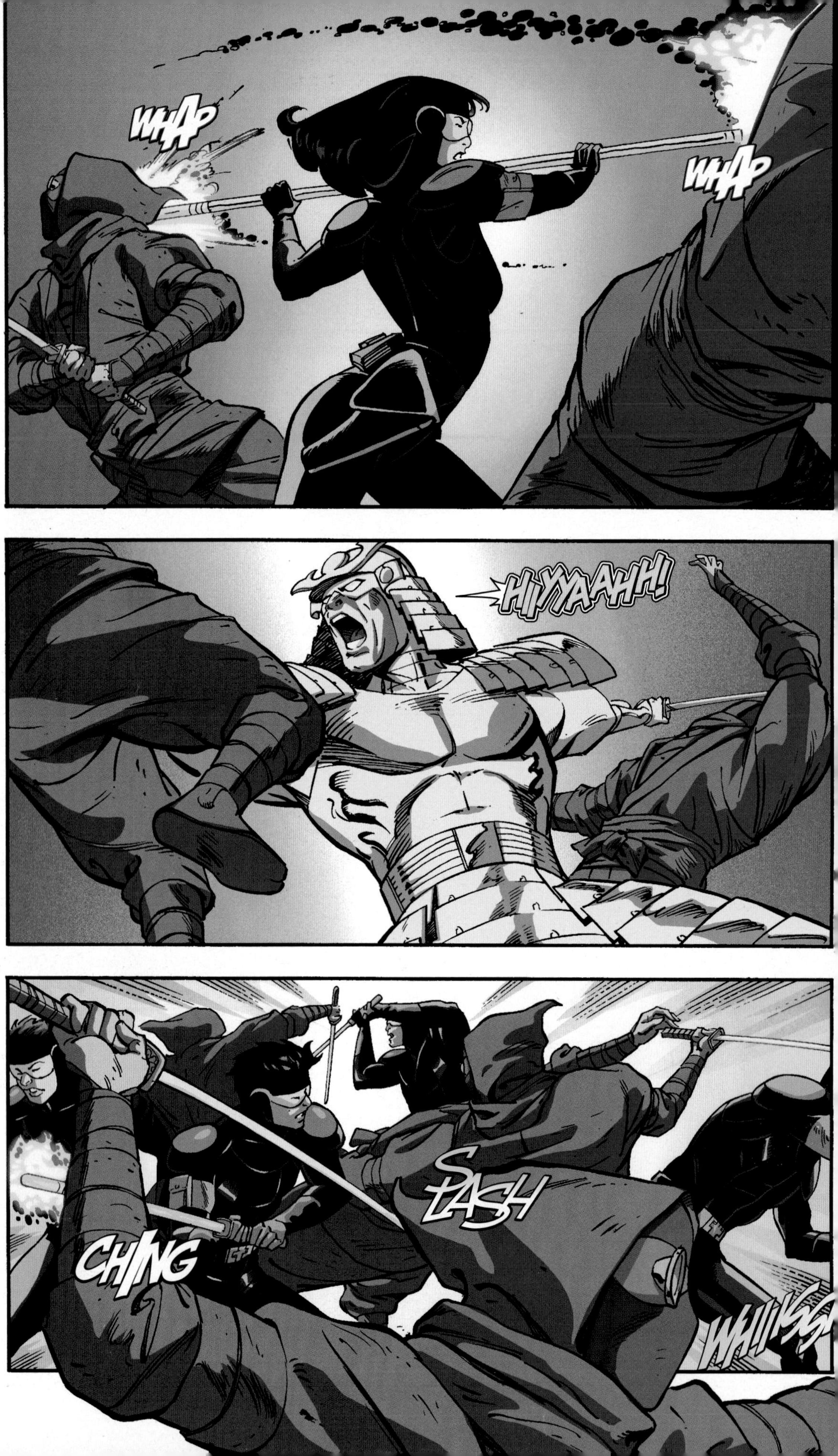
WHAP
WHAP
HIYYAAHH!
SLASH
CHING

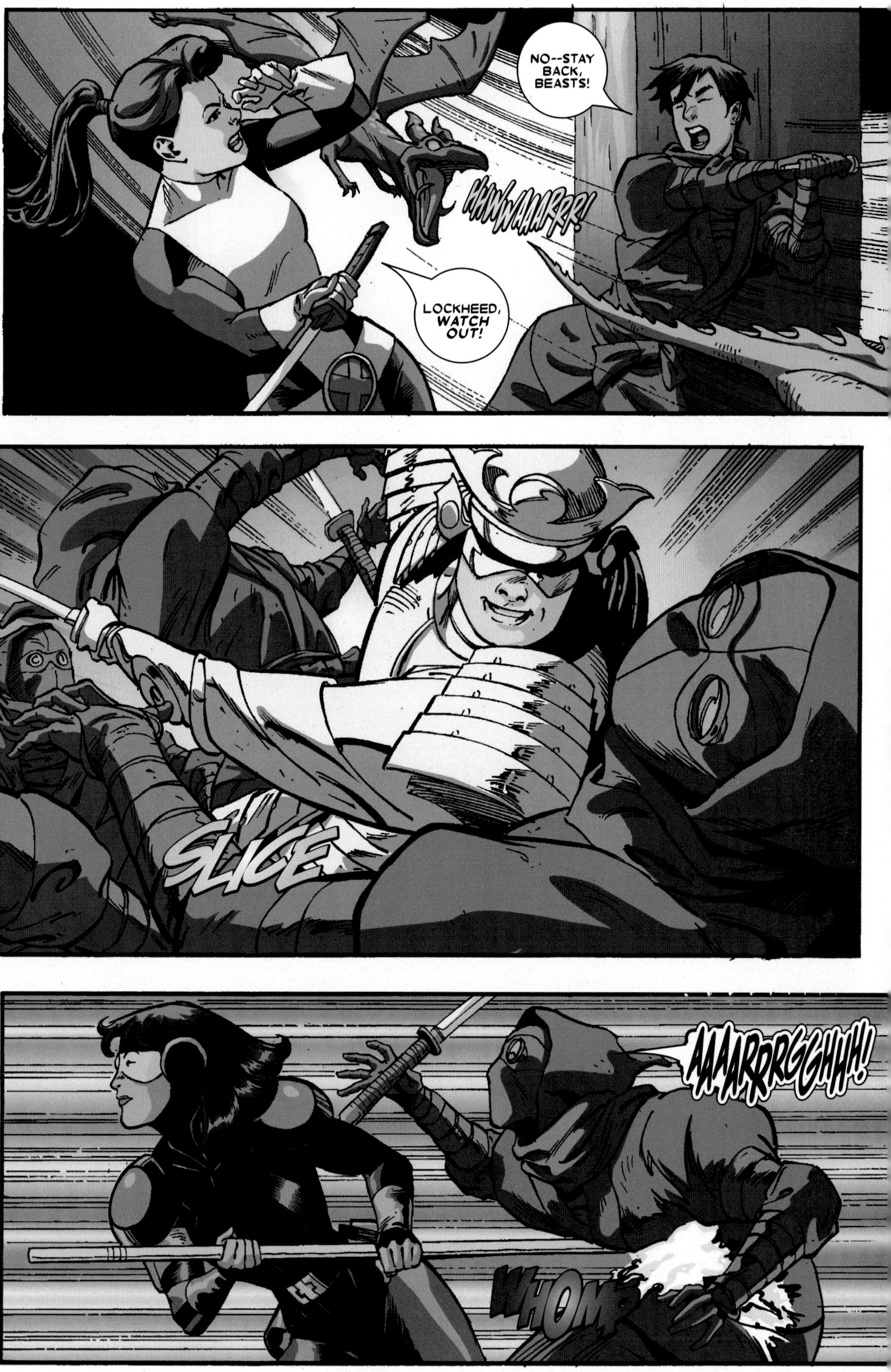
NO--STAY BACK, BEASTS!
HWWAAARRR!
LOCKHEED, WATCH OUT!
SLICE
AAAARRRGHHH!
WHOM

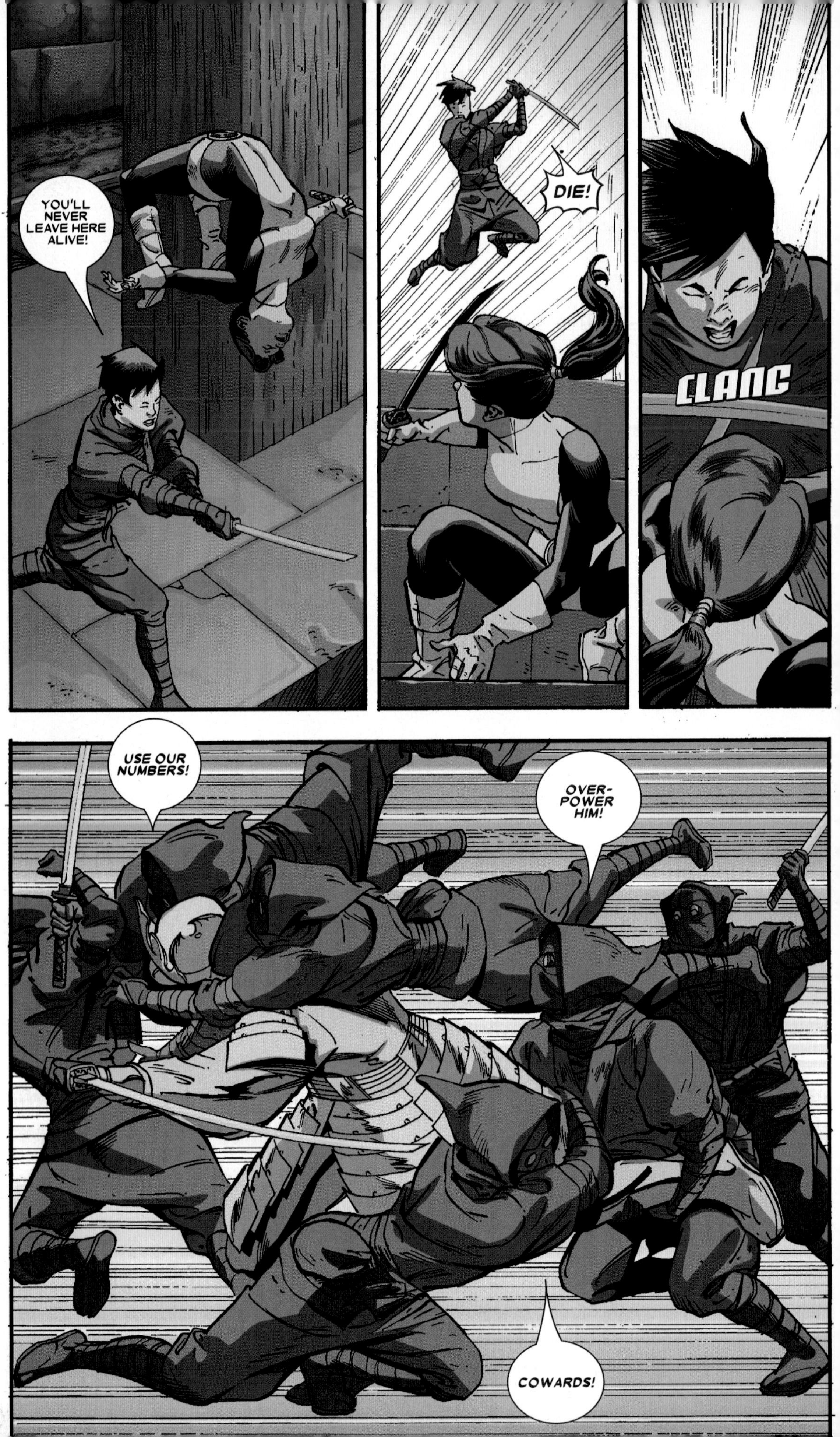
YOU'LL NEVER LEAVE HERE ALIVE!
DIE!
CLANC
USE OUR NUMBERS!
OVER-POWER HIM!
COWARDS!

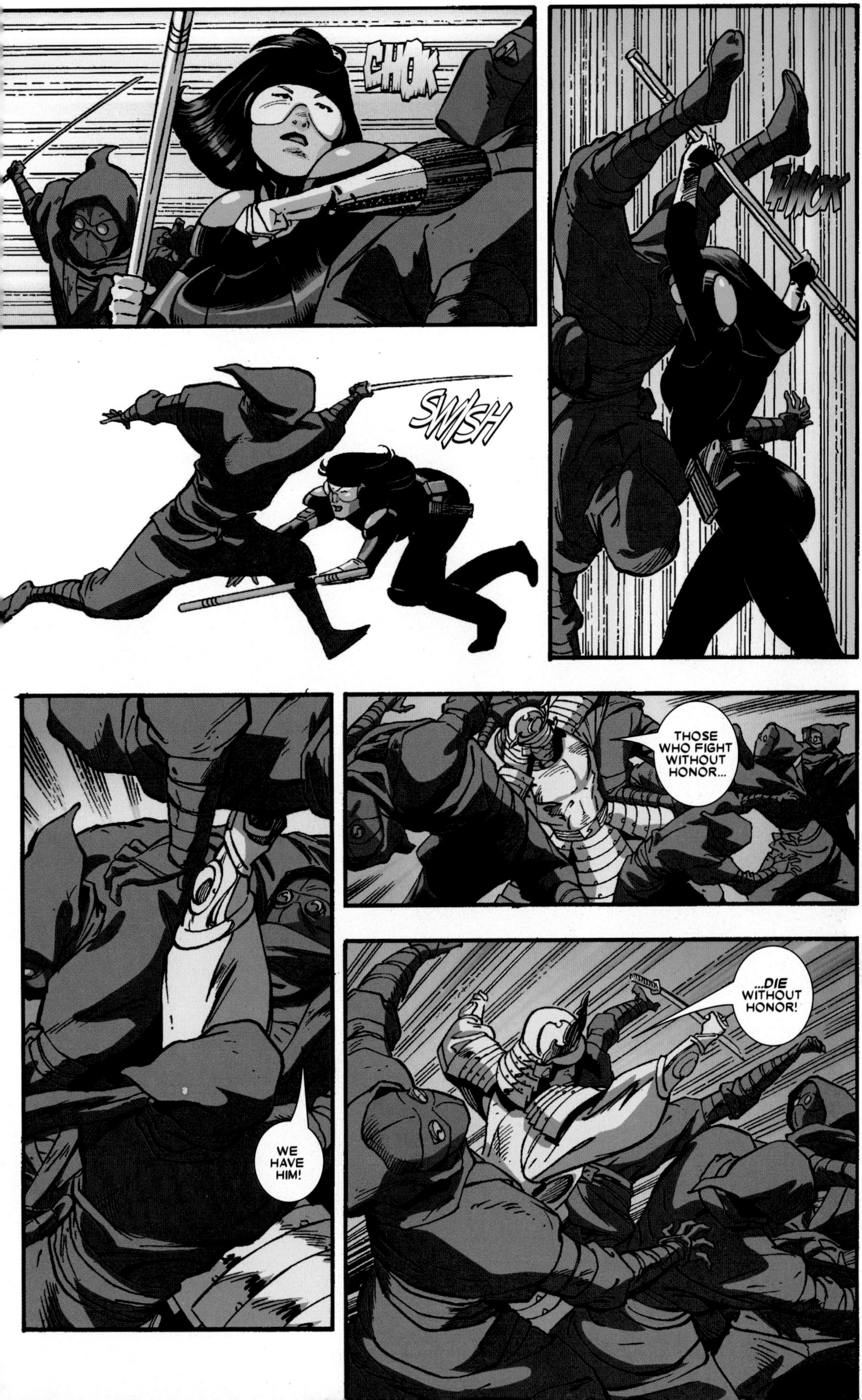
CHOK
THWOK
SWISH
WE HAVE HIM!
THOSE WHO FIGHT WITHOUT HONOR...
...DIE WITHOUT HONOR!

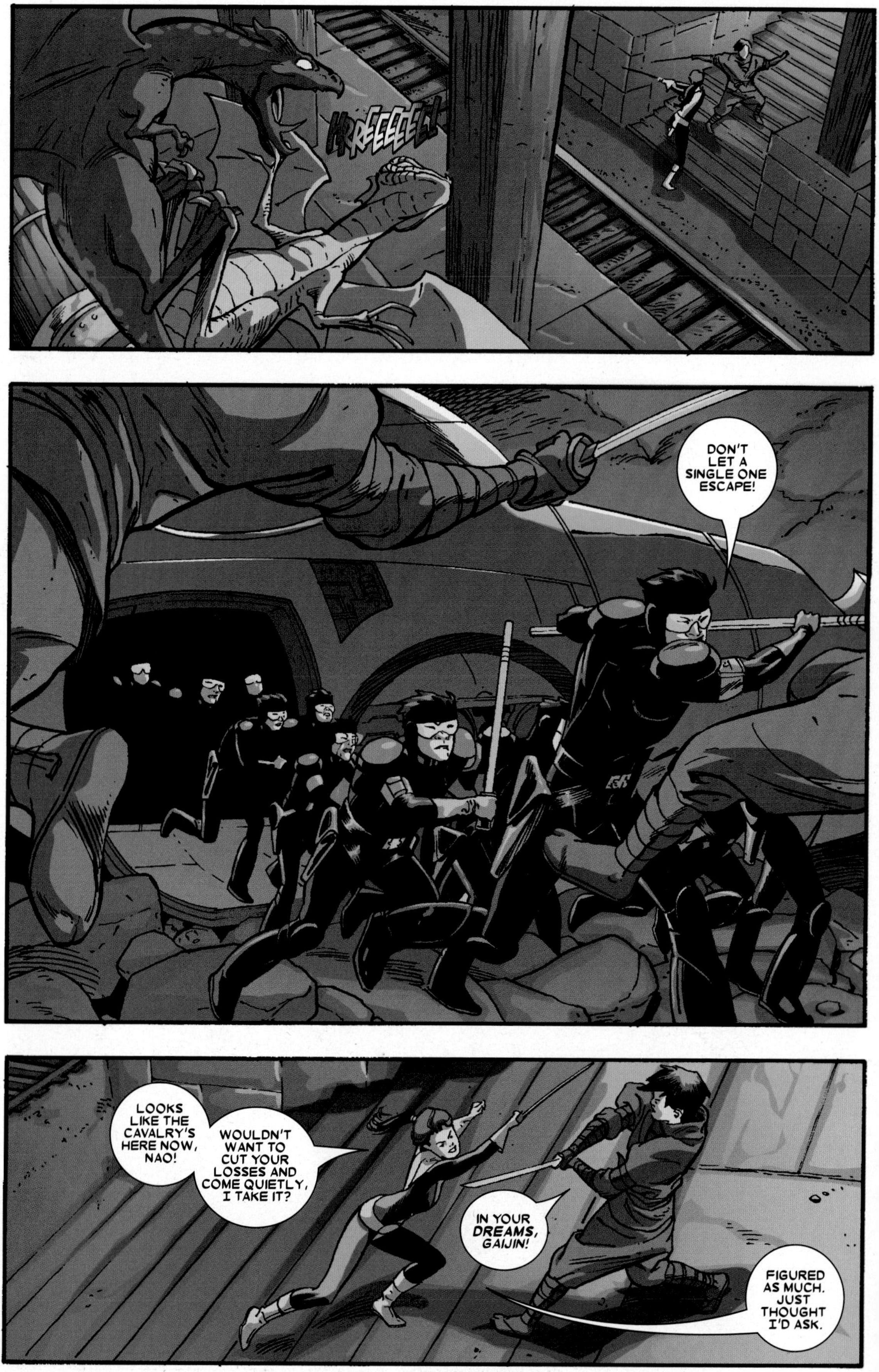
KRREEEEEE!
DON'T LET A SINGLE ONE ESCAPE!
LOOKS LIKE THE CAVALRY'S HERE NOW, NAO!
WOULDN'T WANT TO CUT YOUR LOSSES AND COME QUIETLY, I TAKE IT?
IN YOUR *DREAMS*, GAIJIN!
FIGURED AS MUCH. JUST THOUGHT I'D ASK.

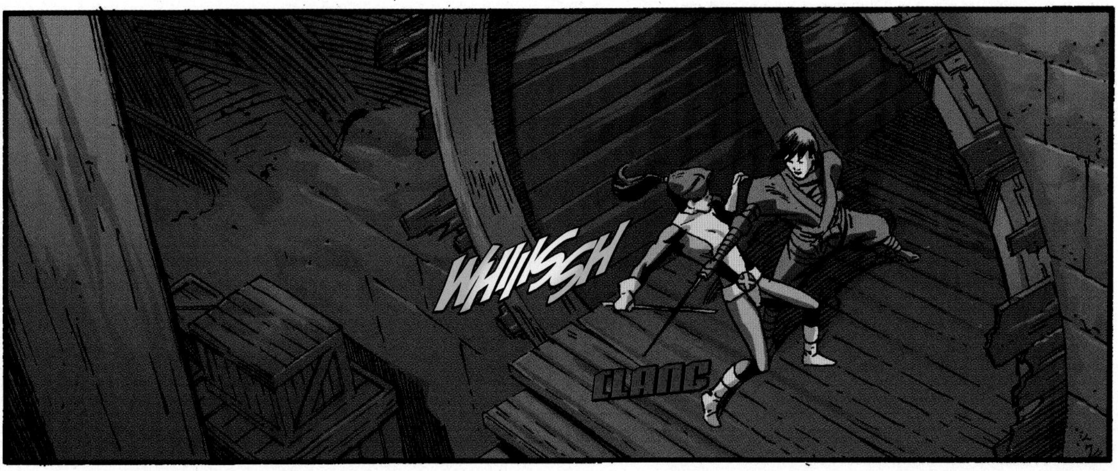
WHIISSH
CLANG

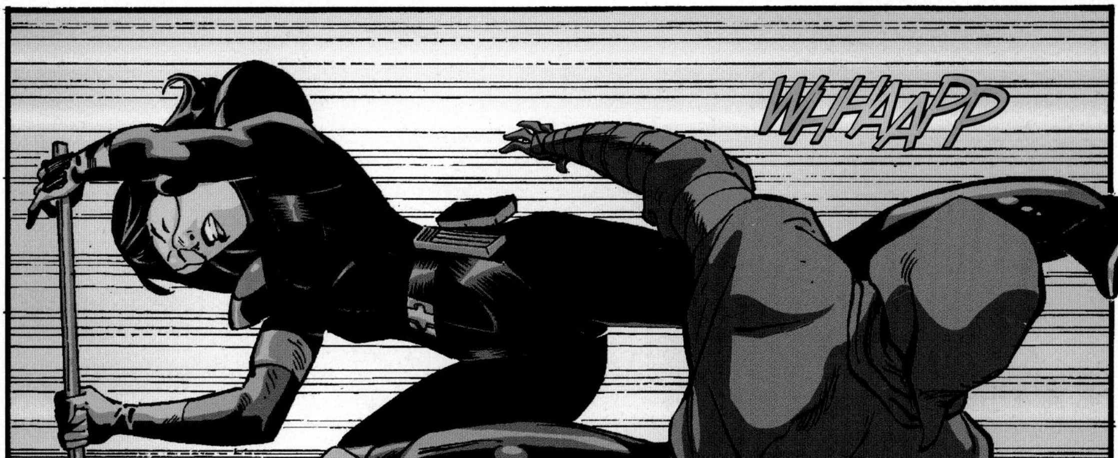
WHHAAPP

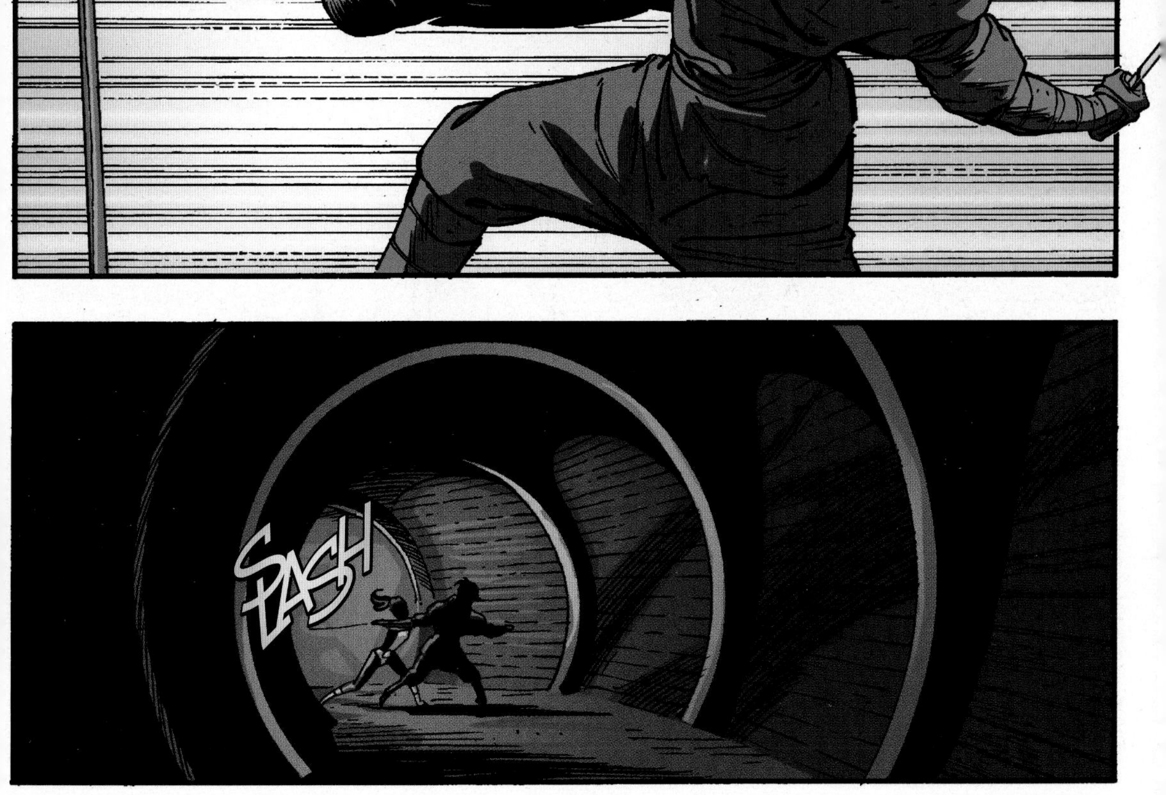
SPASH

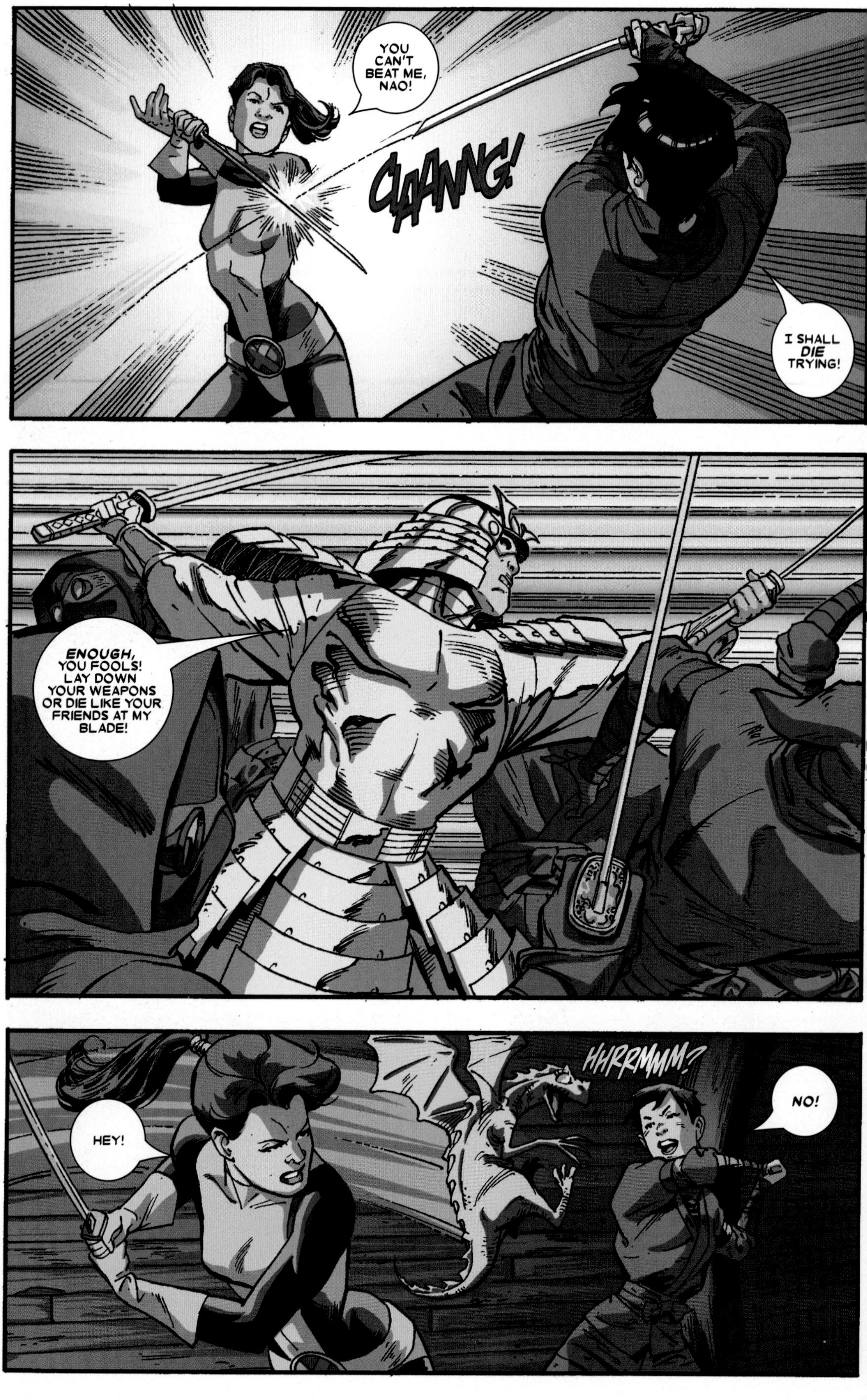
YOU CAN'T BEAT ME, NAO!
CLAANNG!
I SHALL *DIE* TRYING!
ENOUGH, YOU FOOLS! LAY DOWN YOUR WEAPONS OR DIE LIKE YOUR FRIENDS AT MY BLADE!
HEY!
HHRRMMM?
NO!

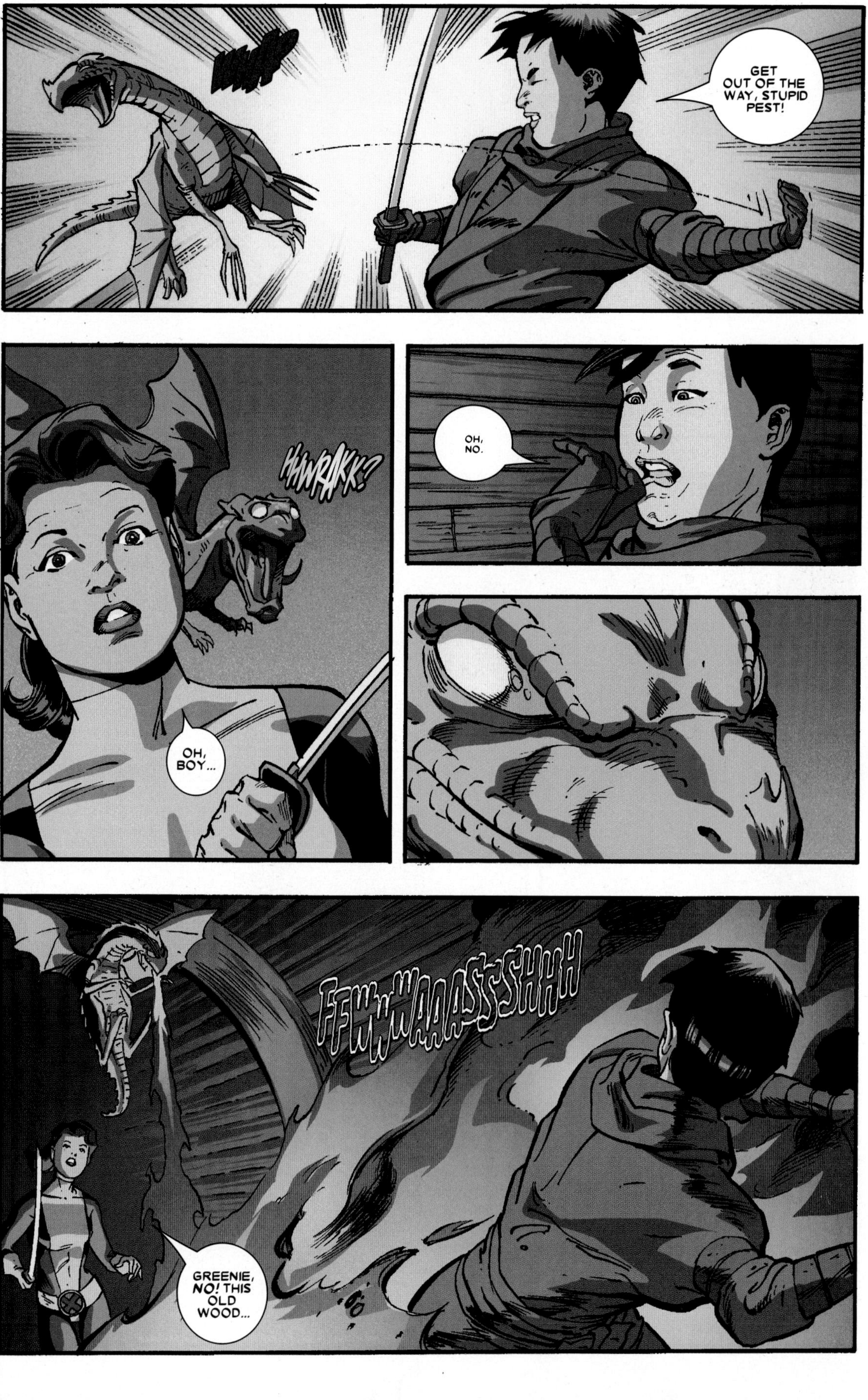

GET OUT OF THE WAY, STUPID PEST!
HWWRAKK?
OH, NO.
OH, BOY...
FFWWWAAASSSHHH
GREENIE, *NO!* THIS OLD WOOD...

NAO, DON'T MOVE! STAY WHERE YOU ARE!
I'VE *GOT* YOU! LET ME GET YOU OUT OF HERE.
NEVER!
IT'S ONE THING TO DIE WITH HONOR. IT'S ANOTHER TO BE *BURNED ALIVE!*
DIFFERENT MEANS TO THE SAME END.
DESTINY WILL DECIDE MY FATE!
NO!
FWOOMM

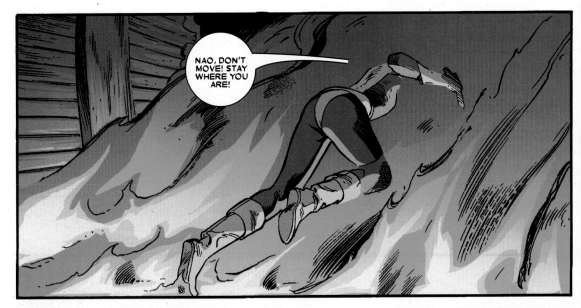

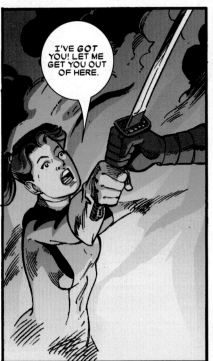

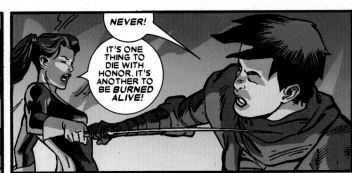

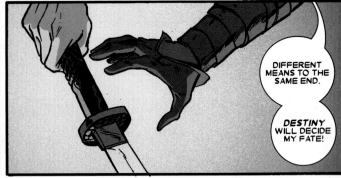

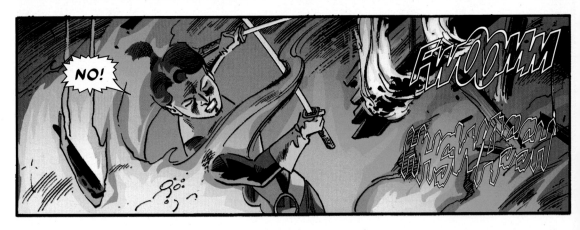

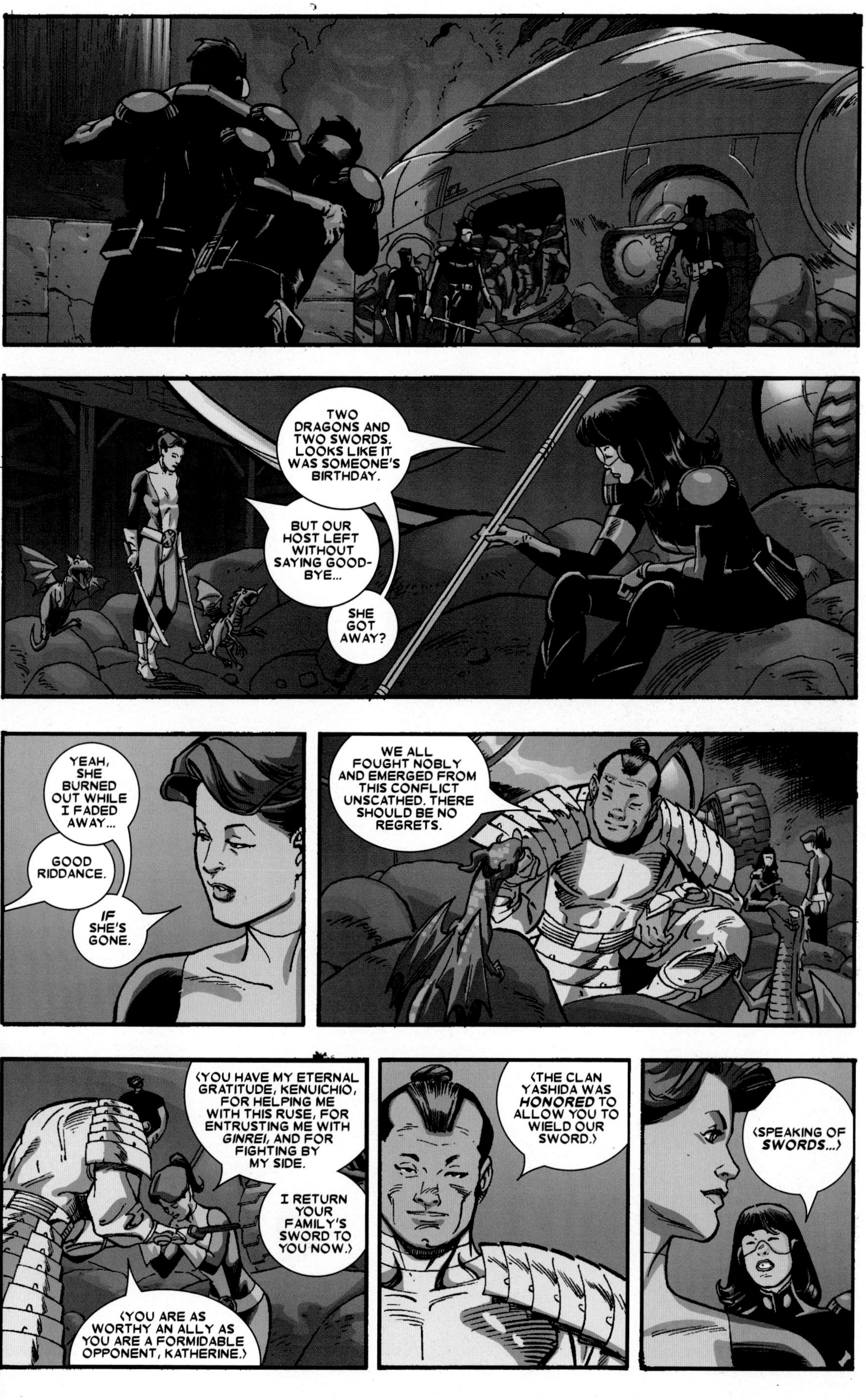
TWO DRAGONS AND TWO SWORDS. LOOKS LIKE IT WAS SOMEONE'S BIRTHDAY.
BUT OUR HOST LEFT WITHOUT SAYING GOOD-BYE...
SHE GOT AWAY?
YEAH, SHE BURNED OUT WHILE I FADED AWAY...
GOOD RIDDANCE.
IF SHE'S GONE.
WE ALL FOUGHT NOBLY AND EMERGED FROM THIS CONFLICT UNSCATHED. THERE SHOULD BE NO REGRETS.
‹YOU HAVE MY ETERNAL GRATITUDE, KENUICHIO, FOR HELPING ME WITH THIS RUSE, FOR ENTRUSTING ME WITH *GINREI*, AND FOR FIGHTING BY MY SIDE.
I RETURN YOUR FAMILY'S SWORD TO YOU NOW.›
‹YOU ARE AS WORTHY AN ALLY AS YOU ARE A FORMIDABLE OPPONENT, KATHERINE.›
‹THE CLAN YASHIDA WAS *HONORED* TO ALLOW YOU TO WIELD OUR SWORD.›
‹SPEAKING OF *SWORDS*...›

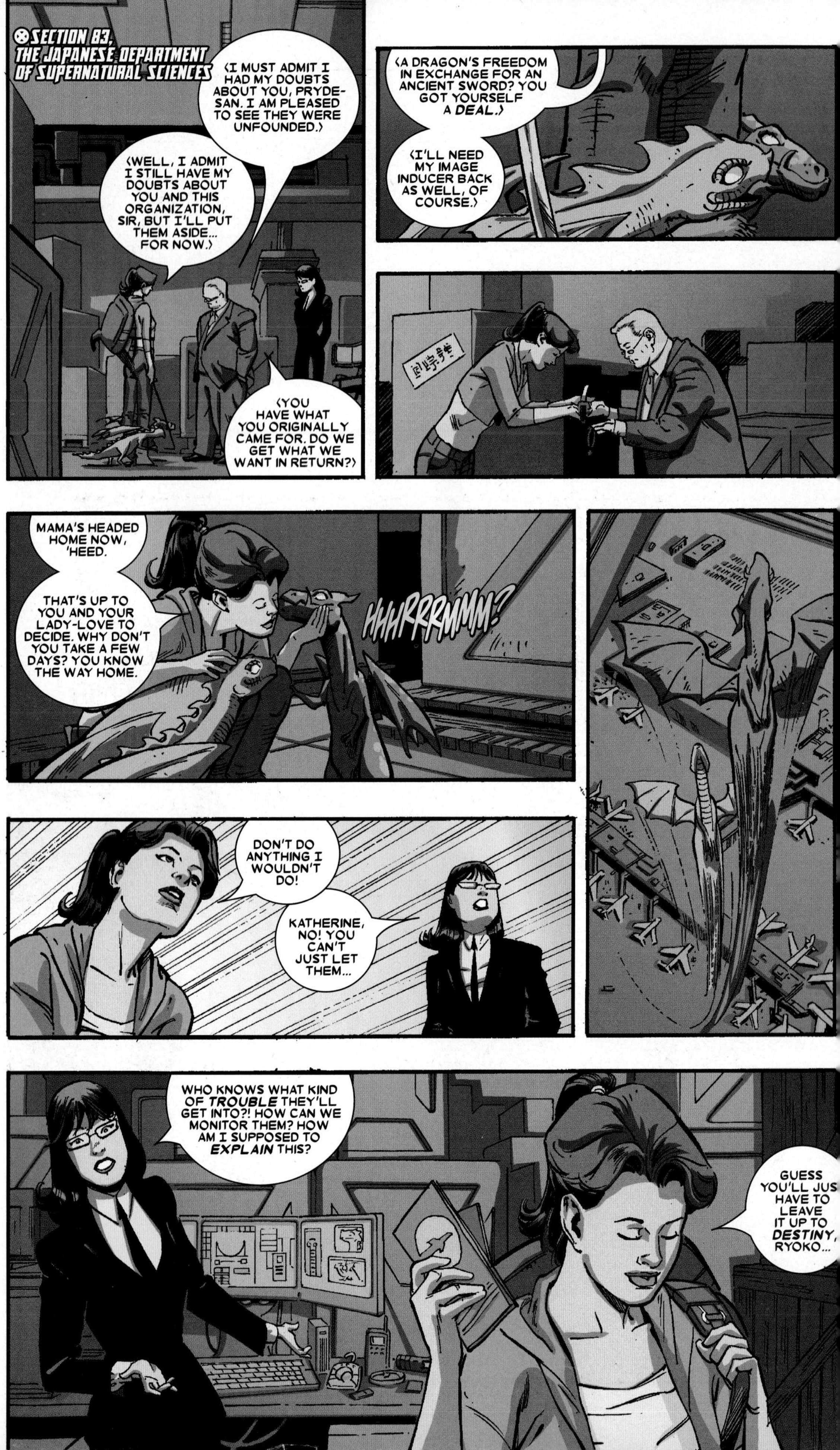
SECTION 83, THE JAPANESE DEPARTMENT OF SUPERNATURAL SCIENCES
‹I MUST ADMIT I HAD MY DOUBTS ABOUT YOU, PRYDE-SAN. I AM PLEASED TO SEE THEY WERE UNFOUNDED.›
‹WELL, I ADMIT I STILL HAVE MY DOUBTS ABOUT YOU AND THIS ORGANIZATION, SIR, BUT I'LL PUT THEM ASIDE... FOR NOW.›
‹YOU HAVE WHAT YOU ORIGINALLY CAME FOR. DO WE GET WHAT WE WANT IN RETURN?›
‹A DRAGON'S FREEDOM IN EXCHANGE FOR AN ANCIENT SWORD? YOU GOT YOURSELF A DEAL.›
‹I'LL NEED MY IMAGE INDUCER BACK AS WELL, OF COURSE.›
MAMA'S HEADED HOME NOW, 'HEED.
HHHRRRMMM?
THAT'S UP TO YOU AND YOUR LADY-LOVE TO DECIDE. WHY DON'T YOU TAKE A FEW DAYS? YOU KNOW THE WAY HOME.
DON'T DO ANYTHING I WOULDN'T DO!
KATHERINE, NO! YOU CAN'T JUST LET THEM...
WHO KNOWS WHAT KIND OF TROUBLE THEY'LL GET INTO?! HOW CAN WE MONITOR THEM? HOW AM I SUPPOSED TO EXPLAIN THIS?
GUESS YOU'LL JUS HAVE TO LEAVE IT UP TO DESTINY, RYOKO...

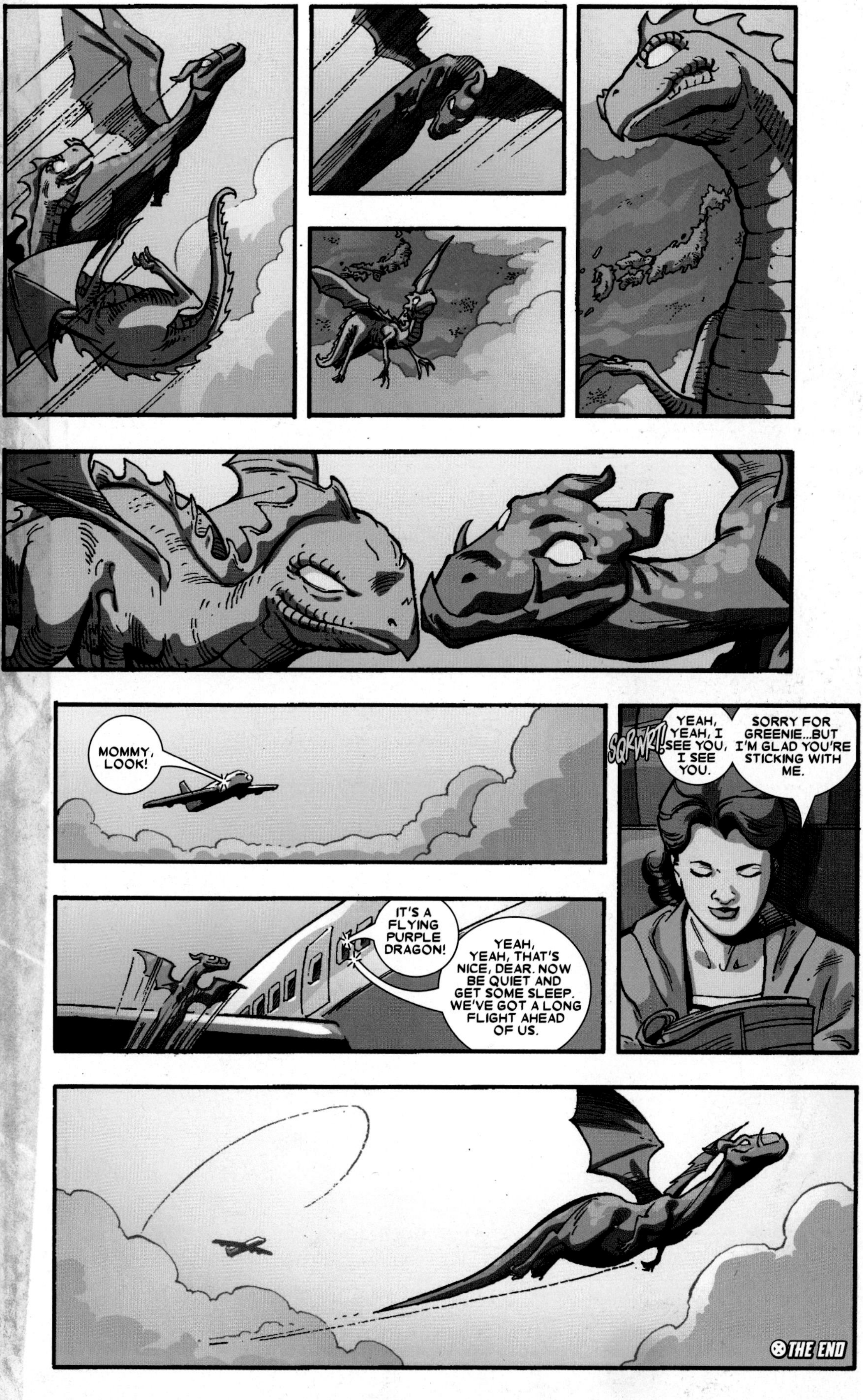
MOMMY, LOOK!
SQRWRT!
YEAH, YEAH, I SEE YOU, I SEE YOU.
SORRY FOR GREENIE...BUT I'M GLAD YOU'RE STICKING WITH ME.
IT'S A FLYING PURPLE DRAGON!
YEAH, YEAH, THAT'S NICE, DEAR. NOW BE QUIET AND GET SOME SLEEP. WE'VE GOT A LONG FLIGHT AHEAD OF US.
THE END

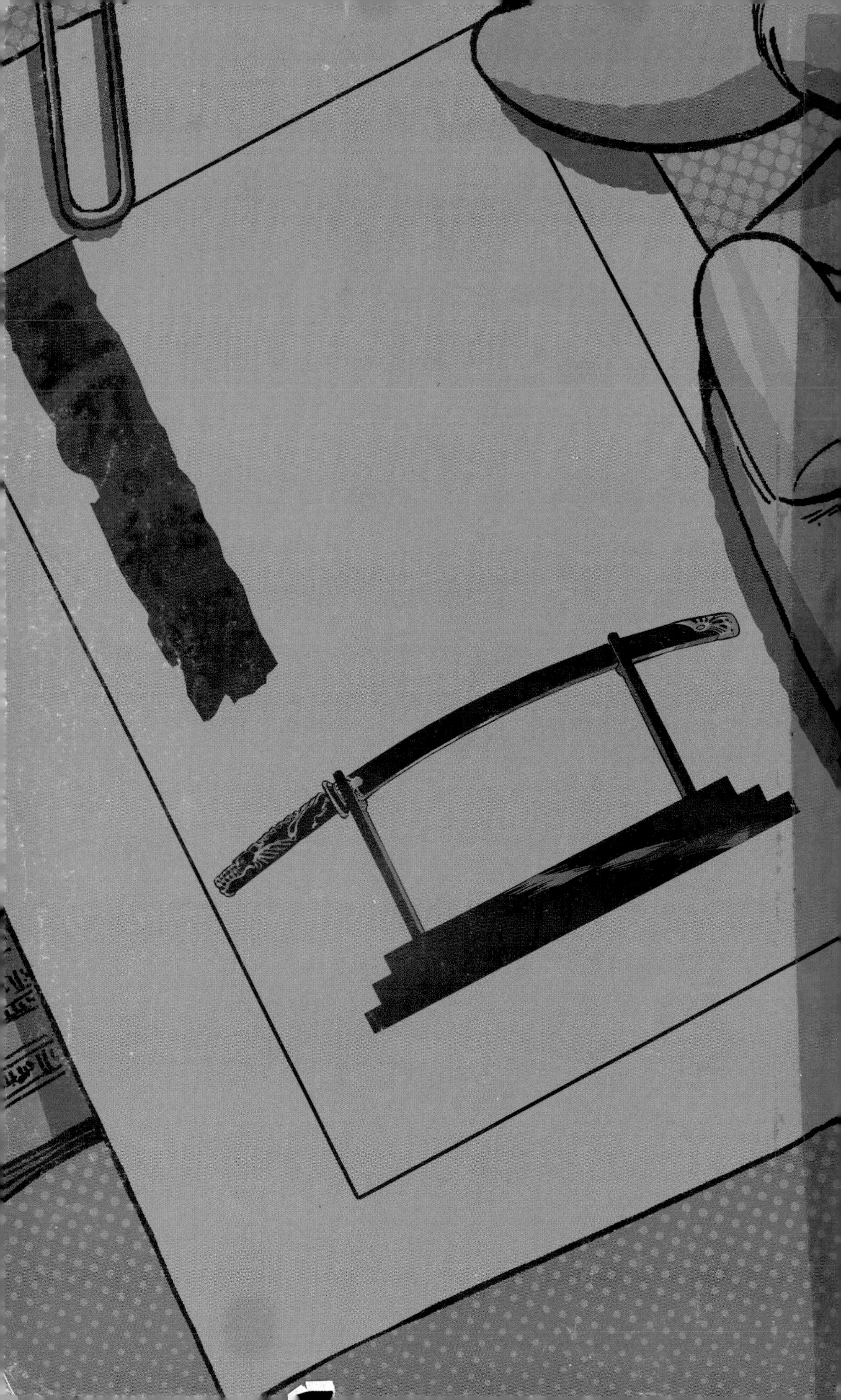